CAMBRIDGE

Brighter Thinking

Tsarist and Communist Russia, 1855–1964

A/AS Level History for AQA Student Book

Hannah Dalton

Series Editors: Michael Fordham and David Smith

CAMBRIDGE
UNIVERSITY PRESS

University Printing House, Cambridge CB2 8BS, United Kingdom

Cambridge University Press is part of the University of Cambridge.

It furthers the University's mission by disseminating knowledge in the pursuit of
education, learning and research at the highest international levels of excellence.

www.cambridge.org
Information on this title: www.cambridge.org/9781107531154 (Paperback)
                             www.cambridge.org/9781107531161 (Cambridge Elevate-enhanced Edition)

First published 2015

A catalogue record for this publication is available from the British Library

ISBN 978-1-107-53115-4 Paperback
ISBN 978-1-107-53116-1 Cambridge Elevate-enhanced Edition

Additional resources for this publication at www.cambridge.org/ukschools

Cambridge University Press has no responsibility for the persistence or accuracy
of URLs for external or third-party internet websites referred to in this publication,
and does not guarantee that any content on such websites is, or will remain,
accurate or appropriate. Information regarding prices, travel timetables, and other
factual information given in this work is correct at the time of first printing but
Cambridge University Press does not guarantee the accuracy of such information
thereafter.

....

Message from AQA

This textbook has been approved by AQA for use with our qualification. This means that we have checked that it broadly covers the specification and we are satisfied with the overall quality. Full details of our approval process can be found on our website.

We approve textbooks because we know how important it is for teachers and students to have the right resources to support their teaching and learning. However, the publisher is ultimately responsible for the editorial control and quality of this book.

Please note that when teaching the A/AS Level History (7041, 7042) course, you must refer to AQA's specification as your definitive source of information. While this book has been written to match the specification, it cannot provide complete coverage of every aspect of the course.

A wide range of other useful resources can be found on the relevant subject pages of our website: www.aqa.org.uk

Contents

[handwritten annotations:]
Tsar Alexander II
Tsar Nicholas + WW ↓ fall of the Romanov
Lenin: NEP.
Stalin: Gulag

About this Series

Cambridge A/AS Level History for AQA is an exciting new series designed to support students in their journey from GCSE to A Level and then on to possible further historical study. The books provide the knowledge, concepts and skills needed for the two-year AQA History A Level course, but it's our intention as series editors that students recognise that their A Level exams are just one step to a potential lifelong relationship with the discipline of history. This book has further readings, extracts from historians' works and links to wider questions and ideas that go beyond the scope of an A Level course. With this series, we have sought to ensure not only that the students are well prepared for their examinations, but also that they gain access to wider debate that characterises historical study.

The series is designed to provide clear and effective support for students as they make the adjustment from GCSE to A Level, and also for teachers, especially those who are not familiar with teaching a two-year linear course. The student books cover the AQA specifications for both A/AS Level. They are intended to appeal to the broadest range of students, and they offer challenge to stretch the top end and additional support for those who need it. Every author in this series is an experienced historian or history teacher, and all have great skill in conveying narratives to readers and asking the kinds of questions that pull those narratives apart.

In addition to high-quality prose, this series also makes extensive use of textual primary sources, maps, diagrams and images, and offers a wide range of activities to encourage students to address historical questions of cause, consequence, change and continuity. Throughout the books there are opportunities to criticise the interpretations of other historians, and to use those interpretations in the construction of students' own accounts of the past. The series aims to ease the transition for those students who move on from A Level to undergraduate study, and the books are written in an engaging style that will encourage those who want to explore the subject further.

Icons used within this book include:

 Key terms

 Developing concepts

 Speak like a historian

 Voices from the past/Hidden voices

 Practice essay questions

 Taking it further

 Chapter summary/ Summary of key events

About Cambridge Elevate

Cambridge Elevate is the platform which hosts a digital version of this Student Book. If you have access to this digital version you can annotate different parts of the book, send and receive messages to and from your teacher and insert weblinks, among other things.

We hope that you enjoy your AS or A Level History course as well as this book, and wish you well for the journey ahead.

Michael Fordham and David L Smith

Series editors

1 Trying to preserve autocracy, 1855–1894

In this section, we will examine the nature of political authority in Russia from 1855 to 1894, considering some of the changes that were taking place and how these changes began to affect the relationship between the people and their Tsar. We will look into:

- the nature of autocracy in Russia, including social divisions and the cultural influences of the Church
- the impact of the Crimean War on Russia
- attempts to reform Russia
- the governance of Russia under Alexander II and Alexander III
- the Tsars' treatment of ethnic minorities
- the growth of opposition
- the economy.

Introduction to Tsarist Russia

Russian political life was overwhelmingly the preserve of social elites in the 19th century under the Romanov dynasty. Ordinary people played almost no role in the institutions that governed Russia and this was to remain the case until 1917 when Tsardom fell. The imposition of **autocracy** on Russia changed little under

Key terms

Radical: someone who believes in drastic change away from traditions or government policy.

Russification: a policy undertaken by the Tsars to assimilate ethnic minorities and different nationalities within Imperial Russia. The policy meant forcing minorities to give up their language and aspects of their culture or religion.

Speak like a historian

Historians often use the word 'backwardness' to describe Russia in the 19th century. The word was first used by an economic theorist called Alexander Gerschenkron, who suggested Russia was 'backward' economically because there was a reliance on agriculture as the main source of income, because banks rather than private investors were relied upon to invest in enterprise, and because new technologies were limited in use.

Alexander II (the 16th Romanov Emperor), who ruled 1855–1881, even as he oversaw the most dramatic domestic reform witnessed in Russia in 200 years: for example, he abolished serfdom, introduced trial by jury and relaxed censorship. He was assassinated in 1881 by a **radical** group that believed his reforms were too conservative, but autocracy survived, the throne successfully passing to his son, Alexander III.

Alexander III did not want to suffer the same fate as his father, and he imposed autocracy even more ruthlessly as police powers were extended and Russia's conservative traditions were reinforced. Especially since an earlier assassination attempt on Alexander II in 1866, ethnic minorities and, in particular, the Jewish community had born the brunt of the imperial government's attempts to affirm the three goals of autocracy, religious orthodoxy and nationality (see the section 'Political authority and the state of Russia: autocracy'). These minorities became targets for discrimination under a policy that became known as **Russification**. This discrimination intensified under Alexander III.

On his deathbed in 1855, Tsar Nicholas I said to his son and heir: 'I am passing command to you that is not in desirable order. I am leaving you many disappointments and cares. Hold it like that!'[1]. At 36 years old, Alexander II was to inherit the largest power in the world – but with it the largest problems. Russia was on the brink of defeat to Britain and France in the Crimean War and couldn't even afford to repay the national debt. The regime was facing increasingly frequent riots by peasants in rural areas and the emergent middle classes were becoming more critical of Russia's evident political and economic 'backwardness'. The 1.5 million subjugated minorities on the fringes of the empire were beginning to call for self-determination and there was genuine fear that the 59 million peasants living in rural Russia were a real threat to the Tsar's authority. It was left to Alexander II to maintain a difficult balancing act: modernising Russia whilst retaining autocratic power.

Political authority and the state of Russia: autocracy

Autocratic rule was not unique to Russia. This system of government, in which solely the sovereign exercises supreme power, had existed in France and Britain, too, but by 1855 Russia was the last great autocratic state in Europe. Tsarist imperial government had been developed under Peter the Great (1682–1725) at a time when there was little alternative to centralised authority. Russia was a vast country; poor roads, no railways and an unfavourable climate meant that mid-17th-century travellers could expect to travel approximately just 50 miles in 24 hours, travelling by horse-drawn carriage. Unprecedented territorial expansion during the 19th century did not alter Russian autocracy; in fact, it only heightened the perceived need for highly centralised authority. In 1900, Italy and France spent more than twice as much per capita as Russia on policing; Russia, whose population was spread thinly over vast areas, possessed only four state officials for every 1000 inhabitants. Lacking a network of state control, the government became reliant upon the infrastructure of the Orthodox Church to enforce its authority. Tsars did not want to see their power curtailed and they were supported by officials whose careers and authority depended on the maintenance of the status quo. This provided a powerful motivation to obstruct change – resulting in systemic inertia.

Therefore, by 1855 little had changed; the Tsars had established a form of autocracy that was uniquely powerful in Europe, and Alexander II's political authority within Russia was virtually unbounded, as it was believed that the Tsar was ordained to his position by God. In 1833 Tsar Nicholas I had set out the doctrine of 'Official Nationality', which was based on autocracy in government, orthodoxy in religion and Russian nationalism. The final three Tsars – Alexander II, Alexander III and Nicholas II – always retained their allegiance to this doctrine, and continued to implement dramatic shifts in policy without popular consent. As the historian Richard Pipes suggests, the final three Tsars seemed to lack any method for resolving political crisis other than repression. Indeed, the styles of government that they imposed seemed to reflect the character of the men themselves.

The concept of autocracy had important implications for the Russian people. For example, the nature of law in Tsarist Russia was very different to the rest of Europe. In the West it became accepted that the monarch was subject to the same laws that governed the behaviour of the population – known as the rule of law. This was never accepted in Russia, where the law was something imposed on the population by the state, embodied by the sovereign. In this sense, the Russian Tsars were above the law. The Tsars' representatives were able to act with impunity in passing judgement on any particular issue or meting out punishments. The historian Peter Waldron (1997) suggests that this system led to widespread corruption. The autocratic system permeated Russian society from the Tsar himself to the lowliest rural tax collector, and every government official at every level knew that they could act without risk of consequence in their dealings as an agent of the state. For Alexander II, this might mean surrendering in a war without taking advice; for a rural bureaucrat, it might mean imprisoning a peasant without evidence.

Figure 1.1: Alexander II c.1860

Orthodoxy and the role of the Church

Autocracy and the preservation of Tsarist authority represented the project at the heart of the Romanov monarchy. However, no regime could rest on politics alone: the Tsars needed to win the hearts of their people. Religion played the crucial role here. The Russian Orthodox Church had been established in the 15th century in a split from the eastern Byzantine Church. The Russian Church reflected the principles of the state, representing that Russia possessed a particular spiritual role in the Christian world. The Church was governed by the Holy Synod, chaired by a government minister, and the Tsar's family had to be members by law. The Tsar had absolute power over Church finance and appointments. The Orthodox Church made spirited efforts to convert people to Orthodoxy from other religions, motivated by the need to integrate new populations into the empire to serve the interests of both Church and state. Orthodoxy played a significant role in legitimising the imperial regime. Nicholas I oversaw the widespread construction of Orthodox churches across the empire and an extension of religious rituals in government, cementing the link between Church and state. Golden domes and minarets still dominate the skylines of many Russian towns.

Nationalism

On 26 December 1825, a group of aristocrats led by Russian army officers, along with about 3000 soldiers, staged a protest in Senate Square, St Petersburg, against Nicholas I's assumption of the throne and in support of his elder brother, Constantine, who in fact had renounced his claim to the throne. The protest was brutally suppressed by Nicholas I, and the five ringleaders of the 'Decembrists' (as the group came to be called) were hanged. These events showed the Tsarist regime that it was not just the peasants they had to fear, but also elements of the aristocracy and the army – traditionally the regime's closest allies. The Romanov tradition was to paint any threat to the regime as 'un-Russian'. This most potent means of bringing people together under the authority of the Tsar was what became known as the doctrine of 'Official Nationality'. The doctrine stood for the application of Orthodoxy and autocracy and suggested the Russian monarchy had a historic destiny to direct the development of its subjects. Linked to this was a belief that Russia and her people were distinctly different to Europeans.

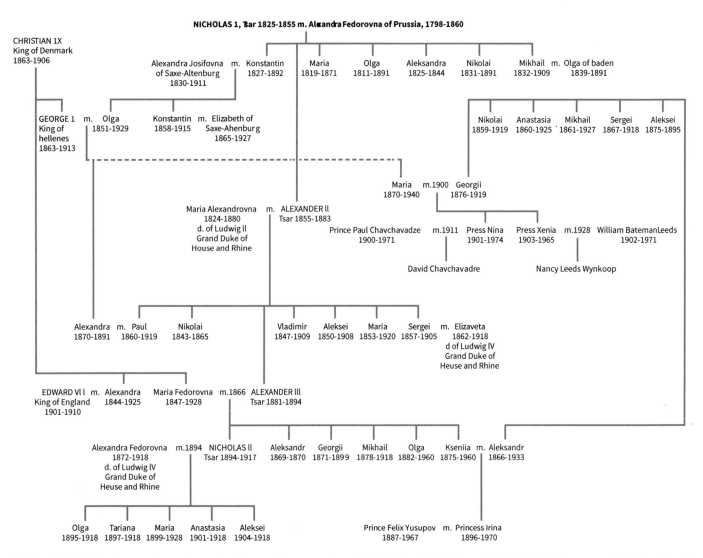

Figure 1.2: The family tree above shows the House of Romanov from Nicholas I to the last Tsar, Nicholas II. The Romanovs had ruled Russia for almost 250 years by the time Alexander II came to the throne.

Figure 1.3 shows a map that gives an impression of the size of the Russian Empire, highlighting the areas where some of the different nationalities lived. The historian Dominic Lieven (1999) has suggested that, of all the borderlands, Ukraine and Belorussia were most crucial to the empire[2]. They lay across the main invasion routes from the West, where Imperial Russia's most powerful and dangerous enemies were. They shielded the empire's capitals and its political and economic heartland.

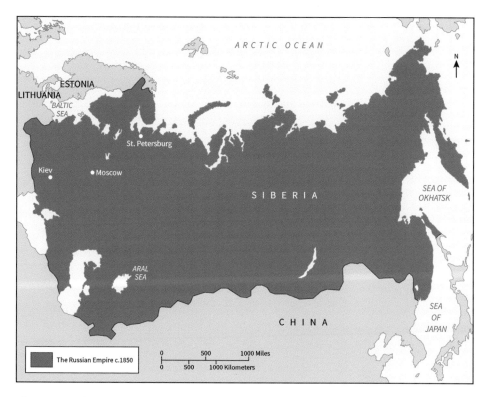

Figure 1.3: The Russian Empire c.1850.

Russia was a state dominated by the rural world and this was fundamental to her identity. 'Slavophiles' embodied this belief, emphasising Russian uniqueness and rejecting Western socio-economic development. This view dominated intellectual thought until the 19th century, when a new ideology started to infiltrate Russia from the West. The Russian empire had expanded so much by the 1850s that people in the western states now lived 4500 miles away from those living on the empire's Pacific coastline. Ultimately, Russia could not remain immune from the wider processes of industrialisation that had been sweeping through Europe since the 1750s. 'Westernisers' (or *progressives* to use common parlance) started to argue that Russia needed to imitate Europe and industrialise, encouraging peasants to move to the cities. They argued that Russia was lagging behind due to 'Slavophile' (reactionary) beliefs. To what extent Russia should engage with European ideas was a dilemma Alexander II could not ignore when he took the throne in 1855.

When studying Russia during this period, it is important to note the European context. European states, above all Britain and France had begun industrialisation to varying degrees during the 18th century, but the process had begun to accelerate in the first half of the 19th century. Russia could not maintain her status as a major power without industrialising. To an extent, this problem plagued every Russian leader up to the end of this study in 1964.

The political, social and economic condition of Russia in 1855

When Alexander II succeeded to the throne the nobility were almost exclusively responsible for the administration of the governance of Russia. The Tsarist government was made up of an Imperial State Council and 13 ministries, which oversaw areas such as education, internal affairs, the military, and the economy. The State Council was no more than an advisory body in reality, and was often referred to as a comfortable place for civil servants to retire to. The 13 ministries were often in competition with each other, and they relied upon the autocratic Tsar to authorise policies, as they reported directly to him. This meant the efficiency of government depended largely on the strength of the Tsar's commitment to governing. With no representative body, popular participation in politics was non-existent and there was no single institution to co-ordinate the work of government, which made governing a complex and tiresome task for the Tsar. In efforts to control his administration, Nicholas I asked for reports from the ministries every year. In 1849, it was recorded that the Ministry of the Interior alone produced 31,122,211 official papers, 165,000 of them 'urgent'. This cumbersome, bureaucratic machine meant that progress was at best slow and at worst non-existent. Alexander II had worked on the Imperial State Council for 10 years prior to becoming Tsar. He was acutely aware of the deficiencies of the system of government, as well as the calls for more representative government from 'Westernisers', who witnessed Western Europeans being granted participation in their 'enlightened' political systems and began to demand similar change in Russia.

This pattern was mirrored in local government, where institutions were largely disparate and inefficient. Local government existed on three levels: province, district and rural district. Russia was divided into 50 provinces, each province being divided into 20 districts. Each province had a governor who was directly responsible to the Tsar. He could deal with up to 100 000 documents a year if he completed his work diligently. Unsurprisingly, the quality and amount of work produced by governors varied greatly. No such chain of command existed in the districts, which were led by a 'marshal of the nobility', who oversaw approximately 200 000 people and was elected by fellow nobles. Although the system of government was incredibly inefficient, it did ensure that the nobility were loyal to the regime and exercised control in the provinces on behalf of the Tsar.

The Third Section

The third element of Russian government, the 'Third Section', was responsible for political security. It conducted surveillance and gathered information on political dissidents, religious schismatics (objectors) and foreigners. It had the power to banish suspected political criminals to remote regions and also operated prisons. It was furthermore responsible for prosecuting counterfeiters of money and official documents, and for conducting censorship. The Third Section functioned in conjunction with the Corps of Gendarmes (formed in 1836), a well-organised military force that operated throughout the empire, and a network of anonymous spies and informers. It became a particularly repressive institution under Nicholas I and was feared throughout Russia by the educated elite, who wanted to be able to discuss ideas without state retribution.

Peasants and serfs

European Russia's population stood at about 65 million in 1855; of this, around 59 million were peasants or serfs. Peasants and serfs had varied obligations as a consequence of subordination to different kinds of landlords, which makes it difficult to generalise about their conditions. At the risk of oversimplification, state-owned peasants were deprived of the right to own private property, although they were allowed to move to find jobs. They were also deprived of any individual legal rights. Thirty million people were classified as 'state peasants' by 1850. Conversely, serfs, numbering 21 million or so, were privately owned by nobles and prohibited from leaving their landowners' estates, and therefore bonded to the land they worked on. They had to provide their lords with labour services (*barschina*) or cash payments or payments in kind (*obrok*), and sometimes both. (A payment in kind in this case would have been a share of crops grown.) The dominance of *obrok* or *barschina* varied by region. For example, in Ukraine, 98 per cent of serf obligations were met by *barschina*. The level of payment increased throughout the 19th century and by 1855 it is estimated that the average payment expected by landowners amounted to over one third of peasant/serf incomes and production. Lastly, household or 'personal' serfs were subject to the whims of their owners, with no allotment of land and no way of supporting themselves; they numbered approximately 8 million. All peasants and serfs had to pay taxes and provide for themselves and their families. The limit of their world was the boundary of their village. They were largely uneducated and illiterate and knew little of politics. Life expectancy was only about 35 years by the 1850s and many found their only solace in the Church or in vodka.

Little had changed in rural areas for hundreds of years, as the motivation for modernisation had been nullified by the practice of serfdom. Landlords had free labour and serfs had nobody to whom they could sell excess goods. The system of serfdom was intended to give the landowning elites a large income by enabling them to exploit the peasantry, but it also provided a useful way of deterring uprisings in the countryside, as punishments could be very severe indeed. Although landlords were not allowed to kill or maim serfs, corporal punishment, such as whipping, was commonplace. It is important to note that uprisings did occur; even the iron-fisted Nicholas I experienced over 1400 different uprisings in the first half of the 19th century. The 'masses', as they were referred to, were genuinely feared as a primary source of revolution when Alexander II assumed the throne in 1855.

ACTIVITY 1.1

Part of becoming a historian is learning to use historically specific terms with accuracy. To understand the context in which Alexander II was ruling, you need to be able to discuss Russian society, which was starkly differentiated from the rest of Europe. Some words you will have come across before, but their meaning is distinctive when referring to Russia in the 19th century. Some key words are: serf, nobility, elite, intelligentsia, peasant. Draw a diagram to see if you can show how these groups of people related to each other.

Figure 1.4: A group of serfs at a rare social event, St Petersburg, Russia, 1890s. One man plays the flute in the background while two younger serfs dance.

The nobility

The Russian nobility also bore a burden of service, based on the 'Table of Ranks' system imposed by Peter the Great in 1722. This had made state service compulsory for every noble male from the age of 15 until overcome by disability or death; this mostly meant becoming an officer in the military, although the luckier ones might secure a position in the state bureaucracy. Military service was universally unpopular amongst noble families as it took men away from running their estates. Becoming a civil servant was a far more attractive proposition to many, with the state providing a regular salary and an education. From 1762 state service was no longer obligatory, but especially the poorer nobles usually stayed on: it is important to note that the Russian nobility was neither universally wealthy nor universally educated. Nobles in rural areas were particularly disadvantaged; in 1858, 40 per cent of all landowners owned fewer than 20 serfs and scraped a meagre living from the land.

A very small number of landowners owned vast estates; for example, Count D.N. Sheremetev had 300 000 serfs working on his land when Alexander II took the throne. Many of the wealthier nobles took on cultural pursuits: the leading figures in the so-called 'Golden Age' of Russian literature and art belonged almost exclusively to the noble elite, including Pushkin, Gogol, Tolstoy and Dostoevsky. The intellectual nobility was often progressive and pushed for reforms on behalf of the peasantry. Most nobles, however, were happy to run Russia for the Romanovs as long as the arrangement remained mutually beneficial, and remained loyal to the regime. Power still lay with the Tsar, who could discipline any nobles who were seen to be neglecting their duties or were deemed less than supportive. Calls for an end to Russia's system of serfdom had been heard since the time of Nicholas I; such a move, however, would threaten the very structure of society upon which the regime was based, and jeopardise the Tsars' authority over their people.

The intelligentsia

Historians tend to refer to 'the intelligentsia' (educated elite) as a group distinct from the nobility or peasants; many students of Russian history therefore make the mistake of assuming it was part of the 'middle classes'. In fact, Russia had only a small middle class of professionals in the mid-19th century, though it was a growing economic force, its members tending to pursue cultural, educational and legal professions. The intelligentsia was socially diverse, although in numerical terms nobles dominated. Those not part of the nobility were sometimes termed *raznochintsy* – or 'people of mixed ranks' – and were often the children of minor officials, clergy and merchants. What was distinct about a member of the intelligentsia was not necessarily their level of education, but that, as Richard Pipes (1995) puts it, they were 'someone not wholly preoccupied with his personal well-being but at least as much and preferably much more concerned with that of society at large, and willing, to the best of his ability, to work on society's behalf' (page 253).

Figure 1.5: A group of nobles in 1849, several of whom became world-renowned writers. From left to right: (top) Leo Tolstoy, Dimitri Grigorovich; (bottom) Ivan Goncharov, Ivan Turgenev, Alexander Druzhinin and Alexander Ostrovsky

Saunders (1992) suggests that the educated elite came to dominate the intelligentsia because they were being 'marginalised' as early as the 1780s, as there were not enough important or prestigious jobs to employ the growing number of educated men. Alexander Pushkin – perhaps Russia's greatest poet – wrote *Eugene Onegin* (his now classic novel in verse, published in serial form 1825–32) based on this theme. Onegin, Pushkin's fictional protagonist, was a talented and highly educated aristocrat who did not feel at home in the society to which he belonged. Many noble and middle class families allowed their children to complete their university studies abroad in Germany or Britain, while others travelled from Russia after their studies to experience 'new Western ideas'. Men such as Bakunin, Herzen, Turgenev, and even Lenin, were members of an educated elite who absorbed ideas from abroad. Their travels distanced them from their Russian traditions and left them contemplating the future of their nation. The improvements in Russia's education system meant that by the 1840s approximately 20 000 non-nobles (predominantly from the middle classes but also including some peasants) had been educated to university level. This, in turn, meant the growth of a 'market for ideas', a new generation thirsty for change.

Economic conditions: agriculture

Russia was undoubtedly the most economically backward of the great European powers in 1855, and this deficiency was most pronounced in the countryside. Tsarist Russia was an agricultural economy where 90 per cent of the population lived in rural areas, the majority being peasants and serfs. Farming in Russia was based on communal structures. The peasant commune (*mir*) was the body that was responsible for ensuring the peasants fulfilled their obligations. The commune could redistribute land after deaths in the village and ensured fairness in the quality of distribution. This system caused huge inefficiencies: the *mir* operated a system of strip farming and crop rotation, and redistribution prevented any investment from the peasants; peasants would often refuse to manure the land the year before repartition because they knew they would have to surrender it. These policies discouraged new agricultural techniques and contributed to the underdeveloped nature of the agrarian sector. Serfdom was not merely a symptom of Russian backwardness but one of its major causes. Low yields were a persistent problem and Russia compared very poorly with other European powers. By the 1850s, Russian grain production per hectare was less than half that of British, Prussian or French farms. As the population was growing at an alarming rate throughout the 19th century, almost doubling towards the latter half, while grain still accounted for 40 per cent of total Russian exports (at a time when the price of grain was decreasing), it became clear Russia needed to reform her economy. One reason Russia had not yet industrialised was because serfdom meant the pool of labour needed for the new industries was tied to the land. Coupled with this problem was the fact that Russia's underdeveloped banking system made it difficult for foreigners to invest.

The costs of war

Russia's finances were frequently put under significant stress due to war and the continual expansion of the empire during the 1800s, particularly as warfare became more technologically demanding, thus requiring ever-greater resources. The Russian state had absorbed new lands into its domains in an almost continuous process for almost 150 years up to 1850. This process had been so successful that the various peoples now incorporated into the Russian empire together accounted for the greatest variety of languages and religions of any state on earth. Yet it had required massive amounts of money and men.

In 1855 Russia was at war with Britain and France in the Crimea. The war had already been ruinously expensive, consuming up to 45 per cent of government expenditure in 1854 and requiring the levying of local taxes in the south to provide fuel, candles and straw for the army. The state's first reaction to the conflict had been to print more money to cover the expenditure, doubling the amount of money in circulation by 1855. However, accustomed methods of dealing with deficits were stretched to the limit. Russia's debts to the banks had grown from 166 million rubles in 1845 to 441 million just 15 years later, and Russian foreign debts reached 360 million rubles. Even landlords were mortgaged beyond their means to pay for lifestyles to which they felt entitled. According to the historian Orlando Figes (1997), one third of the land and two thirds of the peasants were mortgaged to the State Bank or other noble banks by 1859. Many estates were run by managers and bailiffs rather than the noble families themselves. It was clear to Alexander II that Russia was in a financial crisis: this time, the question of abolishing serfdom had to be addressed.

The impact of the Crimean War (1853–56)

Nicholas I died on 2 March 1855 after contracting pneumonia whilst inspecting his troops on the front line. His death came just after Russia's loss of Sevastopol, her most precious fortified base, once thought to be invincible, to an alliance of Britain, France and Turkey. Over 25 million men were subject to military service but Russia's standing army was only 1.4 million. Even of this number, some were exempted due to poor health; others were unavailable for the Crimea as they were needed to maintain the peace elsewhere in the empire. Furthermore, poor infrastructure meant it was difficult to transport soldiers safely. But not only the lack of railways and roads hampered the Russian army: the industrialised armies of Britain and France had modern equipment like steamships and rifled muskets, while the Russians were still using the same weaponry that had been used in the Napoleonic Wars 40 years earlier.

Figure 1.6: 'The Relief of the Light Brigade' by Richard Caton Woodville (1897). The painting shows the Battle of Balaclava, which was part of the British and French attempt to take the port of Sevastopol. This was one of the few battles won by the Russians during the war, due to tactical errors on the part of the British generals.

It is estimated that about 800 000 men (2% of the European-Russian population) went to the Crimea to serve, and casualties were very high. About 250 000 died, very often not in the fighting but from disease and illness. In 1854–5 Russia spent the equivalent of three years' income on the war, covering the deficit by printing more money, which accelerated inflation. The war itself might not have been so devastating had it not been for the significant pressures already facing the regime; as it was, the war exacerbated existing problems. Miliutin, Alexander's Minister of War, predicted that if the war ended badly all Russia's sacrifices would represent nothing more than 'the futile exhaustion of her last resources'[3].

Nicholas's death may have prolonged Russia's involvement in the war, as Alexander II did not want to be seen to capitulate too easily. However, by January 1856 he had no choice but to surrender to Britain and France, and he signed the humiliating Treaty of Paris on 30 March, in which Russia agreed to remove her forces from the Danubian provinces, completely restoring power in the region to the Turks. Russian battleships were banned from sailing in the Black Sea, which drastically decreased the influence of Russia's only warm-water port (considering Russia's other ports were frozen for most of the year, this access in the south had always been important for trading and defensive purposes). After the Treaty the Tsar also needed to contend with a stretched economy and a restless people unhappy with the way in which the war had been executed. Even those conservative intellectuals who had supported Official Nationality were calling for change. Alexander's hand was being forced: he would have to restructure Russia's army, taxation system and economy; more importantly, he had to abolish serfdom.

Political authority and attempts at reform

Alexander II

Alexander II had had a fairly liberal education for an heir to the Russian throne and was relatively well prepared for the role when it came in 1855. As a teenager, Alexander was taken on a six-month tour of Russia, visiting 20 provinces in the country. He also visited many prominent Western European countries. As Tsarevich (heir to the throne), Alexander became the first Romanov heir to visit Siberia. When he was 24 he sat on the State Council and Committee of Ministers and oversaw the construction of the railways between Moscow and St Petersburg. Yet, as Tsar, Alexander II was neither liked nor seen as particularly bright; to all around him, he seemed quite different to the strong-willed man his father had been. In fact, many described him as wholly irresolute (lacking in conviction). Alexander was a cautious man; although the abolition of serfdom occurred only six years into his reign, in reality it could have been realised more quickly had the Tsar committed himself to it.

Emancipation of the serfs: a liberation?

Emancipation had been discussed as early as the 1760s in the reign of Catherine the Great. Catherine had suggested serfdom was immoral and unjust, yet during her reign it spread more widely and became more deeply entrenched across Russia, including the territory Catherine conquered, mainly in Poland. The expansion of the Tsarina's lands matched her increased political power over her subjects. To assuage grievances over poverty and lack of land, every land conquest was followed by hand-outs and peasant colonisation, helping Catherine secure her position. Nicholas I had experimented with reform in Ukrainian Russia, but these projects had caused some 300 peasant disturbances in the countryside and were widely considered a failure. He also changed the status of some state peasants (mainly in Siberia and the north-east) to 'free agriculturalists', but in reality this simply meant they paid tax on land instead of property; they were given no new rights. The nobility also resented this measure, as they were forced to relinquish their rights to free labour without compensation. If the two great monarchs who preceded Alexander II had failed to emancipate the serfs, how would this indecisive man, with no special intellectual gifts, succeed?

As early as 1856, Alexander had said to his ministers:

(…) rumours have spread among you of my intention to abolish serfdom. To refute any groundless gossip on so important a subject I consider it necessary to inform you that I have no intention of doing so immediately. But, of course, and you yourselves

realise it, the existing system of serf owning cannot remain unchanged. It is better to begin abolishing serfdom from above than to wait for it to begin to abolish itself from below. I ask you, gentlemen, to think of ways of doing this. Pass on my words to the nobles for consideration.[4]

Alexander tentatively started secret discussions in a committee on emancipation in 1857. In reality, this was an act of necessity because of the level of domestic disquiet, both in the countryside (there were 250 disturbances recorded that year) and in university towns such as Moscow, where Slavophiles and Westernisers were circulating handwritten memoranda on the question of emancipation. The European-wide banking crisis in 1857, caused by high inflation and fragile economies, forced Alexander to publicly announce his intention to emancipate the serfs, in order to maintain public order. There was now a state of fiscal (financial) urgency, as the state banks could not function without stability in the banking system. The government needed new ways to raise revenue through direct taxation because they could no longer rely on borrowing – it was just too risky.

After more than 409 meetings of the Emancipation Commission over 18 months, the Emancipation *Ukase* (statute) was finally signed by the Tsar on 3 March 1861. Alexander himself was well aware that the laws would fall a long way short of many groups' expectations, and delayed the publication of the bill to 18 March, fearing peasant unrest. There were 19 acts in total, which divided Russia into regions, then sub-regions; in short, the legislation was extremely complex. However, the main principles were as follows:

- Serfs were free to marry whomsoever they wished, own property and set up their own businesses.
- All serfs were to become 'obligated peasants' for two years whilst charters were drawn up to decide the portions of arable land to be given to them. While the charters were being drawn up, existing relations between serfs and nobles were to remain in place.
- After two years, 'obligated peasants' could buy their homes and land if the owner wanted to sell it. Nobles were largely accommodating and, by 1881, 85 per cent of former serfs had become owners of their allotments.
- Peasants were restricted by a maximum allowance of land they could buy. This allowed landowners to trim their holdings so that 75 per cent of allotments bought were less than four dessyatinas (about 11 acres). The minimum land required to feed a peasant family was five dessyatinas, so peasants were farming about 20 per cent less land than before, on average.
- Peasants had to pay 'redemption dues' annually for 49 years at 6 per cent interest. These were effectively mortgages on their land and were calculated not on acreage, but on the obligations they had paid to nobles before 1861. These had never been recorded before and so many nobles managed to inflate the obligations owed to them. Redemption dues were a way for the Tsarist regime to reimburse nobles for the loss of free labour.
- The village commune (*mir*) was made responsible for collecting redemption dues and peasants were only released from the commune (*mir*) when redemptions were fully paid, which would take 49 years.

- State peasants received slightly better treatment as they were given plots of land twice the size of privately owned serfs, although they had to wait until 1866 for their freedom.
- Household or 'personal' serfs were the most poorly treated. They received no land, just their freedom from domestic servitude.

Alexander II has been called 'the Tsar Liberator', and many historians have seen the *Ukase* of 1861 as an epochal event. However, the immediate aftermath suggests quite the contrary. Michael Lynch (2013) explains that peasants – 'dark masses' according to some at court – were seen as a threat throughout Alexander II's reign: 'Beneath the generous words in which emancipation had been couched was a belief that the common people of Russia, unless controlled and directed, were a very real threat to the existing order of things. Whatever emancipation may have offered to the peasants, it was not genuine liberty.' (http://www.historytoday.com/michael-lynch/emancipation-russian-serfs-1861-charter-freedom-or-act-betrayal)

The so-called 'emancipation' legislation had in fact reduced the land available to peasants and therefore perpetuated their dependence upon the nobility; it compelled them to work for the nobility under conditions that had much in common with those of serfdom, as peasants still needed to use nobles' land to earn enough money to make a living. The redemption payments, along with the historic payments peasants had to make to nobles in order to use their land, put an enormous strain on the rural economy. Serfs who had been supposedly 'freed' were now economically enslaved in many cases. For them, this was not 'emancipation', even though serfdom had been abolished; now, instead of paying the landlord, they were simply paying the state. Formerly state-owned peasants gained slightly greater benefits in legislation of 1866 and many became **kulaks**, that is, wealthier peasants who were able to hire labourers to work on their land and then sell their goods for profit.

There was deep resentment among peasants as it was felt that the abolition statutes had not freed everyone equally. There were 647 peasant disturbances in 1861 and the army had to be mobilised to restore order in 449 of them. In Bezdna, peasants rose up against their landlords and around 100 were killed when soldiers were ordered to fire into the crowds. Many radical critics, who had argued that the peasants should be given the land they worked on for free, felt vindicated not only on moral grounds, but on practical ones. The ***Ukase*** had completely ignored the peasant belief that land belonged to those who worked on it. The newly 'freed' peasants couldn't afford to meet the fiscal demands now placed on them and consequently many fell into arrears.

The abolition of serfdom was deeply disturbing for the landed nobility, too. Compensation granted to them via redemption payments was not sufficient to prevent a steady decline in noble landownership following 1861. Historians such as Acton (1995) and Smith (2012) agree that a growing proportion of the nobility began to lose their land altogether; Smith suggests that between 1861 and 1905 the rural nobility lost up to 1 per cent of its land per year[5]. This contributed to growing disillusionment with the regime. Rural nobles were also increasingly threatened by a growing professionalism in the army and civil service. Even nobles

Key term

Kulaks: a class of relatively affluent farmers that emerged after Prime Minister Stolypin's reforms of 1866 (see the section 'Stolypin's land reforms'). According to Marxist-Leninist philosophy, they were class enemies of the poorer peasants; under Lenin, *kulaks* meant anyone who refused to hand over grain during requisitioning. Under Stalin these farmers were terrorised during collectivisation.

who retained their land often resented the government's greater investments in heavy industry following 1861; they felt they were being left to deal with mounting peasant disturbances on their own. Many in the province of Tula called for greater involvement in local government, partly to shore up the influence of their class and partly to express their frustration with the inadequacies of provincial administration. The nobles of Tver went further, suggesting that the new laws were slipshod and that the only way to remedy them was to create an assembly of elected representatives with the specific purpose of solving the problems emancipation had created.

Attempts at domestic and military reform

Changes to the military

Alexander II's attitude to tradition was clearly different to that of his father's, who believed in preserving Russian traditions at all costs. Nowhere was this more apparent than in the military reforms he passed almost immediately after the signing of the Treaty of Paris in 1856. Many soldiers were demobilised (taken out of active service) as Alexander realised that Russia needed more men in reserve in case of war, rather than such an extensive standing army. By 1858, all military colonies had been dissolved and in 1859 Alexander reduced military service from 25 years to 15.

Alexander then appointed Dmitrii Miliutin as Minister of War in 1861, and the changes introduced by Miliutin, a former army officer turned reform-minded bureaucrat, proved to be the most far-reaching army reforms ever carried out in Russia. Firstly, he made every male Russian liable for military service (this would have been impossible before the emancipation of the serfs), while reducing the period of service for the educated classes to six years' active service and 14½ years in the reserves; this stopped the nobility from feeling they were being conscripted like peasants. Consequently, the size of the army actually increased because fewer men tried to opt out; by 1877, the Russians were able to call up more than 750 000 reserve troops to fight in a war that broke out with Turkey. Miliutin also established *gymnasia* (schools that focused on academic learning) for aspiring officers and military personnel, where the curriculum was similar to that of contemporary secondary schools, in an effort to produce more well-rounded officers.

Financial reform

The Minister of Finance, Mikhail von Reutern, took his lead from Miliutin and accelerated the introduction of changes at the Ministry of Finance. He suggested that all ministries set budgets a year in advance; auditors could then compare past budgets with projections. This reflective system would make it easier for the regime to borrow money from abroad like other European countries, as it would help inspire trust. Large loans were made available to industrialists and, as a result, railway building expanded twenty-fold. Reutern also presided over the abolition of tax-farming, a system where the state transferred the right of collection to private individuals called 'tax farmers' in exchange for a certain fee. Under this system, the tax farmers became very rich and only about a third of the revenue collected made it into the Treasury coffers. A particular area of success was vodka, where the excise tax that replaced the old farming method actually made the liquor cheaper and allowed retail merchants to invest in railways, banks and mines. It was also a victory for the average peasant, who could now regularly afford this small luxury.

Educational reform: universities

Soon after ascending to the throne, Alexander had relaxed constraints on universities that had been imposed by his father Nicholas I. The Ministry of Education started to allow women to attend lectures, stopped monitoring

 Voices from the past

Anna Karenina by Leo Tolstoy is a classic novel written against the backdrop of the sweeping changes taking place throughout Russia in this period. A key theme in the novel is the contrast between the old patriarchal values sustaining the landowning aristocracy and the new, liberal values of the Westernisers. Here, the character of Levin is talking to another landowner:

'Well, and how is your land doing?' asked Levin.

'Oh, still just the same, always at a loss,' the landowner answered with a resigned smile, but with an expression of serenity and conviction that so it must be. 'And how do you come to be in our province?' he asked. 'Come to take part in our coup d'état?' he said, confidently pronouncing the French words with a bad accent. 'All Russia's here – gentlemen of the bedchamber, and everything short of the ministry.' He pointed to the imposing figure of Stepan Arkadyevitch in white trousers and his court uniform, walking by with a general.

'I ought to own that I don't very well understand the drift of the provincial elections,' said Levin.

The landowner looked at him.

'Why, what is there to understand? There's no meaning in it at all. It's a decaying institution that goes on running only by the force of inertia. Just look, the very uniforms tell you that it's an assembly of justices of the peace, permanent members of the court, and so on, but not of noblemen.'

'Then why do you come?' asked Levin.

'From habit, nothing else. Then, too, one must keep up connections. It's a moral obligation of a sort. And then, to tell the truth, there's one's own interests. My son-in-law wants to stand as a permanent member; they're not rich people, and he must be brought forward.

These gentlemen, now, what do they come for?' he said, pointing to the malignant gentleman, who was talking at the high table.

'That's the new generation of nobility.'

'New it may be, but nobility it isn't. They're proprietors of a sort, but we're the landowners. As noblemen, they're cutting their own throats.'

'But you say it's an institution that's served its time.'

'That it may be, but still it ought to be treated a little more respectfully. ... We may be of use, or we may not, but we're the growth of a thousand years. If we're laying out a garden, planning one before the house, you know, and there you've a tree that's stood for centuries in the very spot ... Old and gnarled it may be, and yet you don't cut down the old fellow to make room for the flowerbeds, but lay out your beds so as to take advantage of the tree. You won't grow him again in a year,' he said cautiously, and he immediately changed the conversation. 'Well, and how is your land doing?'

'Oh, not very well. I make five per cent.'

Anna Karenina – Oxford World Classics, with an introduction by Malcolm Bradbury 1999. Part 6: Chapter 29, page 802.

Discussion points:
1. What are the key problems facing the landowning classes according to Levin?
2. Levin and the other landowner seem to be lamenting the rise of the new nobility. Why could this be?
3. Some have suggested Tolstoy is making a political point in this section about working for the public good being an avoidance of seeking personal fulfilment first. Can you provide evidence from the text to support this view?

students' behaviour off campus, introduced contentious subjects that involved students questioning ideas, such as the history of philosophy and law, abolished entry quotas and abolished fees for the less well off. Significantly, the Ministry also allowed forward-looking professors to teach in Russia's universities; one example was Konstantin Kavelin, who was employed at St Petersburg in 1861 and was a prime advocate of conferring land as well as liberty on the peasants. Although the student body remained small (just under 5000 by 1860) the removal of entry quotas meant young people who had been denied access to university under Nicholas I could now attend. Consequently, the average age of students increased (nowadays they would be referred to as 'mature students'), and these older students tended to be more politically engaged. The government's 'liberal' approach had thus helped turn universities into a powder-keg. Staff and students became more outspoken and organised, serving to increase political instability.

Local government

After the Emancipation *Ukase*, perhaps the most important changes carried out in Russia were those made to local government in 1863. Severing the link between the nobility and peasants left an administrative vacuum in the countryside. The first solution proposed was to put military commanders in control of the provinces and appoint 'district captains' to enact their decrees. Large numbers of the rural nobility were appalled, including Nikolai Miliutin, the brother of Dimitrii, Minister of War, who launched vocal opposition in newspaper columns. Miliutin was put in charge of local government reform, and began to consider how the countryside could be kept under control by the state. In 1861 a new level of local administration was added, the *volosti,* which were bodies that grouped together *mirs* (peasant communes) to provide administrative and judicial units. The executive board was elected by the peasantry whom they served, and they were therefore representative bodies; really, however, the *volosti* were principally intended to make it easier for St Petersburg to pressurise rural communities. Because they were peasant-only institutions, the *volosti* served to widen the gap between peasants and the privileged; therefore, new assemblies had to be created to ensure the new social orders interacted with each other. These new local assemblies – **zemstva**, as they came to be known – were implemented in 1864 and seemed not only to represent provincial society but to possess considerable authority. The men who joined the *zemstva* were primarily from the professional classes and the nobility; by 1900, about 70 000 doctors, lawyers, teachers and agronomists had joined their ranks. It could be argued that historians have placed too much significance on the formation of local government institutions, as only 43 out of 70 provinces had *zemstva* assemblies by 1900. However, where they existed the *zemstva* had the power to raise taxes and the right to oversee local education, medical care, prisons and road maintenance; even though they did not have the power to enforce their decisions, had no jurisdiction over the *volosti*, and were watched closely by the central administration, they represented a step towards representative government: the delegates were elected by all members of the district for a term of three years from among the local landowners and *volosti* delegates.

Educational reform: schools

Private individuals made immediate huge difference to primary education around 1860, as Sunday schools were set up by volunteers to educate the illiterate peasantry. Over 500 had sprung up by 1862, providing lessons in History, French, German and basic reading. The Third Section believed the schools to be hotbeds of sedition and by June 1862 they had been closed down. In 1863, statutes to expand primary education were passed, but with severe limitations: attendance would be voluntary and subject to a fee, and curricula had to be centrally managed by the state. Primary education was to cover reading and writing (in Russian only), religion and arithmetic. There was a lack of willingness on behalf of the government to promote education amongst the peasantry. Despite this, over 1 000 000 children attended primary school by 1878 (up from 450 000 in 1856). *Gymnasia* were introduced at secondary level: these were very academic institutions, from which pupils could move on to university if they passed the final exams. Traditional curricula were maintained here, too, and Greek and Latin were stressed over the sciences.

Judicial reforms

The statutes that brought emancipation to an end in 1861 also stimulated the introduction of *volost* courts, which dealt exclusively with the peasantry. In this respect, peasants did not achieve legal parity with the rest of society and in this sense, too, were not truly 'liberated'. The nobility would have to wait until 1864 to benefit from legal reform.

The old legal system was at best slow and at worst corrupt: in criminal cases the defendant was guilty until proven innocent and there were no juries or lawyers. Judges sat behind closed doors relying only upon police evidence and court cases were not open to the public. To combat corruption and deliver a more efficient judicial system, five tiers of courts were created in 1864, modelled on Western European legal systems. The *zemstva* would elect Justices of the Peace (JPs) to deal with minor offences, and joint JP sessions constituted the second tier. Judges were appointed at the remaining levels, which were: circuit courts, including magistrates and district courts, which generally heard criminal cases; judicial tribunals, modelled on the French system; and the Senate, the highest of all courts, which acted as a court of appeal. Judges' pay was increased to make them less likely to take bribes, and the profession of barrister was introduced, so that trials became much more like British trials. Juries were also introduced so that trials were open and more fairly practised at all levels.

These legal reforms caused the regime a great deal of trouble, however. The most famous case is that of Vera Zasulich, daughter of an army captain, who shot Fyodor Trepov (Governor of the City of St Petersburg) in 1878, allegedly because he had given an order to flog a political prisoner for rude behaviour. Zasulich was charged with attempted murder and put before a jury in St Petersburg. At her widely publicised trial the sympathetic jury found Zasulich not guilty, demonstrating the courts' ability to stand up to the authorities. This outcome was influenced by Zasulich's very good lawyer, who turned the case on its head so that, as Ulam (1977) notes, it 'very soon became obvious that it was Colonel Trepov rather than his would-be assassin who was really being tried.'[6]

Censorship

In 1855, Alexander II abolished the censorship committee, demonstrating his willingness to allow a certain amount of freedom of the press. He never considered abolishing censorship altogether and no one really expected him to. After 1855 responsibility for censorship fell jointly on the Minister of Education and the Minister of Internal Affairs; in 1863 the latter was given full control. In 1865, Alexander issued the 'Temporary Rules' on press freedom, which remained in place until 1905, allowing periodicals to print materials without gaining prior approval. However, editors were made personally responsible for any printed materials and could be punished either by court trial or directly by the Minister of Internal Affairs. A flurry of texts and journals were published the same year as the 'spirit of reform' swept through Russia; once texts had been circulated they were much harder to control.

The censorship reforms of 1865 finally exhausted Alexander II's drive for change: the last 16 years of his reign were almost absent of government innovation. The death of Alexander's eldest son in 1865 and the first attempt on his life in 1866 had a significant impact on the Tsar. He replaced many of the reform-minded ministers with old conservatives, most notably at the Ministries of Education (Tolstoy replaced Golovnin) and Internal Affairs (Timashev replaced Valuev) and the Third Section (Shuvalov replaced Dolgorukov). That Alexander felt he had done enough by 1865 supports the assertion that his reputation as the 'Tsar Liberator', as he became known, is ill deserved: he was not keen on reform at first, but was pressured by the effects of the Crimean War and the reform-minded ministers around him.

ACTIVITY 1.2

Use your notes to complete a table like the one below on the reforms during the reign of Alexander II.

	Improvements	Weaknesses
Education: universities		
Financial reforms		
Local government		
Education: schools		
Judicial reforms		
Censorship		

Government and Tsars

Alexander II and Alexander III as rulers; attitudes to and imposition of autocracy; key developments

Reforms under Alexander II: assessment

The new era of conservatism only highlighted the weaknesses of some of the reforms made in the first 10 years of Alexander II's reign. It took the regime 10 years to force the nobility into military service. It took Reutern six years to reorganise the state's collection of revenue and he failed to extend the new auditing system to cover the state's investment in railways. The policies of the new ministers after 1865 often exacerbated inherent weaknesses. Dimitri Tolstoy at the Ministry of Education did create teacher-training colleges but state expenditure on education was limited to six per cent (compared to 40 per cent expenditure on the military). Tolstoy also had an additional role as **Procurator of the Holy Synod**, reasserting the influence of the Church on education. He made it impossible for students to attend university unless they had studied a certain amount of Latin and Greek, and reduced the time allowed for all other subjects. Although universities were educating 60 per cent more students in 1880 than in 1859, the general population had grown at the same rate in that period.

What most undermined Alexander II's reforms was his outright refusal to allow a representative national assembly. Even his brother, Grand Duke Konstantin Nikolaievich, returned to the subject constantly. But Alexander, on this issue at least, was resolute: he wanted to maintain autocracy and so he had to remain the central authority in Russia. As Hugh Seton-Watson (1967) argues, this attitude was perhaps his biggest failing: the *zemstva* had given the nobility and the peasantry a taste of participation in politics and they wanted more. After 1866 and the first attempt on his life, Alexander was forced to concede that he would have to introduce a new political institution that might satisfy both the liberal nobles on the *zemstva* and the radicals who tried to take his life. Count M.T. Loris-Melikov was given the enormous task of creating a new cabinet-like advisory body that would resemble the constitutional institution the Tsar's critics wanted. The proposals he developed were nothing like the national assembly that the *zemstva* or the radicals wanted but they might have opened the way for more concessions later if they had ever been approved. Loris-Melikov was successful in securing the Tsar's agreement to the disbandment of the hated Third Section: it is perhaps ironic that Alexander's assassination on 13 March 1866 came just after the police force entrusted with state security had been abolished.

It could be argued that the nobility were the biggest losers after emancipation, despite retaining the greatest share of the best land, receiving compensation for land lost, and dominating the new assemblies (the *zemstva*). By 1905 they owned 40 per cent less land than they had in 1861, mostly because they could no longer run their estates profitably now they had to pay for labour. Even the expanding civil service was no longer reserved just for the nobility, as more and more members of an educated middle-class graduated from university. The members of the growing numbers of organised opposition parties that flourished under Alexander II were drawn from the nobility and educated elite, groups that for different reasons were disillusioned with emancipation and the impact of the reforms. Alexander II ultimately failed to convince the radical intelligentsia that political pressure or even assassination attempts would persuade him to concede his ultimate authority. The peasants, despite the economic burdens they incurred in emancipation, now had access to education and legal rights, and so their prospects did improve under Alexander II. As Saunders (1992) suggests, 'there can be little doubt that they [the reforms] marked a radical break with the past'[7].

Alexander III: unshakeable autocracy?

On 13 March 1881 Tsar Alexander II was assassinated in broad daylight on his way to the Winter Palace. His son, now Alexander III, had no intention of falling victim to the same fate and wanted to demonstrate to Russia that he was decisive and strong-willed, unlike his father. His instincts were opposed to his father's liberal path. He surrounded himself with conservatives such as the journalist Mikhail Katkov, who blamed liberals for Alexander II's death. Konstantin Pobedonostsev, who had been Alexander III's tutor and was to become Minister of Internal Affairs, said Loris-Melikov's proposals had been 'a deception based on a foreign model that is unsuitable for Russia'[8]. Pobedonostsev published a *Manifesto on Unshakable Autocracy* on 29 April 1881, in which he suggested that Russian monarchs should rule 'with faith in the strength and truth of the autocratic power that we have been called upon to affirm and safeguard for the popular good from any infringement'. Four ministers who had served Alexander II, including Loris-Melikov, resigned the following day. Alexander III set about implementing reforms to counter those of his father, setting the tone for his reign. A crackdown on dissidents began immediately, with the execution of the five assassins (see the section 'Radicals'), a nationwide police offensive and 10 000 arrests.

Re-establishing control

Yet for all of Alexander III's reactionary policies aimed at preventing opposition, the Tsar was of the opinion that Russia needed to industrialise rapidly (see the section 'Economic and social developments'). He needed peace to allow this to happen and this was his justification for keeping Russia under such oppressive control. Therefore, the first decade of his reign was aimed at curbing the forces of sedition by augmenting the power of the autocratic state.

The *Okhrana*

Alexander III introduced a new instrument of control and repression, which came to be known as the *Okhrana*. This force took over many of the duties of the old Third Section secret police, though at first it was fairly small. Its main target for surveillance was the educated class: newspaper editors, teachers, university professors and students. However, whole towns or even provinces could be designated 'areas of subversion' under supposedly temporary legislation, and provincial governors were given extraordinary powers to search, fine, arrest or deport individuals within such areas without evidence. Between 1881 and 1894 the Ministry of Internal Affairs approved the exile of 5000 'dissidents', mostly to Siberia. In 1882 one 'temporary law' tightened censorship, making it difficult to distribute or sell publications that were seen to be critical of the government in any way; editors were threatened with life bans if found guilty of publishing 'harmful' works. In 1884 a new statute was passed that completely destroyed any autonomy enjoyed by university professors in terms of what was taught and

Nationalism was a potent force in this period. The strong nation-states of France and Great Britain inspired jealousy throughout the rest of Europe. This led groups elsewhere in Europe, such as German intellectuals, to argue that there existed a 'national spirit' that could unify a people. Many subjugated European language groups argued in the 19th century that they should have their own nation-state. In Eastern Europe, Polish nationalism led to the Polish Revolt of 1863; in Austria, the Magyars' claim to an independent Kingdom of Hungary was one cause of the 1848 revolution there. A particularly compelling nationalist force known as Pan-Slavism also began to circulate among various Slavic groups in Russia, Poland and Austria. Tsar Alexander III was easily swept up in these currents, given his own beliefs about the supremacy of Russian culture.

who was teaching. By 1887, the Church had begun to take back full control over primary education and significant financial barriers had been put in place to deter young peasants from entering education.

Local government

In 1889, Alexander III wanted to reward the nobles who had remained loyal to the regime and to reinforce the traditional social structures in Russia. He introduced 'Land Captains', who could exercise substantial administrative (especially tax collection), judicial and police authority over peasants in the district. It was an unprecedented assertion of Tsarist authority in the countryside, and the role of Land Captain effectively replaced that of the elected Justice of the Peace established in 1864.

In 1890 the *zemstvo* were restructured, giving the peasantry fewer voting rights in the election of members, cementing noble dominance. In addition to the new voting procedures, every elected member now had to be approved by the Minister of the Interior. Some of these measures must be seen as Alexander III attempting to get a grip on the questions of tax collection and absenteeism from assembly meetings, which his father had never managed to do. However, newly established 'closed' courts and more severe conditions in prison demonstrated the regime's determination to control dissent at all levels of society. The historian Chubarov (1999) has described Alexander III's reign as being characterised by 'continuous reaction … political stagnation with growing aggressiveness'[9] towards any attempt to undermine the autocratic power of the monarch. If Alexander III really wanted to modernise Russia through industrialisation, he would also have to modernise the country's institutions. He did not do so and therefore failed to stamp out opposition as he had wished.

Political authority in action

There was an extensive gulf between the mythology of autocracy as imagined by Russia's inhabitants, where the Tsar wielded unrestricted power as head of state, and the complexities of dealing with such a vast empire on a daily basis. This was nowhere more evident than in Alexander III's approach to ethnic minorities. Nationalism was a potent idea sweeping throughout Europe in the 19th century. Alexander III combined it with his grandfather's old doctrine of 'Official Nationality' to push a vision of 'Russian' national characteristics as superior to those of the nations subjugated within the Russian Empire, as well as Russia's European neighbours. Nationality became an increasingly divisive issue across the empire and would weaken the Russian state by antagonising non-Russians, engendering hatred for the Tsarist regime.

Russification

The idea that all things Russian were superior led to a particularly pernicious policy under Alexander III called 'Russification'. The policy was not so much intended to cement the unity of the empire as to bring the 'dangerous' elements on its fringes under state control. A whole battery of discriminatory legislation was devised that aimed to suppress all manifestations of 'non-Russian' identity, as well as to crush any non-Orthodox religious practices.

This approach was in contrast to that of Alexander II, who had taken a slightly more liberal approach to the empire's ethnic and national minorities during his reign. He had allowed the publication of the first Ukrainian-language journal and the setting up of societies called *bromady* that celebrated Ukrainian culture. Alexander II had also allowed Jews – historically the most harshly treated of all the minorities – into universities and government service. Some Jews were allowed to settle outside the 'Pale of Settlement' (an area which today covers central Poland and Ukraine), where they had been forced to live for centuries. The Finns were given their own parliament (*Diet*) and could use their own currency by the 1860s. Poland was granted its own Archbishop, and in 1857 Polish intellectuals were permitted to found the 'Agricultural Society', which became a forum for debating political ideas. However, in 1863 when 200 000 Poles rose up to demand self-determination Alexander II acted decisively in putting down the rebellion, and limited any further freedoms for minorities. By 1876, schools could no longer teach children in Ukrainian (or, as the edict insultingly referred to it, 'Little Russian').

Treatment of ethnic minorities and Jews

Alexander III sought to use religion as a way of homogenising the empire. In the Baltic regions, land was given to the landless if they became Orthodox and financial support was made available to schools that agreed to be placed under the control of the Orthodox Church. It is estimated that 37 000 Lutherans had undergone conversion to Orthodoxy by 1894 (though many returned to Lutheranism after laws were relaxed in 1905). Catholic monasteries were closed down in Poland and an 'All-Russian Orthodox Missionary Society' was established. By 1894 the society claimed that 60 000 'heathens' and Muslims had become Orthodox as a result of its work.

The Jewish population suffered the most direct religious discrimination. Alexander III was openly anti-Semitic at court and under his rule special legislation was passed to restrict the rights of Jewish people. Their choice of employment was severely limited and they were no longer allowed to enter government service. Jewish access to education was limited by quotas: in the Pale of Settlement, only 10 per cent of schoolchildren could come from Jewish families, and this was reduced to five per cent across the rest of the empire. There were also increased **pogroms** on Jewish communities (violent attacks on property, synagogues and individuals); Tsarist authorities almost always turned a blind eye to these attacks. It is perhaps unsurprising that many radical revolutionary groups found it easy to recruit young Jewish men to their ranks after the 1870s.

Opposition

Both Alexander II and Alexander III faced opposition during their reigns. What was striking about the hostility that developed from 1855 onwards was that it came from circles that had traditionally been loyal to the Tsars. Apart from when the Decembrists had attempted a *coup d'état* against Nicholas I in St Petersburg in 1825, the gentry had usually acted as a reliable agent of the monarch. Nicholas I had hanged the ring leaders of the Decembrist uprising and exiled their associates, but the idea they had expounded – that Russia needed to change – was not lost

Summary of key events

- Alexander II had instigated some reforms in 1861 and in the years that followed, but they were too limited in scope to satisfy radicals, who assassinated him in 1881.

- Alexander III was a reactionary Tsar who feared being assassinated like his father; he therefore ensured that as little liberalisation as possible occurred and instigated widespread repression.

- Alexander III implemented a ruthless policy of Russification in an attempt to suppress the different nationalities and ethnicities within the empire. His policies placed 'Russianness' above any other cultural identity.

amongst the younger generation, who often saw these men as heroes. This next generation spawned Alexander II's killers and would continue to be a thorn in the side of Alexander III.

Liberal and radical groups

Liberals

Though the *zemstva* were 'all-class' institutions, they were dominated by fairly conservative nobility and professionals; they were not the tireless champions of the peoples' rights that some have claimed. They began to emerge in the 1880s as centres of opposition to the bureaucracy, and eventually to the autocracy as well. They began to resist Alexander III's encroachments on their activities and funds. In 1890, Ivan Durnovo, the new Minister of the Interior, limited the power of the zemstva by making appointments the responsibility of the governor and giving him the power of veto over their decisions. Despite these restrictions, the *zemstva* increased their work in health, education, welfare and agriculture from 1890 onwards as expenditure doubled. Alexander's interference had benefited neither the state nor the *zemstva*, provoking only new tensions.

Radicals

According to Chubarov (1999), the Russian intelligentsia in this period can be characterised as having a strong social consciousness and an 'anti-bourgeois' mentality, as well as a sense of alienation from the state. Perhaps the two most influential members of the intelligentsia in the 1860s were Alexander Herzen and Nicholas Chernychevsky. They believed that the village commune (*mir*) could become the best social structure for the realisation of the collectivist instincts of the individual. Herzen was particularly fervent in his insistence that Russians must find a solution within her peasant institutions; he believed that due to Russia's unique social make-up it would be out of the peasant commune that the revolution would emerge. Chernychevsky was influenced by Russian authors such as Ivan Turgenev, whose novel *Fathers and Sons* (1862) featured a nihilist called Bazarov. Nihilists rejected Russian institutions and believed the empire needed radical change. In 1863, Chernychevsky wrote *What is to be done?*. It was a work of fiction and so slipped past the censors, but it gave some stirring descriptions of co-operative workers' associations of the future. It caused a sensation amongst university students, and heroes of the novel such as Rakhmentov – who sleeps on wooden planks studded with nails to steel himself for the revolution – became prototypes upon whom generations of radicals consciously modelled themselves. Years later, a schoolboy from Simbirsk, Vladimir Ulianov, better known as Lenin, would read the novel, and he later set down his own ideas about revolution in a book with the same title: *What is to be done?*.

The writings of Herzen and Chernychevsky helped lay the foundations for the ideas of Mikhail Bakunin (1814–76) and the Narodniks (*narod* in Russian means 'the people', and 'Narodniks' can be translated as **Populists**). The Populists believed Russia would inevitably reach socialism (a society of equals) through the survival of the *mir*, because the *mir* was founded on egalitarian principles, thus ensuring basic equality of wealth and a smooth transition into a new social order. They proposed the transition would occur through transferring all land to the peasants, lifting the burdens of taxation and removing administrative and police controls. Bakunin hoped this would ultimately be achieved by a spontaneous peasant uprising, helped along by small groups that would help villagers believe in the need to unite in the struggle for their liberation. Sergei Nechaev was an intellectual who participated in the 'conspiratorial trend' that emerged within the intelligentsia during the 1860s, in which radicals plotted assassination attempts to bring down the regime. He wrote *Catechism of a Revolutionary* (1869), in which he explained the code of rules by which the revolutionaries should be guided. He said revolutionaries should sever all ties with society and give up their interests and even feelings, thereby devoting themselves to a single thought: the revolution. This amoral approach led him to murder one of his circle after a disagreement; he died in prison for his crime. It is important to note that some of the intelligentsia rejected Nechaev's amoralism. The Tchaikovsky Circle was one such group. The Circle was founded in St Petersburg during the student unrest of 1868–9 as a literary society for self-education. Its initial purpose was to share books and knowledge that had been banned in the Russian empire; other main tasks came to include linking students in St Petersburg with students in other cities and conducting propaganda among workers and peasants with the purpose of fomenting a social revolution. This project included smuggling copies of Marx's *Das Kapital* into Russia.

By the 1870s, a number of groups under the ideological influence of Bakunin, Nechaev and others initiated the so-called 'going to the people' movement, whereby hundreds of students donned peasant clothing and went into the countryside to educate the peasantry about their plight, with hopes of sparking a revolution. They found the people wholly unreceptive, loyal to their Tsar and to God; they were suspicious of these non-peasant outsiders who had tried to mimic their accents. One such populist, Mikhail Romas, sailed 30 miles down the Volga River to a small village to set up a co-operative store. He hoped to rescue the peasants from merchants by selling them cheap manufactured goods. The peasants could not understand why his prices were so cheap and they refused to buy from him, ultimately murdering one of his assistants and setting light to the store. Romas was then blamed for the fire and forced to flee for his life.

The 'going to the people' movement failed miserably, and split the revolutionaries between those who wanted to continue with propaganda and agitation, working with the peasants (this group became 'Black Partition'), and those who wanted to use terrorism to stage a political coup. The latter became known as 'People's Will' and consisted of about 30 intellectuals who resolved to bring down the oppressive regime by assassinating the key political leaders, including Tsar Alexander II. Others had tried to assassinate the Tsar, but those attempts had been in response to particular events. For example, Dmitrii Karakosov, who carried out the first assassination attempt in 1866, shot at the Tsar out of revenge for the deception of the peasants after emancipation. People's Will was the first group to seek the Tsar's assassination as a means of achieving social transformation. After a number of attempts, Ignacy Hryniewiecki, a member of the group, was finally successful in killing the Tsar. The popular response to the assassination included anti-Semitic pogroms in Ukraine (Jews were often scapegoats for dreadful events). Alexander III sentenced his father's assassins to death by public hanging. As it turned out, the effect of the assassination was not to destroy autocracy but rather to lead the system to adopt even more repressive policies.

Opposition: ideas and ideologies: Marxism, individuals and radical groups

The Communist Manifesto

Born on 5 May 1818 into a middle-class Jewish family in Germany, Karl Heinrich Marx was probably the most influential political philosopher of the 19th and 20th centuries. His message is most clearly set out in the pamphlet he wrote in 1848 with Friedrich Engels: *The Communist Manifesto*. He was the first to set out the far-reaching powers of modern industry and chart the astounding transformation of society under the emergence of global capitalism. He was also the first to recognise the inherent tendency within capitalism to invent new needs and the means to satisfy them, not only subverting but obliterating cultural practices and hierarchies, turning everything into an object for sale. Stedman-Jones (1967) argues that what was unique about Marx's *Manifesto* was 'its unflinchingly modernist vision, in which the capitalist world market was not simply identified with destabilisation and exploitation but also with a liberating power, the power to release people from backwardness and tradition-bound experience'[10].

His unique vision has attracted many thousands of young people all over the world. The *Manifesto* presents Marx's analysis in the form of predictions, not principles, and in this way it convinced his early followers that revolution was inevitable. Marx introduces his theory of socialism as a scientific discovery based on his materialist conception of history. Historical materialism looks for the causes of developments and changes in human society in the means by which humans collectively produce the necessities of life. Contemporary economic activity goes hand in hand with social classes, which are interrelated with the political structures and ways of thinking in society. The key to Marx's vision of history is the control of the means of production by a particular social class that could then use this control to exploit the labour of the rest. As one class becomes dominant, it establishes its own political, religious and cultural institutions that reflect its own self-interest. The supremacy of this class, however, can never be permanent because it will always be overthrown by the oppressed. Thus, history proceeds as a continuing struggle between classes. Using this approach, Marx singles out five socio-economic formations: primitive society, slavery, feudalism, capitalism and communism. The central idea in Marx's analysis of capitalism was that the present phase of history, dominated by the bourgeoisie, had brought a remarkable 'acceleration' in global development.

The starting point of *The Communist Manifesto* is an evaluation of the declared antagonist, the bourgeoisie (those who own most of society's wealth and the means of production). Unexpectedly, Marx writes that their achievement in creating 'productive forces' is greater than the building of the Egyptian pyramids. Yet for him the end is nigh for this triumphant class; it will be destroyed by the 'proletariat' – the modern working class – that it has created.

'*The weapons with which the bourgeoisie felled feudalism to the ground are now turned against the bourgeoisie itself. But not only has the bourgeoisie forged the weapons that bring death to itself; it has also called into existence the men who are to wield those weapons — the modern working class — the proletarians.*' Stedman-Jones GS. Introduction. In Marx K. and Engels F. *The Communist Manifesto*, Penguin; 1967, p.226.

The sequence of events was inexorable: the bourgeoisie would antagonise the proletariat by driving it to utter destitution and poverty, thus provoking an uprising that would destroy capitalism altogether, leading to an egalitarian society of the workers. But Russia hadn't been affected by industrialisation until the 1880s, and so the earlier radical groups, such as the Populists and university students, had largely ignored Marx's theory as applicable for Western Europeans, not Russians. They accepted his criticisms of capitalism and the bourgeoisie, but

 Hidden voices

Extract from *The Communist Manifesto*

Modern bourgeois society, with its relations of production, of exchange and of property, a society that has conjured up such gigantic means of production and of exchange, is like the sorcerer who is no longer able to control the powers of the nether world whom he has called up by his spells. For many a decade past, the history of industry and commerce is but the history of the revolt of modern productive forces against modern conditions of production, against the property relations that are the conditions for the existence of the bourgeois and of its rule. It is enough to mention the commercial crises that by their periodical return put the existence of the entire bourgeois society on its trial, each time more threateningly. In these crises, a great part not only of the existing products, but also of the previously created productive forces, are periodically destroyed. In these crises, there breaks out an epidemic that, in all earlier epochs, would have seemed an absurdity – the epidemic of over-production. Society suddenly finds itself put back into a state of momentary barbarism; it appears as if a famine, a universal war of devastation, had cut off the supply of every means of subsistence; industry and commerce seem to be destroyed; and why? Because there is too much civilisation, too much means of subsistence, too much industry, too much commerce. The productive forces at the disposal of society no longer tend to further the development of the conditions of bourgeois property; on the contrary, they have

become too powerful for these conditions, by which they are fettered, and so soon as they overcome these fetters, they bring disorder into the whole of bourgeois society, endanger the existence of bourgeois property. The conditions of bourgeois society are too narrow to comprise the wealth created by them. And how does the bourgeoisie get over these crises? On the one hand, by enforced destruction of a mass of productive forces; on the other, by the conquest of new markets, and by the more thorough exploitation of the old ones. That is to say, by paving the way for more extensive and more destructive crises, and by diminishing the means whereby crises are prevented.

The weapons with which the bourgeoisie felled feudalism to the ground are now turned against the bourgeoisie itself.

But not only has the bourgeoisie forged the weapons that bring death to itself; it has also called into existence the men who are to wield those weapons – the modern working class – the proletarians.

Discussion points:

1. 'What the bourgeoisie, therefore, produces, above all, is its own gravediggers.' Using the extract and your own knowledge, explain this quote from Marx.
2. According to Marx, why is it not possible to eliminate class antagonisms through political reforms that improve the workers' quality of life?
3. What is Marx's theory of history?

rejected his doctrine that Russia must follow a capitalist path where peasants would become factory hands or proletarians (workers). The famine of 1891–93 would help change this attitude, illustrating to many that the peasantry as a class was literally 'dying out'. This, coupled with the great strides that were beginning to be made in industrialisation and the associated growth of the towns, signalled to some that capitalism was coming to Russia.

The emergence of Russian Marxism

In the wake of the Populists' disastrous campaigns, **Marxists** emerged as a distinct group within the intelligentsia.

It is no coincidence that the resurgence of radicalism in Russia coincided with the great famine that began in 1891 (see the section 'Economic and social developments: industrial developments and the land issue; social divisions; nobles, landowners and the position of the peasantry'), and the consequent epidemics of cholera and typhus. The disaster was a reminder to many educated Russians that the country was economically backward and that industrial-scale change was necessary. Confronted by a regime that included staunch 'anti-modernists' such as Pobedonostsev (see the section 'Alexander III: unshakeable autocracy?'), who was determined to maintain the social order through brutal repression whilst facing the emergence of an industrialised proletariat, it is perhaps not surprising that many of the more radical members of the intelligentsia found Marx's political philosophy so appealing.

The first Russian Marxist group had been set up in Switzerland in 1883 by Georgi Plekhanov. The members of his small organisation, 'Emancipation of Labour', had been active *Narodniks* (see the section 'Radicals') in the past, but the failures of the 1870s had led them to re-evaluate their ideology. They now identified the urban working class as their base of support and Russia's main potential for revolution. (This was set against their former populist ideology, which had focused on Russia's rural peasantry.) Plekhanov analysed the situation in Russia from a Marxist perspective and wrote *Socialism and Political Struggle* (1883) to attract the intelligentsia to the revolutionary cause. He mapped out a two-stage revolutionary strategy: Russia was at the start of the capitalist stage, and a democratic movement by the workers in alliance with the bourgeoisie was needed before the socialist stage could commence. For decades, revolutionaries had rejected capitalism, but Marx's views, as explained by Plekhanov, began to gain ground with young radicals, as they appeared to prove in a scientific way that socialism was inevitable: history was on the side of the proletariat.

The Tsarist reaction to radicalism

On the face of it, Alexander II's regime had overestimated the security threats it faced in the earlier stages of his reign, as peasant disturbances had all but fallen away by 1863. This was perhaps because peasants found it easier to avoid paying taxes to the state than to a landlord, or because emancipation had removed day-to-day friction between landlords and serfs. A rash of illegally printed revolutionary pamphlets had been produced in 1862 and several fires had broken out across several cities, including the capital, which were believed to have been started by a group of university students calling themselves 'Young Russia'. Yet

Key term

Marxists: Followers of the political and economic theory expounded by Karl Marx and Friedrich Engels. Their theory placed class struggle at the centre of historical development.

those believed responsible were arrested swiftly and pressure from the nobility calling for a constitution sharply abated. The real turning points came in 1863, when the Polish revolted against imperial rule, and then in April 1866 with the attempt on the Tsar's life by an emotionally unstable radical student named Dmitrii Karakosov. These events severely shook the Tsar's advisers' confidence in liberal reforms. The assassination attempt seemed to instigate a rapid broadening of the ranks of educated public opinion outside officialdom. The attempt had followed the Populists' 'mad summer' of 'going to the people' (see the section 'Radicals') and it was felt that some political change should be made before mass propaganda could be circulated amongst the peasantry. The Vera Zasulich acquittal in 1878 (see the section 'Judicial reforms') had already helped undermine the regime's authority, but the Treaty of Berlin, signed to end the Russo-Turkish war in 1878, was even more humiliating and dealt a severe blow to Alexander II. The war had been fought against the Ottoman Empire to try and recoup territory and pride lost in the Crimean War. Russia had won the war but Britain and France had made her accept revised peace terms. This was quickly followed by the creation of 'People's Will' in 1879 (see the section 'Radicals'), which pronounced a death sentence on the Tsar himself, inducing near panic at government level.

There was no clear strategy about how to deal with the radical pressures facing the government, and leadership was not forthcoming from Alexander, who had been retreating ever further from public life to spend time with his mistress Catherine Dolgorukaya since his wife had fallen ill. This had caused a division not only in the royal family but in high society too, between those who supported the Tsar and those who sided with his dying wife. The traditional conservatives had sided with his wife, which left Alexander with the support of progressive-minded ministers such as General M.T. Loris-Melikov. It was Melikov's idea to broaden the base of support for the government by proposing that some representatives from outside government could sit on the State Council as advisers. This was not a constitution, but the move seemed to signal that autocracy was unsustainable and would inexorably lead to some form of constitutional monarchy. As usual, the Tsar hesitated at first, but did eventually accept consultative commissions on the issue on the same day he was assassinated.

Alexander III's attitude towards opposition was much more hostile. He reinstated the secret police, this time with extended powers, in order to 'pacify' the growing numbers of radicals seeking to undermine the Tsarist regime (see the section 'The Okhrana'). The major players in the revolutionary movements could no longer operate inside Russia because the *Okhrana* had agents in almost every building: even caretakers now became authorised government agents, required to report suspected illegal activities. Even this fearsome organisation, however, could not provide genuine permanent protection from the threat of revolutionaries, for it was riddled with incompetence, corruption and dishonesty – like many Russian institutions of the period. For example, Police Chief Krementskii had a national reputation for efficiency, each year successfully closing down three or four illegal printing presses; eventually, however, it was revealed that it was he who had ordered the presses to be set up in the first place, in order that he might then 'discover' them. The *Okhrana* used factory 'informers' to watch out for early signs of unrest by observing workers' conditions. However, they spent most of their time looking for the instigators of strikes, even though during 1886–94 there were on average only 33 strikes per year. By 1903, this had increased to 550 strikes, involving 138 877 workers.

In Alexander III's last four years on the throne, Russia seemed to be heading for more turmoil. In November 1890, four terrorists with links to Swiss bomb-makers were hanged. The 1891 famine increased revolutionary activity as peasants started to respond to calls for land redistribution. The trial and execution of Lenin's brother, Alexander Ulyanov, and his accomplices attracted attention to the revolutionary cause. By the time Alexander III, aged 49, died of a kidney complaint on 1 November 1894, his repressive policies seemed to have proven ineffectual at dampening hostility towards the regime in radical circles.

Economic and social developments

Industrial developments and the land issue

The defeat in the Crimean War had driven home the problem of Russia's economic backwardness. In 1860, she was the least economically developed country of the European powers, with only about 860 000 of her 74 million inhabitants employed in industry and a heavy reliance on the agricultural sector for national income. The reforms begun in 1861 formed a foundation for industrialisation, making mobilisation of money and men much easier and establishing a legal framework for securing property rights. Nonetheless, industrial growth remained slow for the following 25 years due to the regime's failure to lay down a clear economic policy.

Reutern's influence

Mikhail von Reutern, Minister of Finance under Alexander II (1862–78) oversaw a transition from Russia's traditional agriculturalist economy towards the industrialist economy that Sergei Witte, Minister of Finance under Nicholas II, would embrace fully upon taking office in 1892. Reutern had been extremely impressed by a visit to America and lamented the fact that enterprise had not yet swept through Russia as it had evidently swept through nations in the West. He wanted to secure the conditions to encourage private initiative (which had not been widespread in Russia) and planned to implement fiscal (economic) reform so that Russia would once again have a balanced budget with a new taxation system and stable currency. He had a huge task ahead of him, as state debt had reached 566 million rubles by 1857 and the Crimean War had caused a deficit of 64 million rubles, putting unsustainable strain on the banking system.

Reutern published a list of revenues and expenses in 1862 and introduced a government-wide system of accounting and book-keeping in the hope that this openness would encourage trust from foreign investors. Reutern was also successful in introducing the State Bank in 1860, which became the hub of private commercial banking, and abolishing the tax farming of vodka in 1863, which gave the state more control of vodka revenues and also helped peasants access cheaper alcohol (see the section 'Financial reform'). Reutern managed to bring state spending under control, particularly in military affairs. He only allowed major state investment in railways (by guaranteeing annual dividends to foreign investors whether or not lines were profitable). By 1883, common-carrier railways covered

14 700 miles, compared to 3000 in 1866. Industry underwent notable expansion, especially in textiles and metallurgy (due to British investment in particular), as areas such as the Donets Basin were developed in the 1860s as centres of iron and steel production. The Nobel brothers invested money in Baku in 1873 to found oil refineries, eventually establishing technical chemical research centres to complement their work there.

Even though private investment increased and the development of railways tied Russian agriculture to the international grain market, very little was done in the agricultural sector, and this accounted for Reutern's overall failure to stabilise the ruble (Russia's currency).

Reforms under Bunge

Nikolai Bunge, Minister of Finance under Alexander III (1881–87) undertook a number of reforms with the aim of modernising the Russian economy. He believed the country would be best served by making the peasants better producers of crops and wealth as well as turning them into consumers who would spend more. For these reasons, he consolidated the banking system and founded the Peasants' Land Bank in 1883, which helped peasants to purchase land (although it should be noted that the bank only helped in 20% of most peasant land purchases). He also introduced important changes to tax law because he wanted to shift dependence away from direct taxation and enhance the importance of indirect levies. The government had been slow to reform taxation during the 1860s–70s because they were wary of the upheaval caused by emancipation; it was only during the 1880s that they felt confident enough to make major financial reforms. To achieve this, Bunge reduced the poll tax that had been established under Peter the Great as a tax on households, eventually abolishing it altogether in 1886, despite the fact it had brought in 60 million rubles annually during the 1870s. Abolishing the poll tax reduced the tax burden on the peasantry, although at the same time Bunge reformed the system of cash payments due from former state peasants, converting them to full redemption payments in 1886 (20 years after their emancipation), which increased state income from this source by 30 per cent to 43 million rubles annually by 1890.

Bunge's policies towards the Russian industries were extremely protectionist. He introduced tariffs on imported goods in 1878, which increased until 1891 when duties reached 30 per cent of the value of raw materials. This supported the iron industry in southern Russia particularly. Bunge also promoted the construction of railways (by 1885, there were 17 000 miles of track) and spearheaded the first Russian labour laws, some of them aimed at reducing child labour. He managed to resist the demands of colleagues in the Ministries of War, the Navy and Transport for substantial sums of money to maintain the empire's military standing among the great powers. He could not avoid government borrowing and in 1887, under pressure from conservative deputies accusing him of incompetence and incapability of overcoming the budget deficit due to continued problems of state capital, Bunge resigned.

Economic reform under Vyshnegradsky

Bunge's successor, Ivan Vyshnegradsky (1887–92) took a different view of policy. Vyshnegradsky's policy can be summed up by the following quote: 'We shall ourselves not eat, but we shall export'[11]. He thought that by curbing consumption, imports and state expenditure he could boost gold reserves, create a surplus and encourage investment in Russian industry. He increased indirect taxes on consumer goods, raised tariffs (taxes) on imports even more than Bunge had, and pushed the collection of redemption payments, all of which increased the financial burden on the peasantry. He was able to negotiate French loans and Russia's gold reserves almost doubled, enabling him to claim some success in his period in office. However, a bad harvest in 1891 demonstrated the risks of Vyshnegradsky's approach: many peasants had been left with insufficient grain to survive a crop failure because they had sold off increasing amounts to be able to afford everyday goods. The famine that ensued in 1891–2 hit 17 of Russia's 39 provinces. The heir to the throne, the future Nicholas II, was appointed to oversee famine relief and sought to coordinate charitable efforts to help those suffering. The government made a reasonable job of limiting what could have been a complete disaster by giving aid to 13 million peasants (out of the 35 million affected). The imposition of Land Captains on rural areas and the restriction of the powers of the *zemstva* (under the 1890 statute) had made co-operation almost impossible, but this national calamity did bring officials together. Despite their efforts, and those of individuals such as the writer, Leo Tolstoy, who opened a soup kitchen, around 400 000 peasants died (many of them from a simultaneous cholera epidemic). Although Vyshnegradsky's export policies thus cost Russia dearly, on average grain production continued to expand by 2.1 per cent annually between 1883 and 1914. The famine, however, forced Vyshnegradsky to retire in disgrace in the summer of 1892. His policies had helped to politicise Russia, and resurgence in opposition to the government had become inevitable.

Alexander III had placed a stronger emphasis on industrial growth than his father, preferring to maintain the status quo in rural areas, where he saw law and order as a primary concern. However, as both Tsars neglected the burdens of redemption payments and inertia caused by repartition exercised by the *mir*, grain productivity only grew at a slow if steady rate. This slow agricultural growth starkly contrasted with the rate of growth of the rural population, and it was clear by the 1890s that 'land hunger' would be a huge issue for the next Tsar to settle. Unfortunately for the peasants, Alexander III's reign saw huge energy being diverted towards industrialisation, although even this did not really develop until the 1890s.

Social divisions

Two distinct attitudes were held within the educated class that came to be known as the 'intelligentsia'. One group sought to reconcile themselves with the Tsarist regime as 'new nobility'; this group was largely drawn from the increasing numbers of bureaucrats in the civil service, which had ballooned as a result of the reforms. The second group was highly critical of the regime and had been influenced by the ideas of the Western European Enlightenment. Increasingly radically inclined, this group began to understand Russia's system of serfdom as nothing less than a moral scandal. The radicals sought a change in the power structure of Russia through constitutional development; they often had no vested interests in the current system but everything to gain in a more accessible one. This group came to provide the main threat to the Tsarist regime.

Nobles, landowners and the position of the peasantry

Autocratic power was founded on the total control of every aspect of Russian state and society. But the *Ukase* of 1861 dismantled one of the crucial elements of autocracy in severing links between the regime and the nobility, ultimately undermining control of the rural population. Between 1877 and 1905, the amount of land owned by peasants grew from 6 million to 21.6 million hectares, and noble landholdings fell by half. The nobility needed a new role in society, and this might have been achieved if Alexander II's reforms had continued apace as they had begun. However, conservative reaction and further tightening of control under Alexander III meant that many younger members of the noble class never found a reason to be loyal to the autocratic regime. The regime itself was helping to plant the seeds of its own downfall.

The statutes of 1861 had stopped well short of awarding the peasants full freedom, in order to maintain stability across the empire. The Tsar and his ministers were fearful of a mass influx of peasants into the cities through the creation of a landless proletariat, which would be dangerous for law and order. Consequently, reinforcing old ties to the *mir* was necessary, though this time through redemption payments rather than serfdom. Whilst leaving villages permanently was impossible, many peasants did start to travel to towns and cities for temporary work to keep up with redemption demands. Seasonal labourers, such as those who moved from the central rural villages to the Donbass mines, could be away for months at a time, only returning for harvest. In 1900, almost 8.5 million peasants took out passports for seasonal work in St Petersburg and the central industrial regions. As Fitzpatrick (2008) explains, 'Many peasants were in fact living with one foot in the traditional village world and the other in the quite different world of the modern industrial town'[12].

The Orthodox Church was made responsible for elementary education in the 1860s due to fears that radical intellectuals would gain influence over the masses after emancipation. However, Dmitri Tolstoy (as Procurator of the Holy Synod 1865–80 and Minister of Education 1866–1880) showed little interest in educating the masses in religious instruction, spending only 6 per cent of the education budget on schools. Despite this, primary education expanded rapidly, as did peasants' appetite for reading fiction, and book production went up 400 per cent between 1855 and 1881. This perhaps signals that, despite the deprivation suffered in the post-emancipation period, peasants were aspirational in a way they hadn't been before. It should be noted that, in 1897, literacy was still only at 21 per cent according to the national census, perhaps because by 1895 government spending on primary schooling was only 2 million rubles, but literacy was growing in both rural and urban areas, particularly amongst the younger generation. The education of the masses could have been a positive development for Russia; however, in the long term it was to stir up more discontent and make it easier for radicals to spread new ideas about how Russia should be governed.

By the 1890s, both the nobility and the peasantry found themselves in a seemingly never-ending maze of debts and arrears due to relative land shortage because of a growing population and low productivity. Both Alexander II and Alexander III had failed to offer remedies for fear of diverting resources away from industrial

ACTIVITY 1.3

This is a basic timeline for the reign of Alexander II. Go back through your notes and use them to annotate the timeline (which follows) with more detail.

development and security. Whereas between 1871–90 relief expenditure (i.e. money spent on emergency food and shelter) had been 12 million rubles, in 1891 the exchequer handed out 144 million, with another 95 million rubles spent in the following decade (1893–1902) on relief.

The cultural influence of the Church

The Russian Orthodox Church was not a popular institution even during the reign of Catherine the Great (1762–96). Richard Pipes (1974) writes that 'what popularity it had it steadily lost'[13] most probably because of its extremely conservative outlook, which to many in the intelligentsia seemed 'anti-intellectual'. Adding to this, the Procurators of the Holy Synod had remained silent in the debates over the abolition of serfdom, thus appearing indifferent to what was increasingly understood as a social injustice. Many in the intelligentsia felt that the Church thus showed a lack of Christian ethics, and it is perhaps no wonder that many younger nobles from the 1860s began to fill the spiritual vacuum with secular ideologies that promised to realise social and political justice.

However, it would be absurd to suggest that Orthodoxy and religious custom did not permeate life in the Russian countryside. It is said that every Russian peasant home had a 'red corner' where religious icons were kept, which were brought out for births, marriages, deaths, and the beginning of war. Religious events also determined state holidays, of which there were up to 90 annually. For many Russians there was a strong element of mysticism in their religious beliefs. Many fasted regularly and consulted 'holy men' for advice about solving all manner of problems. Some 'holy men' wandered around Russia like beggars, relying on the charity of believers to support them. Some claimed they had healing powers. Some engaged in debauchery, teaching that only after great sin could one truly repent to God.

Simon Dixon (1999) has suggested that the Orthodox Church was torn for much of the 19th century between assimilating its rivals' techniques from across the multinational empire whilst seeking to differentiate its own doctrinal identity. In practice, this meant making sure that churches were warm in the winter, and periodically redecorating them. This became increasingly important during the 19th century as Russia extended her borders so that Finns, Ukrainians, Poles, Germans, Lithuanians and Latvians were incorporated into the empire. Archbishops insisted liturgies (services) remained ritualistic to preserve the mystical element, for Orthodoxy relied heavily on aesthetics to attract worshippers.

Conclusion

It is tempting to assume, along with many historians such as Richard Pipes (1995), that 'the trappings of imperial omnipotence (after 1762) served merely to conceal the monarchy's desperate weakness'[14] This view focuses on the weaknesses of autocracy; however, the accessions to the throne of Tsars Nicholas I, Alexander II and Alexander III were all smooth, and their coronations saw great public outpourings of joy and celebration. Of course, there were underlying weaknesses: Russia's rulers had to allow controlled modernisation of the economy while at the same time seeking to halt or even reverse social and political modernisation – an

 Developing concepts

The following concepts have been very important in this section. For each one, write a definition of the concept and give an example of what it means in the context of Russian society 1855–94.

- Autocracy
- Nobility
- Intelligentsia
- Serfs
- Peasants
- Russification
- Orthodoxy
- Official Nationality

impossible task. Opposition was growing and Russia needed a strong Tsar to hold back the tide; instead, what they got was Nicholas II.

Timeline: key events during the reign of Alexander II.

Year	Events
1855	Crimean War ends with Russia's defeat
1861	Emancipation Act is announced
1862	Mikhail von Reutern becomes Minister of Finance
	Dmitrii Miliutin becomes Minister of Defence and begins military reforms
1863	Censorship laws relaxed
	Polish revolt
1864	*Zemstva* created; legal reforms implemented
1866	State serfs freed
	First assassination attempt, by Dmitrii Karakosov
1869	*Catechism of a Revolutionary* by Nechaev is published
1876	Russification: Ukrainian schools could not teach in native language
1877	Russo-Turkish War
1878	Russo-Turkish War ends
	Vesa Zasulich case
1879	The People's Will group is formed
1881	Assassination of Alexander II; People's Will smashed
	Alexander III becomes Tsar
	Unshakable Autocracy by Pobedonostsev is published
	Bunge becomes Minister of Finance
1882	Censorship laws
1883	Peasant Land Bank established
	Georgi Plekhanov writes *Emancipation of Labour*
1884	Law against university autonomy
1887	Bunge resigns; Vyshnegradsky becomes Minister of Finance
	Church regains control of primary education
	Lenin's brother is hanged for revolutionary activity
1889	Land Captains are introduced

Year	Events
1890	Four terrorists hanged for plot against the Tsar

Act passed limiting power of the *zemstva*; peasant voting rights restricted in *zemstvo* elections |
| 1891–1893 | Famine |
| 1894 | Tsar Alexander III dies of kidney disease

Nicholas Romanov becomes Tsar Nicholas II of Russia |

Practice essay questions

1. Alexander II was more successful than Alexander III in coping with the economic problems he inherited. Assess the validity of this view.
2. 'The most repressive of their policies.' To what extent do you agree with this assessment of both Alexander II's and Alexander III's policies towards non-Russian national groups living within the empire?
3. To what extent had Tsarist autocracy been weakened by 1894?
4. With reference to these extracts and your understanding of the historical context, which of these two extracts provides the more convincing interpretation of growth of opposition to Tsarism during the reign of Alexander II? **(AS Level)**

Extract A

Non-Russian peoples were governed in a contradictory system that involved indirect rule in some places, direct military government through local elites assimilated into the Russian administrative system in others, and various forms of constitutionalism (in the Grand Duchy of Finland and, until 1863, the Kingdom of Poland). Among the effects of tsarism was the imposition of a new state order on societies that had little contact with strong state structures, new regulations and laws, the spread of serfdom to certain regions, such as Georgia, and the enforcement of new taxation. This administrative 'Russification', the extension of bureaucratic absolutism over non-Russian subjects, was accompanied by a spontaneous self-Russification that many non-Russians found advantageous in the first two-thirds of the nineteenth century. But after 1881, when the government adopted a more stridently anti-national and anti-semitic policies that threatened forced cultural homogenisation, even ethnicities which had been Russophilic, such as the Armenians, turned hostile to the tsarist regime.

Suny RG. Nationality Policies. In Acton E, Cherniaev V, Rosenberg WG. (eds.) *Critical Companion to the Russian Revolution*. Arnold; 1997. p.660

Extract B

The Tsar's support for emancipation must be understood within the broader context of the state's role in a serf-based society. That role involved two primary and overriding responsibilities: to guarantee domestic and foreign security. The head of the Third Section had explicitly warned Nicholas that friction between serf and master constituted a time-bomb which threatened the whole empire. Peasant disturbances grew ominously in number and intensity as each decade passed, and outbreaks were overwhelmingly concentrated on private estates. Confronted by noble resistance and alarmed by foreign upheaval, Nicholas had shelved the issue and committed himself to upholding the status quo at home and abroad. It was the catastrophe of the Crimean War which rendered this commitment untenable. Humiliated on her own doorstep, Russia's ability to influence Western affairs was sharply curtailed. The whole framework within which Nicholas had viewed the options before him broke down. Moreover, the war rudely brought home the military cost of social and economic backwardness. The Treasury had run up a huge deficit. Russian forces had been incomparably less well armed than those of Britain and France. Supply problems during the war made it seem madness to postpone further the steps necessary to improve communications and construct strategic railways. The correlation between serfdom and economic backwardness was now conventional wisdom, vague though the economic analysis on which it was based might be. The case for following the Western example of reducing the costly standing army by building a reserve of trained men became incontrovertible. Yet as long as serfdom remained, so did the objection that it was not safe to return hundreds of thousands of trained men into the countryside. Serfdom was becoming a dire threat to both domestic and foreign security.

It is this conjuncture which explains why a state rooted in the social and economic dominance of the serf-owning nobility should have undertaken emancipation. It also explains why the Tsar was able to secure the acquiescence of the nobility. The sense of urgency over the issue took time to spread. It was not at first shared by most serf-owners in the provinces, or indeed by most of the great landowners among senior officials. Individual noblemen had of course learned to their cost of both peasant fury and Russia's military decline. A minority, responding to a combination of moral conviction, economic incentive, frustration at the cost and difficulty with overcoming the inefficiency and petty subordination of serf labour, and fear, might favour some sort of emancipation. But the majority preferred to live with the moral problem and forgo the reputed advantages of freely hired labour rather than contemplate the abolition of their traditional rights over their peasants. Yet should their own government, run by fellow noblemen and dedicated to their security, conclude that serfdom was too dangerous to perpetuate, they would bow to the inevitable. And it was this message which, haltingly, the Tsar and some of his ministers began to communicate.

Acton E, Russia: The Tsarist and Soviet Legacy. Routledge; 1995. pp. 68–69

 Taking it further

Daniel Saunders ends his book *Russia in the Age of Reaction and Reform 1801–1881* (1992) with this statement: 'Terrorism made compromise impossible.' How far do you agree with this statement?

Further reading
David Saunders provides a thoroughly researched overview of the reforms undertaken by Alexander II and their impact in *Russia in Russia in the Age of Reaction and Reform 1801–1881* (1992). This is a very good place to start if you would like to know more about the reasons why Alexander II launched his programme of reform and why so many compromises were made.

Edvard Radzinsky, the author of *Alexander II: The Last Tsar* (2006), is a playwright as well as a historian, and it shows in this engaging book about Alexander II. Full of interesting stories about the Tsar's childhood and life at court, this is an illuminating and enjoyable read.

The most comprehensive study of Russia in the 19th century is probably *Russia under the Old Regime* by Richard Pipes (1995). Though quite a challenging read in places, the study is extremely detailed.

 Chapter summary

After studying this period, you should be able to:

- describe political, economic and social conditions in Russia in 1855
- evaluate Alexander II's domestic and military reforms
- compare how Russian autocracy was imposed differently under the two Alexanders
- explain the increasing discrimination against ethnic minorities and Jews.

End notes
1   Radzinsky E. *Alexander II: The Last Tsar*. Simon and Schuster; 2006.
2   Lieven D. *Russia as empire: a comparative perspective*. In: Hosking G and Service R (eds.) *Reinterpreting Russia*. Edward Arnold; 1991. p.212. In: Hosking G and Service R (eds.) *Reinterpreting Russia*. Edward Arnold; 1991. p.212
3   Saunders D. *Russia in the Age of Reaction and Reform 1801-1881*. Longman; 1992.
4   Saunders D. *Russia in the Age of Reaction and Reform 1801-1881*. Longman; 1992.
5   Smith D. *Former People: the Last Days of the Russian Aristocracy*. Macmillan; 2012.
6   Ulam A. *In the Name of the People: Prophets and Conspirators in Prerevolutionary Russia*. Viking; 1977.
7   Saunders D. *Russia in the age of reaction and reform 1801-1881*. Longman; 1992.
8   Peretts EA. *Dnevnik gosudarstvennogo sekretaria (1880–1883)*. Moscow and Leningrad; 1927. Cited in Polunov A. *Russia in the Nineteenth Century: Autocracy, Reform and Social Change 1814-1914*. Armonk; 2005.
9   Chubarov A. *Fragile Empire: A History of Imperial Russia*. Continuum; 1999.
10 Stedman-Jones G. Introduction. In Marx K. and Engels F. *The Communist Manifesto*. Penguin; 1967.
11 Cited in Mosse WE. *An Economic History of Russia 1856-1914*. I. B Tauris; 1996.
12 Fitzpatrick S. *The Russian Revolution*. Oxford University Press; 2008.
13 Pipes R. *Russia Under the Old Regime*. Penguin; 1995.
14 Pipes R. *Russia Under the Old Regime*. Penguin; 1995.

2 The collapse of autocracy, 1894–1917

In this section, we will examine the political authority of Nicholas II, Russia's last Tsar, who reigned from 1894 to 1917. We will consider some of the changes that were taking place in this period and how these began to sour the relationship between Nicholas and the people of Russia. We will look into:

- political developments: political tension until 1905 and the constitutional experiment of 1906–14
- industrial growth and agricultural change to 1917
- growth of opposition to the regime, 1894–1917
- social developments in Russia, 1894–1917
- political developments of 1917
- Bolshevik takeover and the establishment of Bolshevik government.

Introduction

Nicholas II inherited a vast, largely peaceful empire. Perhaps the most important attitudes he took from his father related to his perspective on leadership. Nicholas's idealised view of Tsarism, and of his father in particular, was such that it led him to commission a huge bronze statue of Alexander III. The immense figure of Alexander riding a substantial horse – the 'Hippopotamus', as it became known – was supposed to be symbolic of the state's own steadfast immovability; it was one of the first St Petersburg landmarks to be mutilated when the revolution began in February 1917. Nicholas II believed it his mission to emulate his father's autocratic rule, but after Alexander's premature death (he was only 49 when he died) his son wept 'I am not prepared to be a Tsar'; he was 26 upon inheriting the throne. He was to prove himself right by showing little readiness to respond to liberal demands to move Russia towards a constitutional order.

The industrialisation of the 1890s brought profound demographic and social changes to Russia. A generation of young, literate peasants became local activists of the Russian Revolution as the Tsarist regime failed to concede to their political demands, struggling to reconcile itself with the new and dynamic society. However, war would be the biggest threat to the regime in this period: in 1904 against the Japanese and then against Germany in the First World War. The outbreak of the First World War in 1914 both exposed and increased the vulnerability of the regime. Nicholas II was lucky to end the Russo-Japanese war in 1905 and escape with the concession of a **Duma** (national assembly); he wasn't so lucky in February 1917, when he was forced to sign to his abdication from power.

Political authority: government and Tsar

Nicholas II as ruler

Russia's last Tsar acceded to the throne upon his father's death on 1 November 1894. He is regarded by most historians as a reluctant ruler at best, who lacked a distinct political identity. At worst, according to Edward Acton, he was 'breathtakingly insensitive'; Orlando Figes (1997) provides an even harsher assessment: 'If there was a vacuum at the centre of the ruling system, then he was the empty space'[1]. Even at his coronation, the usual celebrations were marred by disaster: around 1300 people died at Khodynka when panic overtook the traditional distribution of coronation keepsakes. Many blamed the police's heavy-handed attempts to control the crowds, but anger was widespread when the people learned that Tsar Nicholas attended a ball at the French embassy the same night. It was a poor first impression.

Early mistakes were compounded Nicholas II rebuked several *zemstvo* delegates who asked whether one day their views might 'reach the heights of the throne' (cited in Manning, 1982, page 40). He referred to this notion as 'senseless dreams', in the manner his father might have done. This incident was an early demonstration of his lack of political judgement: Nicholas was not the commanding figure that Alexander III had been, and he often appeared disconnected from his people. His general views were influenced by Constantine Pobedonostsev, who had been his tutor as a young boy and had served Alexander III as de facto head of the Russian Orthodox Church. Pobedonostsev saw autocracy, the Church and the peasantry in village communities as unique institutions to be vigorously defended against liberalism and democracy. He imagined the biggest threat to Russia would come from the educated aristocrats who were obsessed by Western Europe. But on the whole Nicholas was bored by politics, and although he grew in confidence throughout his reign he never gained the necessary skills to rule Russia from his autocratic position. Nicholas did work hard as an administrator of the empire; in this role he clearly felt comfortable, even if he did not want to consider broader policy implications. Figes (1997) writes that Nicholas II spent hours each day typing up and signing documents, as a secretary might do; in other words, he preferred to focus on the minutiae of processing legislation at the expense of the pressing issues facing Russia, which deprived the government of effective leadership. As Figes (1997) puts it, the regime became an 'autocracy without an autocrat'.

Political developments to 1914

1905: The People's Revolution

The Revolution of 1905 is widely regarded as a watershed in the history of imperial Russia. It was not initiated by revolutionary groups, but by a prison chaplain called Father Gapon and the workers of St Petersburg. It was an event that thrust the Tsarist regime into its first constitutional experiment, forcing the unwilling Nicholas II to relinquish part of his power to an elected body and to grant civil rights to Russian subjects. It was also, though, an opportunity for the regime to regain the initiative while moving towards a constitutional system like those that existed in other parts of Europe. Tsar Nicholas's reluctance to accept change to the autocratic system would contribute greatly to the regime's collapse in 1917.

The Russo-Japanese War

Richard Pipes (1997) lays the blame for the Russo-Japanese War firmly at Russia's door. The story begins with the building of Prime Minister Witte's Trans-Siberian Railway, which needed to run its final segment through Chinese Manchuria to connect Lake Baikal with Vladivostock. The Chinese acquiesced on the strict understanding that their sovereignty in this region was recognised. By January 1903, however, Russia had stationed military garrisons there as a prelude to invasion; this led the Japanese, who also had designs on the area, to propose that Japan and Russia split Manchuria between them. Since Nicholas's youth, when he had been shot at in Japan, he had referred to the Japanese as '*malaki*' (apes), and he refused to negotiate with them. He had assumed the Japanese would be intimidated by Russia's military might, and so the Russian approach to negotiations, according to Acton (1995), was 'complacent in the extreme'[2]. On 8 February 1904, the Japanese took the initiative (probably emboldened by an alliance with Britain that had been struck in 1902) and launched an attack on Port Arthur, neutralising the Russian Pacific fleet by sinking several ships, thus securing mastery over the China Sea. A land campaign followed in Manchuria, which was made difficult for the Russians because the area was thousands of miles from the capital St Petersburg; since the Trans-Siberian railway was still incomplete, this caused immense logistical problems.

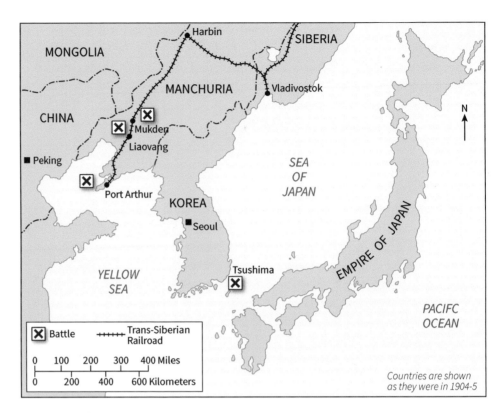

Figure 2.1: The Russo-Japanese War, 1904–5.

Six months into the war, turmoil at home increased: the Social Revolutionaries (SRs) had a major success in their terror campaign (see the section 'Opposition'), assassinating the hated Minister of the Interior, Plehve. Meanwhile, the Union of Liberation (see the section 'Liberals') had been organising 'banquets' on a national scale to pass resolutions calling for a national parliament or **constituent assembly**. Slightly panicked, in October 1904 Nicholas decided to try and win back liberal support (which was waning due to the Union of Liberation movement and lack of enthusiasm for the war) by sending the Baltic fleet halfway around the world to retrieve Port Arthur. Whilst the fleet was en route, the telegraphs brought bad news: Port Arthur surrendered in December 1904 and 25 000 prisoners were taken.

Mistakes: Bloody Sunday

Up until 1905, workers and peasants had not participated in the political turmoil surrounding the war. The demands for constitutional change had almost exclusively come from university students and the *zemstvo* gentry. That was to change on what came to be known as 'Bloody Sunday' – 22 January 1905 – when a St Petersburg priest, Father Gapon, led 120 000 men, women and children to the Winter Palace. Gapon had applied the Head of the Okhrana, Zubatov's principles (see the section 'Trade Unions') with success in St Petersburg, not only to aid the regime but also to put pressure on it to change for the good of the people. He had conferred with liberals in the Union of Liberation and his appeal to the Tsar incorporated parts of their programme. The workers, waving religious banners and icons, appealed to their Tsar for a living wage, more humane working conditions and civil and political rights – but were met with a hail of bullets. Gapon had specifically forbidden red banners on the march, so that the authorities could not mistake the workers for revolutionaries. But the authorities appeared to take no notice. It is estimated that between 150 and 200 protestors were killed and a further 800 wounded after the Tsar's soldiers opened fire in the belief that the crowd was refusing to disperse. At once, the myth of Nicholas II as the 'Little Father' of Russia, kept in ignorance of the people's suffering, was shattered, and disbelief turned to unabated anger. The ultra-conservative *Novoe Vremia* (New Times) newspaper coined a slogan that echoed across Russia during 1905: 'It is no longer possible to live in this way'. Many of the rights demanded by the workers on Bloody Sunday corresponded to the goals of even some of the conservative-minded liberals, and this helps to explain why so many of the gentry were willing to support the non-economic demands of striking workers in the ensuing months.

Figure 2.2: Artist's impression of Bloody Sunday, 22 January 1905, St Petersburg; the Imperial Guard shoot at unarmed demonstrators outside the Winter Palace.

Revulsion over the massacre of peaceful demonstrators reverberated across Russia and caused what the historian Ascher (1988) has called 'disarray'. In January 1905 alone, over 400 000 workers went out on strike, representing the largest single labour protest in Russian history. St Petersburg was placed under martial law, and Governor-General Trepov pacified workers with brutal repression. Mensheviks and Bolsheviks played no part in the workers' march to the Winter Palace, but claimed it as a victory for Marxist theory and suggested a revolution would follow.

Both groups had only approximately 2000 worker members between them and their leaders were in exile, unable to exert great influence on the direction of the revolution. They did, however, aid the creation of illegal trade unions and strike committees. **Soviets** (workers' councils) began to appear in 1905, the most significant being founded in St Petersburg. However, it was the reaction of the

Key terms

Mensheviks: originally part of the Russian Social-Democratic Labour Party, the Mensheviks (the word means 'minority') were formed after a split in the Party between Julius Martov and Vladimir Lenin, leader of the Bolsheviks, which occurred at the Second Congress of 1903. The Mensheviks opposed Lenin's idea of a vanguard party and wanted broad-based support.

Bolsheviks: led by Lenin, the Bolsheviks (the word means 'majority') would seize control of the government of Russia in 1917.

Key term

Soviets: in late imperial Russia, 'soviets' were workers' councils, the earliest being formed in St Petersburg in 1905. They were formed as part of a movement of workers independent of the government-sponsored 'Zubatov unions' (see the section 'Trade unions').

liberal middle classes and the gentry that would turn the events of Bloody Sunday into a revolutionary crisis.

Spontaneous revolution

After the massacre at the Winter Palace, Nicholas II, never a decisive leader even in normal circumstances, wavered. After much hesitation he agreed to launch a commission led by N.V. Shidlovskii, a member of the State Council, to investigate labour problems in St Petersburg. The commission collapsed after its first meeting on 16 February 1905 when Shidlovskii refused to guarantee that workers demanding political change would not be arrested. Waves of strikes followed as trust in the regime was further eroded, but still the Tsar failed to perceive the severity of the mounting crisis. The liberals, encouraged by the continuing wave of strikes, formed a Union of Unions, which brought together many professional associations, such as lawyers, physicians and teachers, as well as the Union of Liberation. They now began to demand a constituent assembly, elected by universal, direct and equal suffrage, and this goal was also embraced by the newly formed All-Russian Peasants' Union (see below).

In response, Nicholas II issued a manifesto ordering the people to unite behind the throne and send their proposals for improvements to the government. Thousands of grievances and petitions flooded in from all over Russia over the next four months, giving expression to the evolving politicisation of the masses. Alexander Bulygin, who had replaced Prince Sviatopolk-Mirskii on 20 January 1905 as Minister of the Interior, was tasked with creating a limited consultative Duma: the demands expressed in petitions for constitutional monarchy were far too radical for Nicholas II. But the Bulygin Duma was far too little, far too late. Under the proposals less than 1 per cent of St Petersburg's adult population would qualify to vote. Widespread civil disobedience in the form of strikes and, on occasion, riots, ensued among all but the most moderate of reformers.

Tsar Nicholas's regime survived this spontaneous outburst of discontent, perhaps because rural turbulence didn't erupt until later on in the year, when the cities had largely been brought under some semblance of control. The peasants in the countryside reacted to news from the cities, disastrous reports from the battlefields, **Socialist Revolutionary** (SR) pamphlets and nationalism in the borderlands, and their anger grew as the year wore on. Peasants expressed their anger as they had always done, burning and looting 3000 former landlords' manors and attacking members of the gentry; the army was deployed no less than 2700 times to quell peasant disturbances. However, peasants were increasingly

Hidden voices

Textile workers

The increase in the hiring of female labour after 1905 was because of the relative cheapness of female workers and their supposedly more tranquil character. However, as Ian Thatcher (2005) writes, the most strike-prone industries employed a higher number of

women. In some ways women suffered more than men in factories. For example, the daily body searches that took place to check for stolen items were not just humiliating but could be combined with sexual abuse.

politically articulate. In May 1905, approximately 100 delegates representing peasants from 22 provinces across Russia met in Moscow. They called themselves the All-Russian Peasants' Union and represented a substantial body of opinion. There was nothing new about their claims that the land belonged to those who worked it; what was new were the proposals for a constituent assembly elected by direct universal suffrage. It was becoming clear to Nicholas and his advisers that the peasants were no longer the loyal, conservative majority they had always assumed.

The sinking of the Baltic fleet at Tsushima (see the section 'Political authority: opposition and the state of Russia in wartime') provoked a general political strike, organised by the Union of Unions in October 1905, which aimed to bring the country to a standstill and force the monarchy to acquiesce to their demands. This came after Moscow printers, railroad personnel and university students had all launched massive strikes throughout September. The workers had begun to adopt Menshevik slogans such as 'To arms!' and 'Revolutionary self-government!', though they had not yet become conscious that revolution was their goal. The regime shuddered as it became impossible to move troops to the necessary areas due to paralysed railways. Orlando Figes (1997) writes that Nicholas II remained oblivious to the crisis, filling his diaries during this time with trivial notes about the weather and hunting. Historian Abraham Ascher (1988) suggests the politicisation of the working class, and Nicholas's remaining oblivious to it, were the principal reasons for the shift to the left across the country. In October 1905, Sergei Witte, one of the Tsar's ministers, submitted to the Tsar a survey of the situation, which outlined just how drastically the political situation had transformed since January. Witte's memorandum seemed to indicate his acceptance of liberal demands: 'Russia has outgrown the existing regime and is striving for an order based on civic liberty.' He suggested to the Tsar that he could either appoint a military dictator or make political concessions, urging him to grant liberal demands for a legislative parliament and introduce liberties such as freedom of speech and assembly.

Even in these desperate times the Tsar hesitated, exploring more repressive alternatives and telling the Governor-General of St Petersburg, Trepov, 'not to use blanks [or] to spare bullets'[4] in dealing with protestors. However, the military seemed reluctant to face the crowds and events were spiralling out of control. On 13 October, a strike committee in St Petersburg that was formed of Mensheviks and workers adopted the name 'Soviet of Workers' Deputies'. It began to publish its own newspaper, *Izvestia*, to keep strikers informed of developments, organised a militia and distributed food supplies. It was led by Leon Trotsky The workers were organising and even Nicholas's military advisers warned him of the need to act. Eventually, he gave in: on 30 October, the Tsar presented Russia with the October Manifesto.

The regime regains the initiative: the October Manifesto

The October Manifesto represented the end of traditional autocracy in Russia and it was met with jubilation outside the Winter Palace, where the events of Bloody Sunday had taken place. Even officers and members of the gentry held red banners and sang the *Marseillaise* in solidarity with workers and students. The Manifesto served to split the opposition, however, as the liberals who had led many of the protests against the regime now felt they had achieved their aims.

Key term

A **curia** was a division a district's population was divided into for elections. The first curia consisted of those who possessed 200 or more desiatinas of land (about 540 acres), or other land worth at least 15 000 rubles; these comprised nobles and other landlords. The second curia consisted of those with a yearly income of at least 6000 rubles. The third curia consisted mainly of representatives of village societies and peasants who did not require a special possession permit.

Voices from the past

The October Manifesto

The oath which We took as Tsar compels Us to use all Our strength, intelligence and power to put a speedy end to this unrest which is so dangerous for the State. The relevant authorities have been ordered to take measures to deal with direct outbreaks of disorder and violence and to protect people who only want to go about their daily business in peace. However, in view of the need to speedily implement earlier measures to pacify the country, we have decided that the work of the government must be unified.

We have therefore ordered the government to take the following measures in fulfilment of our unbending will:

1. Fundamental civil freedoms will be granted to the population, including real personal inviolability, freedom of conscience, speech assembly and association.

2. Participation in the Duma will be granted to those classes of the population which are at present deprived of voting powers, insofar as is possible in the short period before the convocation of the Duma, and this will lead to the development of a universal franchise. There will be no delay to the Duma elections which have already been organized.

3. It is established as an unshakeable rule that no law can come into force without approval by the State Duma and that the elected representatives of the people will be given the opportunity to play a real part in the supervision of the legality of the activities of government bodies.

We call upon all true sons of Russia to remember their duty to their homeland, to help put a stop to this unprecedented unrest and, together with this, to devote all their strength to the restoration of peace to their native land.

Discussion points

1. Underline any words or phrases where Nicholas is trying to assert his authority.
2. Does the Manifesto represent the end of autocratic rule in Russia?
3. This extract only shows part of the Manifesto. Research the full document; what else did Nicholas promise?
4. Trotsky (a Menshevik) said the October Manifesto was 'a whip wrapped in the parchment of a constitution'. Why might he have thought this?

A loose alliance of industrialists and gentry created a Union – the **Octobrists** – to work with the Tsar on the basis on the Manifesto. Other liberals thought the Manifesto should only be seen as a stepping stone to full parliamentary democracy, and so formed the **Constitutional Democratic Party – the Kadets** – although they agreed to accept the Tsar's offerings for now. Nicholas added to the Manifesto that he would appoint a Chairman of the Council of Ministers, similar to a Prime Minister. The post was given to Witte, who tried to bring together liberals but failed because too many of them feared assassination, so the cabinet was staffed exclusively by loyal conservative officials.

For the majority of workers, the Manifesto offered nothing to nullify their grievances and soviets continued to spring up across Russia on the model of the Soviet of Workers' Deputies in St Petersburg. So, strikes continued. Peasant disturbances peaked in violence and 211 separate mutinies were recorded in the armed services at the close of 1905, including at Kronstadt outside St Petersburg. Lenin returned to Russia in November, declaring the Manifesto nothing more than a 'scrap of paper', and Trotsky (Vice Chairman of the St Petersburg Soviet) denounced the concessions. In early December 1905, 300 of the St Petersburg deputies were arrested and Trotsky was jailed and then exiled to Siberia. The Bolsheviks dominated the newly formed Moscow soviet and launched a week-long, guerrilla-style uprising against government authorities, which proved fruitless. The authorities had gained the upper hand; between 500 and 1000 were killed in the uprising and martial law was extended to 41 provinces. Nicholas was appalled at the continuing unrest and felt betrayed at having signed the Manifesto in the belief it would pacify the country. His response was brutal: districts such as Presnia in St Petersburg were shelled indiscriminately and summary executions of leading workers were carried out; it was even reported that police administered beatings to workers' children.

Tsarist supporters in Odessa took to the streets on 19–20 October 1905 in an effort to try and halt the unrest. This time the riots began as political protests against the Tsar but turned into a pogrom, people attacking Jews wherever they could be found. By the time the riots were over, 19 Jews had been killed and 56 injured. Jewish self-defence leagues stopped some of the violence but were not wholly successful. The Odessa pogrom was part of a much larger movement of 690 pogroms carried out against Jews that swept through the Russian empire after the October Manifesto of 1905, carried out by nationalist groups calling themselves the 'Black Hundreds'. Throughout the countryside, socialists were also rounded up and imprisoned or exiled. In the Baltic regions, army units began a campaign of terror, executing 1200 people, destroying thousands of buildings and flogging thousands of peasants for their part in the disturbances between December 1905 and May 1906. The regime aimed to break the spirits of the peasants: there is evidence that entire communities were made to prostrate themselves on the ground like serfs before Cossack troops. Mounted soldiers whipped peasants until they surrendered their leaders for execution, without any pretence of a trial. Figes estimates that 15 000 peasants were executed, 20 000 wounded and 45 000 exiled between October 1905 and April 1906. As Pipes (1997) suggests, the 1905 revolution might have changed political institutions, but clearly 'political attitudes had been left untouched'[5].

Conclusions

Perhaps the main reason Tsar Nicholas survived 1905 was that the armed forces mostly remained loyal and were willing to put into effect brutal repression to quell

 Voices from the past

Why were the Russians singing the words of the French national anthem after the announcement of the October Manifesto? The *Marseillaise* was written during the French Revolution in 1792. It was a revolutionary song that called upon the citizens of France to fight against tyranny, using an evocative melody and the refrain 'March on!'. A Russian radical, Pyotr Lavrov, wrote a Russian version of the *Marseillaise* in 1875 that clearly takes inspiration from the original:

'We will go among the suffering brethren, We will go to the hungry people; Together with them we send our curses to the evil-doers, We will call them to struggle with us: Arise, arise, working people! Arise against the enemies, hungry brother! Forward! Let the cry of vengeance, Sound of the people!'

Summary of key events

- Tsar Nicholas II faced spontaneous outbreaks of rioting and strikes throughout 1905.

- The Tsar signed the October Manifesto to assuage striking workers who were paralysing Russia; in doing so, he allowed a national Duma to be created.

- The 1905 Revolution appeased the liberals, but the radicals had to be suppressed using brutal force.

the unrest. But the various opposition movements were also not united politically behind the goal of bringing the government down. The Manifesto split the liberal opposition from the revolutionary circles, which was enough to send moderate trade unions, such as the railway workers, back to work. The flame of revolution that threatened to engulf Russia was extinguished relatively quickly. Soon after signing the Manifesto, Nicholas wrote: 'My dearest Mama, you can't imagine what I went through before that moment … There was no other way out than to cross oneself and give what everyone was asking for.' He had acted out of desperation rather than conviction but it had saved him, for now. The Tsarist government had not escaped unscathed; the Russian people had won freedoms that could not simply be withdrawn. The flourishing of newspapers and journals, the convocation of an elected Duma, the formation of political parties and legality of trade unions ensured that politics was now in the public arena, even if the Tsar retained the real instruments of power.

Duma government

Nicholas II had only allowed the formation of a constitution in Russia in order to appease the moderates and create a loyal parliament that would not interfere with his royal prerogative. The constitution had provided Nicholas with an opportunity to construct a positive, stable working relationship with moderates and win back public opinion with a series of reforms. However, for the most part, he was unwilling to work with them or hear their demands. He had chastised himself for being unnecessarily weak in 1905, and became increasingly stubborn and reluctant to change as a result. In his eyes, there had been no revolution, nor would there be. Historians have fiercely debated whether the Tsarist regime could have survived without the interruption of the First World War, but there is evidence to suggest that by 1914 all but the most conservative elements of the Duma had lost hope of achieving true parliamentary democracy.

Nicholas II issued the **Fundamental Laws** in April 1906, just before the opening of the State Duma, which sought to clarify issues the Tsar had been unhappy with after the October Manifesto. The laws created a two-chamber Parliament: the upper house (State Council), which consisted of members of the Church and nobility; and the lower house (the State Duma), made up of elected representatives chosen by a complex franchise system weighted in favour of the more conservative elements of society, traditionally the peasantry and nobility. All legislation had to have the consent of both chambers before it was put before the monarch, who had the authority to veto. The chambers could question public

Voices from the past

The Black Hundreds were small groups of Russo-centric nationalists who were avid supporters of the Tsar. They denied the existence of a Ukrainian nation and sought to promote the Tsarist ideals of religious orthodoxy, autocracy and nationalism. Members of these organisations came from a wide variety of social strata including landowners, workers, clergymen and merchants. The Tsarist regime provided financial support to the movement and thus condoned its activities, which ranged from holding meetings and demonstrations to terrorist acts against revolutionaries and violent pogroms against Jews.

ministers and authorise budgets; however, the Crown retained the ability to appoint ministers – this would be a source of much friction – and to form foreign policy.

The opening of the first State Duma on 27 April 1906 revealed the true attitudes of both the monarchists and the opposition. One elected deputy from the Crimea recalled: 'The two hostile sides stood confronting each other'[6]. This did not bode well for the new constitutional experiment. When the Tsar arrived, the monarchist side of the hall exploded with rapturous applause whilst the Duma deputies

---

 Voices from the past

Extracts from the Fundamental Laws, 23 April 1906

1 The Russian State is one and indivisible …

3 The Russian language is the general language of the state, and its use is compulsory in the army, the navy and state and public institutions …

4 The All-Russian Emperor possesses the supreme autocratic power. Not only fear and conscience, but God himself, commands obedience to his authority.

7 The Sovereign Emperor exercises power in conjunction with the State Council and the State Duma.

8 The Sovereign Emperor possesses the initiative in all legislative matters. The Fundamental Laws may be subject to revision in the State Council and State Duma only on His initiative. The Sovereign Emperor ratifies the laws. No law can come into force without his approval.

9 The Sovereign Emperor approves laws; and without his approval no legislative measure can become law.

14 The Sovereign Emperor is the Commander-in-Chief of the Russian army and navy.

63 The Emperor who holds the throne of all Russia cannot profess any religion save the Orthodox.

64 The State Council and the State Duma have equal rights in legislative matters.

67 Freedom of religion is accorded, not only to Christians of foreign denominations, but also to Jews, Muslims and heathens.

73 No one can be held under arrest except in cases prescribed by law.

78 Russian subjects have the right to organise meetings for purposes that are not contrary to the laws, peacefully, and without weapons.

79 Everyone may, within the limits of the law, express his ideas orally and in writing and may also disseminate them by means of the press or by other methods.

80 Russian subjects have the right to form societies and associations for purposes that are not in contravention of the laws. …

86 No new law can come into force without the approval of the State Council and State Duma and the ratification of the Sovereign Emperor.

87 If extraordinary circumstances require legislative action whilst the State Duma is in recess, the Council of Ministers may make recommendations direct to the Sovereign Emperor. Such a measure may not, however, introduce changes in the Fundamental Laws, in the statutes of the State Council and State Duma or in the regulations governing elections to the Council and the Duma. Should such a measure not be introduced into the Duma as a bill within two months from the date of its next meeting … it loses force.

106 The State Council and the State Duma possess equal legislative powers.

123 The Chairman of the Council of Ministers and the Ministers … are responsible to the Sovereign Emperor for the general operation of the state administration. Each of them is individually responsible for his own actions and orders.

Source: Svod Zakonov Rossiiskoi Imperii, 3rd series, vol. 1, pt. 1. St Petersburg, 1912, pp. 5–26.

---

remained stony-faced and silent. The Tsar's mother broke down in tears at the sight of so many commoners in the palace and took days to recover from the shock. It was in this tense atmosphere that the parliamentary era of Nicholas's reign began.

The First Duma, April–July 1906: *The Duma of National Hopes*

The make-up of the First Duma was much more radical than the authorities had intended. Even though the SRs and Social Democrats (SDs) stated they would boycott the elections (something they would later regret) they still won seats, which went unfilled for the duration of the First Duma. The majority of the votes were won by the Kadets and by the Trudoviks – a party formed of socialists and some SRs who had decided the time had come to establish an open, legal party to aid peasant deputies elected to the Duma. In the Tsar's eyes the Trudoviks were dangerously radical. The burning issue the opposition deputies wanted to discuss was that of land reform, and a confrontational proposal was put forward that land should be expropriated and shared amongst the peasants, with some compensation for landlords coming from the state. Paul Miliukov used the rostrum of the Duma to lecture ministers on the need for an end to bureaucratic and arbitrary government and the abolition of the Upper Chamber. Ivan Goremykin, an ageing and obedient bureaucrat who had replaced the energetic Witte as Chairman of the Council of Ministers after his resignation, rejected the proposals outright, calling them 'inadmissible'. The Court had already managed to negotiate a loan from France of 2250 million gold francs, nullifying the need for budgetary discussion. Nicholas II was wholly unimpressed both by the discussions amongst the deputies and the way Goremykin dealt with them, so he dismissed the old Prime Minister and dissolved the First Duma in July 1906, just three months after it had opened. He ordered fresh elections. Ivan Goremykin was replaced by Pyotr Stolypin, a former Governor of Saratov, where some of the most brutal repression of the peasantry had been witnessed following the events of October 1905.

In response to the dissolution of the First Duma, 200 delegates, including 120 Kadets withdrew to the Finnish city of Vyborg, beyond the reach of the Russian police. There, they appealed to the peasantry to refuse either to pay taxes or conscript. The Kadets wrote their own Manifesto, which had unexpected consequences. Mutinies erupted at Sveaborg and Kronstadt and some peasants revolted in support of the Kadets. A few radicals even attempted to assassinate Stolypin, injuring two of his children and destroying his house. Stolypin felt forced to establish courts-martial to calm the apparent threat. By April 1907, the courts-martial had passed 683 death sentences and Stolypin had disenfranchised those Kadets who had fled to Vyborg. This deprived the liberals of some of their most outspoken leaders.

The Second Duma, February–June 1907: *The Duma of National Anger*

The Second Duma, which convened in February 1907, proved no more agreeable to Nicholas II than the first. Groups from the extreme left and right replaced the disenfranchised Kadets, heaping criticism on the government for its measures against revolutionary activity (e.g. Stolypin's courts-martial). Stolypin sought to define the state as subject to the will of the monarch alone. His terms would ensure the government retained the initiative and offered no concessions to the

Party	1st Duma April–July 1906	2nd Duma Feb–June 1907	3rd Duma Nov 1907–June 1912	4th Duma Nov 1912–Feb 1917
SDs (Bolsheviks)	—	—	19	15
SDs (Mensheviks)	18	47	—	—
Trudoviks: peasant-based labour group that broke away from the SRs; they had no formal programme but advocated nationalisation of non-peasant land, minimum wage and a constituent assembly.	102	104	13	10
SRs	34	37	—	—
Kadets: led by Paul Miliukov; a central liberal party that favoured constitutional monarchy with parliamentary democracy.	182	91	54	53
Octobrists: led by Alexander Guchkov; a moderate conservative party supported by wealthy industrialists and landowners.	17	42	154	95
Progressists: loose grouping of businessmen who favoured moderate reform.	—	—	28	41
Right-wing groups; Union of Russian People: led by Vladimir Purishkevich; parliamentary arm of the Black Hundreds, anti-Semitic, pro-monarchy/Orthodoxy.	9	10	147	154
National groups: Ukrainians, Poles, Georgians, Muslims; all seeking rights and greater independence.	60	93	26	22

Table 2.1: The parties that formed the Duma and the number of seats they gained during each sitting.

newly elected radicals. Unable to establish any common ground between his land reforms (see the section 'Stolypin's land reforms') and the radical demands of the left, who would accept nothing less than land confiscation, Stolypin dissolved the Duma on 16 June 1907 after a spurious claim emerged that the SDs had conspired to assassinate the Tsar. The SDs had their parliamentary immunity lifted even before the enquiry had established guilt, and rumours circulated that Stolypin had made the claim himself to evoke the emergency powers (Article 87) he needed.

ACTIVITY 2.1

1. What do you notice about the length of the Dumas? Why might this change have occurred?

2. How were the third and fourth Dumas different in composition from the first and second?

This time the Duma had lasted four months. In violation of the Fundamental Laws and in what some historians have referred to as a *coup d'etat*, Stolypin dramatically altered the franchise laws by which future Dumas could be elected. Perhaps unsurprisingly, representation of the urban population, the peasantry and the national minorities was cut right down, allowing the conservative gentry to hold a dominant influence.

Figure 2.3: Members of the First State Duma

The Third Duma, November 1907–June 1912: *The Duma of Lords and Lackeys*

The new electoral laws ensured the production of a co-operative legislature and hastened the retreat from liberalism; consequently, the Third Duma was the only one to serve out its full five-year term. In practice, this meant that members were much more willing to accept and support new legislation and much less likely to demand reform. The Octobrists won the majority of seats in this Duma, led by the wealthy Alexander Guchkov, who, though a conservative-monarchist, still engaged Stolypin in heated debates (particularly around concerns dear to him, such as foreign policy and defence) before agreeing to his laws. The Octobrist-dominated Duma voted on 2571 bills presented by the government and proposed 205 bills of its own. One of its greatest achievements was that, by 1914, the government had established 50 000 additional primary schools, which were administered and financed by the *zemstva*. Despite his respect for Stolypin and his willingness to co-operate, Guchkov created the first major clash between Stolypin and the Duma by pressing the government on naval ship-building programmes and criticising several of Nicholas's relatives for their malignant influence on the army. Despite the progress that had been made, Nicholas II began to lose trust in Stolypin, believing he was being self-aggrandising (promoting his own self-importance) by entertaining Guchkov, rather than acting in the interests of Russia.

Stolypin's second clash with the Duma came with his announcement of sweeping reform to local government to expand *zemstvo* activities and budgets. The *zemstvo* would also be introduced in western Russia, a move that had always been vetoed in the past due to fear of the 'disloyalty' of the Polish or Jewish subjects in the region. The nobility mounted a campaign against the reforms through the State Council, afraid that giving greater powers to the *zemstva* would lead to unsophisticated peasant electors being led astray again. The 'United Nobility' lobby group had won striking concessions from Stolypin by 1911, including a body dominated by nobles that would screen all local government proposals before they were put before the Duma. Stolypin prevailed in ensuring that two of the nobles who had led the campaign were disciplined by the Tsar, but this only served to alienate Nicholas. The Duma ended in disillusionment and suspicion.

As part of celebrations for the 50-year anniversary of the liberation of Russia's serfs, Tsar Nicholas II attended an opera in Kiev along with Prime Minister Stolypin. Dmitri Bogrov, a leftist revolutionary who was also an agent of the secret police, told the authorities there was a plan to assassinate Stolypin in the opera house; however, Bogrov was still allowed to attend carrying a revolver. Bogrov shot Stolypin twice, once in the arm and then again in the chest. After making the sign of the cross towards Nicholas, Stolypin was taken to hospital where he died four days later, on 18 September 1911, aged 49. Suspicion arose that the police had been actively involved in Stolypin's murder; this only increased when the Tsar halted the investigation into Stolypin's death without explanation.

The Fourth Duma, November 1912–February 1917

On the opening of the Fourth Duma, M.V. Rodzianko, who had succeeded Guchkov as president of the lower chamber, declared that its first order of business should be 'the implementation of the Great Manifesto of 17 October'[7]. The Octobrists feared renewed industrial unrest and saw that the government's actions were radicalising the people. As their leader Guchkov had remarked just before he lost his seat, 'with every day the people are losing faith in the state' cited in Rogger, 1983, p. 237. Stolypin's successor, Kokovstsov, suggested the opposite, namely that Russia's troubles were superficial and would pass; the tensions, he argued, existed only in the Duma (this debate has been echoed by historians throughout the last century).

A new party made up of industrialists and headed by the Riabushinkii brothers, whose views were opposed in many ways both to those of the Tsar and to those of the radical intelligentsia, began to dominate discussion in the Duma. One of the only 'progressive' bills passed in this period introduced the considerable expansion of the delivery of health services through the *zemstva;* consequently, in 1912, a system of health insurance for workers was established. However, the regime failed to develop a flexible labour policy, and, as historian R.B. McKean (1992) concludes, evolutionary reformist movements seemed unlikely to survive in Tsarist Russia after 1907. The Duma was plagued by ministers refusing to appear before the elected body, and a general drift towards the right ensued, with proposals even for mild reforms failing to translate into legislation. The only area that united Octobrists, Kadets and the rightist deputies was a rigorous, assertive foreign policy, a policy that in the words of Hans Rogger (1983) would lead to a 'fated drift into the abyss'[8].

Speak like a historian

This extract is taken from Alexander Chubarov's book, *The Fragile Empire,* 2001, page 153.

The social upheavals of 1905 had finally forced out of the government the promise to introduce a constitutional system with an elected parliament. However, Nicholas's reluctance to allow any weakening of his autocratic powers ensured that the government's attempts to devise a workable constitutional framework would be half-hearted and incomplete. When drawing up the Fundamental Laws early in 1906, Nicholas did all he could to limit the powers of the Duma. The electoral system discriminated heavily against peasants and workers; elections were to be indirect and votes were to be cast and counted by separate constituencies (called curios), set up for each class or property group.

Moreover, the powers vested in the new legislative forum were severely limited. Ministers remained responsible solely to the tsar and continued to be appointed and dismissed solely by him. The Duma had the power to reject only parts of the state budget. The new constitution transformed the traditional supreme body within the bureaucracy, the State Council, into an upper house, many of whose members were to be appointed by the tsar or nominated by the government. The tsar retained the power to veto all legislation, while Article 87 of the Fundamental Laws enabled him to rule by decree when the Duma was not in session. In addition, Nicholas insisted on referring to his own authority as 'autocratic', though he agreed to drop the word 'unlimited' from the traditional formula describing the sovereign's power. This now read: 'Supreme autocratic power belongs to the emperor of all Russia.' …

The constitutional reform had failed to bridge the gap between the government and Russia's rapidly changing educated elites. The new upper classes were politically disaffected, antagonised by Nicholas's attempts to stifle the potentially democratic institution of the Duma and his refusal to introduce a Western-style government. Even the backing the regime could expect from its traditional supporters, such as the landed nobility, was hesitant and uncertain. Its power now rested on the bureaucracy and the army alone. The most dangerous aspect of the government's position was the political blindness of the tsar, who still believed in the loyalty of the masses of the peasants, the army and the nobility. Nicholas simply was unable to see how isolated his government was and how narrow was the base of support for a government about to lead its country into a devastating international war.

Discussion points

1. What is Chubarov arguing here with regard to the constitution? Do you agree with him?
2. Can you find evidence in your notes to refute Chubarov's view that Nicholas had no supporters left in 1914?
3. Which groups does Chubarov think the regime needed support from in order to survive?

Using your own knowledge of the context, how convincing is his argument?

ACTIVITY 2.2

Timeline of 1894–1914

Learning the chronological order of events is really important for understanding how political developments unfolded. Use your notes to create a timeline like the one below.

1894–1900	1896 St Petersburg Strike
1900–Mar 1906	1904 Russo-Japanese War begins 1905 Revolution: October Manifesto 1906 Fundamental Laws
Apr–Jul 1906	First Duma
Feb–Jun 1907	Second Duma Electoral Laws
Jun 1907–1912	Third Duma 2571 bills voted on 1911 Stolypin assassinated
1912–1914	Opening of the Fourth Duma 50 000 additional primary schools

Use one colour to identify events that show a strengthening of the Tsarist regime and a second colour for events that show a weakening of the regime.

Economic developments to 1914: industrial and agricultural growth and change

While Alexander III and his son Nicholas II (1894–1917) remained resolutely committed to preserving their divine authority, Russia's traditional social structure underwent a profound transformation. The lead-up to the 1917 revolutions cannot be assessed without evaluating the impact of the rapid industrial development of the period. The Russian government never took an overall view of the consequences of its industrial policies, and historians have argued that these policies had serious repercussions for the stability of the regime at the turn of the century.

Industry

When Sergei Witte took over from the disgraced Vyshnegradsky as Minister of Finance in 1892, it was fairly obvious what his priorities would be. He had spent much of his career in private enterprises, particularly in the administration and management of various railroad lines in Russia, especially in Ukraine, where he was in charge of the Odessa Railway during the 1870s. In 1875, a train on the

Key term

Gold standard: a system of valuing money against fixed quantities of gold.

Odessa Railway derailed at the cost of many lives; for this, Witte was arrested and sentenced to four months in prison. However, while still contesting the case in court, the company made such extraordinary efforts towards the transport of troops and war materials in the Russo-Turkish War (1877–8) that Grand Duke Nikolai Nikolaevich (Alexander II's brother) intervened to have Witte's term reduced to two weeks. Tsar Alexander III appointed Witte acting Minister of Ways and Communications in 1892, and there began an ambitious programme of railway construction, including the famous Trans-Siberian Railway. The Russian Treasury invested 3.5 billion rubles in railroad building, which was a significant impetus for the development of metallurgy (the technology of mixing metals to create alloys) and machinery production. The production of minerals required by the railway programme – iron, coal and oil – almost trebled between 1885 and 1900, and virtually every other sector of industry benefited from the stimulus. Russia's growth rate reached 8 per cent (phenomenal by any standard) in the 1890s, despite her supposed 'backwardness', as investors copied advanced technologies from Western Europe, thus starting to help Russia 'catch up' to Britain and France. By 1914, Russia was the world's fifth largest industrial power (behind Britain, the USA, France and Germany) and fourth largest gold-mining nation.

Assessing the contribution of Sergei Witte

Sergei Witte's vision for Russia was borrowed from the German economist Friedrich List, who advocated a form of 'state capitalism' where the state would use its power and resources to promote a railroad boom that would foster heavy industrial growth, which would in turn lead to greater prosperity amongst the population. Following Vyshnegradsky's goal of improving the budgetary position of the country, Witte introduced a new ruble, which was tied to the gold standard. This was a successful move, as it encouraged foreign investors to put capital into Russia's heavy industries. Witte also took out foreign loans (particularly from the French); foreign debt increased by 1 billion rubles between 1895 and 1900.

Period	Mileage	Kilometres of railway track
1886–1890	1898	22 865
1891–1895	4403	—
1896–1900	10 035	53 234
1900–1913		67 000

Table 2.2: Increments in railroad mileage

Russia's industrialisation programme began with investment in the railways, which helps to explain the miles of track laid down during this time, the most significant of which was the Trans-Siberian Railway (completed in 1917). Witte realised that railways were profitable, and the state started to develop most of the railways without foreign investment; it owned two thirds of all railways in Russia by 1905.

	UK	France	Germany	Austria	Belgium	Russia
1820–4	17	1	1	0.1	—	—
1840–4	34	4	4	0.5	4	—
1860–4	86	10	21	4	10	0.04
1880–4	159	20	66	17	18	4
1900–4	230	33	157	39	23	17

Table 2.3: Output of coal and lignite (in million metric tonnes): selected countries, annual averages

Table 2.3 illustrates that although Russia made significant advances in coal output, so did other European nations and Russia still lagged behind her imperial counterparts, even the tiny nation of Belgium.

	UK	France	Germany	Austria	Belgium	Russia
1781–90	69	141	—	—	—	—
1825–29	669	212	90	85	—	164
1855–59	3583	900	422	306	312	254
1875–79	6484	1462	1770	418	484	424
1900–14	8778	2665	7925	1425	1070	2773

Table 2.4: Output of pig iron (in thousand metric tons): selected countries, annual averages

The development of pig-iron output was one of the areas of greatest success, demonstrating remarkable growth in 1900–14; however, Russia remained a long way behind Britain and Germany.

	UK	France	Germany	Austria	Belgium	Russia
1834	10 000	2500	626	800	200	700 (1840)
1877	39 500	5000	4700	1558	800	2500
1913	55 700	7400	11 186	4909	1492	9212

Source: http://www.fordham.edu/halsall/mod/indrevtabs1.asp
Table 2.5: Growth of the cotton industry in selected countries

The development of heavy industry intensified regional specialisation and increased the dependence of businesses on the state (see 'Speak like a historian' on capitalism). Spectacular expansion took place in coal mining in the Donets Basin, and the oil industry in the Caucasus saw explosive growth in the 1890s, even overtaking that of the United States. Russia's share of world steel output

Speak like a historian

Capitalism can be described as an economic system where the means of production are privately owned, which means there is a free market of private companies competing for profit. State capitalism can be described similarly, except that the state manages or organises the means of production and can dictate wages and organise the management of enterprises. This is why some historians have suggested that businessmen relied on the state, because it was the state that funded much of the enterprise that developed in Russia at the beginning of the 20th century.

rose from 2 per cent to 8 per cent from 1870 to 1900, putting her ahead of France. Russia had concentrated on developing her cotton industry by implanting highly mechanised systems of production around Moscow, which made the country the fourth largest producer of textiles worldwide; unfortunately, at the same time she fell far behind in wool manufacture. In fact, Alec Nove (1969) argues that even whilst Russia caught up with some European states, she was falling still further behind the United States and Germany, which were expanding their economies at a phenomenal rate. Additionally, most industrial equipment was still imported from Germany, and this was to cause a catastrophic shortage of armaments when the First World War broke out in 1914.

Industry 1905–14

The continuous strike activity that characterised much of 1905–6 (see the section 'Spontaneous revolution') also ravaged the industrial programme set up by Witte in 1892. Between 1900 and 1906, average annual rates of growth fell from 8 per cent to just 1.43 per cent: this decline was certainly linked to the political turmoil faced during those years. The regime now faced the difficult task of forcing Russia through another sustained period of industrialisation and growth. Some success was achieved. Between 1909 and 1913, annual industrial growth averaged 6 per cent, (see Table 2.6) in part due to the regime's demand for rearmament to re-equip the army in order to ensure the humiliating losses of the Russo-Japanese War of 1904–5 would never be repeated. Consequently, the coal, iron and steel industries grew, and rearmament renewed the economic impetus that the construction of the railways had provided; heavy industry thus continued to dominate growth figures. High expenditure in industry also benefited the manufacturers of textiles, albeit less dramatically. Russia still relied heavily on foreign investment: over 55 per cent of total capital came from foreign individuals, to the extent that overseas investors owned 54 per cent of heavy industry. Despite successes in continuing industrial growth, the gap between Russia and her European neighbours continued to widen as the Western economies grew even faster. Russia's per capita income had been half the Western average in 1860; by 1913 it had fallen to one third.

	1900	1913
Cotton consumption (million poods*)	16.0	25.7
Imports (million rubles)	626.3	1084.4
Savings accounts (millions)	4 988 000	8 992 000
Budget revenue (million rubles)	1704.1	3417.3
National debt (million rubles)	9 014 000	8 835 000

*A pood is a weight equivalent to 16.39 kg.
Table 2.6: Economic progress up to 1914

Agriculture

Agriculture was slow to develop in the late 19th century; in fact, it is difficult to discern any real change in the methods employed by peasants at all in this period.

Witte largely neglected agriculture, and the conservative voices, such as that of Pobodenostsev, that had the ear Nicholas II convinced him the status quo should be maintained in this area. The most significant change came because of falling grain prices, which forced many nobles to sell their land. The Peasant Land Bank that had been established under Alexander III cut interest rates, making it easier for peasants to take out loans to buy more land. This benefited some, particularly the more wealthy peasants known as *kulaks* (representing about 20% of all peasants) and by 1905 peasants owned 35 per cent of land holdings in Russia, compared to just 13 per cent owned by the nobles. On the other hand, around 10 per cent of all peasants were landless and lived in dire poverty.

Witte had argued that for Russia to maintain political stability, sustained economic growth was necessary. Wholesale modernisation was to prove impossible within an antiquated political structure and few of those at the centre of government understood the massive contradiction between the economic and social policies being pursued by the government. Whilst Witte energetically promoted industrialisation, the Ministry of the Interior (an extremely important body with responsibility for policing, national security and the supervision of local government) led by Ivan Durnovo and influenced by Pobedonostsev, pursued conservative policies that ignored and possibly impeded economic change. This was to prove fatal.

Considerable pressure had been placed on the peasant economy after emancipation. Land prices had begun to fall during the 1880s but increased again after the 1890s until 1914. The proportion of the workforce engaged in agriculture dropped only 2 per cent between 1880 and 1913, but the overall population had nearly doubled, so land shortage became an acute problem. In 1905, following mass peasant disturbances, the regime had decided to cut redemption payments in half for 1906, and abolished them altogether the following year. The ferociousness of the peasant unrest of 1905–6 persuaded the regime that the age-old commune would not guarantee rural stability.

Stolypin's land reforms

Stolypin saw the state of the peasantry as fundamental to the success of the regime. He was convinced of the need to replace communal with private ownership in the countryside and implemented the most significant reforms since

 Hidden voices

Note on statistics

Economic statistics from this period could lead a historian towards both positive and negative assessments of the success of Sergei Witte. Indices of industrial output reveal some progress was made in Russia under Witte and later Pyotr Stolypin (1906–11), but it is important to note that in this period Russia never

really caught up with Britain or the USA in terms of the amount of iron produced or per capita income. Marks (1991) has suggested state capitalism might have held Russia back from more rapid development, as businesses became too accustomed to taking their lead from the state. There is a general consensus amongst historians that the so-called 'Great Spurt' during the 1890s was made easier by the fact that Russia was starting from such a low level.

the abolition of serfdom in 1861. His theories were based on the belief that private ownership would foster initiative to experiment with more modern techniques, as had already happened in industry, and thus create a class of wealthier and therefore satisfied peasants who were loyal to the regime. Dismantling the *mir*, which Stolypin believed had often stoked peasant uprisings rather than controlled them, seemed a much more attractive way of appeasing land hunger than expropriating lands from the gentry.

Stolypin passed legislation that encouraged peasants to register their communal holdings as private property, allowing them to exchange their scattered strips for consolidated farms. Thus, 50 years after the emancipation statute, peasants could finally become sole owners of the land they worked on. Stolypin also created favourable loans and mortgage terms from the Peasant Land Bank to facilitate this process. The more important aspect of the legislation, however, was the discouragement of strip farming, which had continued after the abolition of serfdom. The *mir* had always dispersed allotments in different locations across the commune on a three-year rotation cycle (called 'repartition'); this had ensured fairness, as every family could have their chance at farming the best land at one time or another. However, the system was also wasteful of labour and rendered modern machinery useless. The legislation of 1906 allowed peasants to combine scattered strips into compact and enclosed farmsteads, as long as a two-thirds majority of villagers agreed to this. Consolidation was made automatic as titles were transferred in legislation passed in 1910. By 1915, about one third of peasant households had filed for separation from the *mir* and about 2.6 million (one quarter) completed the process. Some historians have argued that 9 per cent withdrew their applications because they were afraid of how other villagers would react. Approximately 10 per cent of those who applied for separation actually set up consolidated farms; of these, only 320 000 left the communal village to set up their new farmsteads. These peasants became the wealthiest group of *kulaks* and caused much resentment in peasant communities. The reluctance of most peasants to consolidate their farms can be explained by the security the commune offered. Those who did not consolidate merely sold all or part of their allotment land, either through need or simply out of a wish to relocate. As many as 3 million peasants relocated to Siberia to develop the dairy industry. While some peasants became quite wealthy under the new legislation, many fell deeper into poverty.

Agricultural growth under Nicholas II: an assessment

History books quote figures that show Russia's economy grew exponentially during Nicholas II's reign, yet these figures conceal great variations both geographically and from year to year. The population of the empire was growing at an annual rate of 1.5 per cent between 1883 and 1914, with grain production expanding by 2.1 per cent annually. However, around 400 000 died in the famine of 1891–2, and in 1905–8 harvests were poor across much of Russia and grain production fell. It is difficult to make generalisations about the state of the peasantry by 1914, as there were many differences even between peasants living in the same region; however, peasants with smaller allotments certainly suffered more than those with larger plots. Although it can be said that, overall, the agricultural economy avoided crisis in the 50 years following emancipation, it had failed to make the necessary progress by 1914.

Stolypin's reforms were disseminated over the course of five years but would have taken decades to implement. His wager on the 'sturdy and strong', as he called it, was a gamble that might have paid off had the population not continued to grow at such an alarming rate and had Stolypin survived long enough to oversee further reforms. As circumstances dictated, many of his reforms were simply not enacted, and so the sum of his achievements was merely that he bought the monarchy some much needed breathing space before the next crisis.

The difficult economic position of the peasantry and the poor state of agriculture in Russia represented a lasting problem that was faced by every leader dealt with in this study. The sheer scale of the changes that would need to be made, and the peasants' reluctance to break with age-old traditions, were things the Tsarist regime never came to terms with. After Stolypin's reforms it was not until Stalin's **collectivisation** policy that any major change was rolled out in Russian agriculture.

 Key term

Collectivisation: this was a policy introduced by Stalin in 1928 that aimed to consolidate individual land holdings into collective farms (***kolkhozy***) in the hope of increasing production. The human costs of this policy were enormous.

ACTIVITY 2.3

You should now be able to provide a broad assessment of economic developments in Russia across the period 1894–1914. Historians have debated the stability and strength of Russia on the eve of the First World War. The activity below is designed to help you consider your view on this issue. Go back over your notes from the previous section and look for evidence to support both views in the table.

	Industry	Agriculture
Russia had a strong economy in 1914		
Russia had a weak economy in 1914		

Social developments to 1914

Change and conditions of working and living in towns and countryside

Living conditions for industrial workers

The growth of Russia's urban population between 1867 and 1917 was startling. It quadrupled from 6 to 28 million in this relatively short space of time, causing significant social divisions in towns as well as in the countryside. By 1914, three out of four people living in St Petersburg were peasants by birth and over half the city's population had arrived since 1894. It is perhaps no surprise then that the strikes and riots that took place in major conurbations in 1905, 1912 and 1917 in many ways resembled the peasant uprisings in the 1860s. Despite the rapid growth of cities such as Moscow, the rate of modernisation did not always keep up and it was not uncommon to see livestock roaming the streets with peasant markets, such as the one in Red Square in Moscow.

Large-scale employers depended on the Tsarist regime to supply a cheap and malleable workforce and overwhelmingly supportive inspectorates. The industrial workers (numbering only about 2 million by 1900 but 6 million by 1913) suffered from long working hours and an absence of social legislation to protect them from the factory owners, who sometimes treated their employees like serfs. Wages failed to keep pace with inflation, even after the economic depression of 1900–08. Women were particularly poorly paid, despite making up a third of the workforce by 1914. Workers often lived in unsanitary conditions with overcrowded rooms (16 people per apartment and six to a room was common) or dormitories built hastily by factory owners, yet even in these poor conditions rents could consume up to half a worker's wages. Thirty thousand people died in cholera epidemics in St Petersburg during 1908–9 due to cramped and unsanitary conditions and the lack of sewage systems. Some families were even made to sleep on the factory floor itself, putting huge strains on family life. Accidents were common and compensation non-existent; there was no job security and owners could impose fines for the smallest mistakes. The Tsar failed to implement much legislation to improve the workers' lot, fearing that it would raise expectations of wage increases that would discourage foreign investment. By 1897, hours of work had been reduced to 11.5 per day, and after 1903 factories were supposedly subject to inspections relating to working conditions; it was not until 1912, however, that health insurance was implemented for sick workers. These changes meant little for workers who could not expect to provide a better life for their children. It is surely unsurprising that militancy and political consciousness grew within the factory proletariat under these conditions.

The wages of workers in textile and other light industries did not rise throughout the period, remaining low compared to those in the metallurgical industries. Witte placed high tariffs on manufactured consumer goods and thereby increased government revenues, but this weighed heavily on household budgets, both urban and rural. Most workers who had moved to the towns and cities were engaged in small-scale (workshop and artisan) industry. By 1915, small-scale industries employed about 67 per cent of those in the industrial sector, some 5.2 million people. However, it was the workforce in the huge factories in the metallurgical and textile industries (where over 1000 workers could be employed in a single factory) that would become the most dangerous to the Tsarist regime.

Living in the countryside

One of Witte's economic policies from 1894 had been to increase indirect taxation, which disproportionately affected those on the lowest incomes, namely the peasants, who were already making redemption payments for inadequate landholdings under the Emancipation Ukase of 1861 (see the section 'Emancipation of the serfs – a liberation?'), and their arrears (debts) accumulated. Witte had also continued Vyshnegradsky's grain export policy despite the famine of 1891 and grain prices continued to fall globally, which meant peasants were yielding lower returns on their holdings during the 1890s. Pressure on the land was mounting as the rural population exploded by 25 per cent between 1877 and 1905, reaching well over 100 million by 1910. Despite Stolypin's reforms (see the section 'Agriculture') the 'solcha', or wooden plough, was still used by many peasants, and ration systems dating back to medieval times were still practised, which were wasteful and discouraged productivity.

Many of those peasants who relocated to work in the cities, particularly before 1905, did so only for temporary periods and usually returned to the countryside in time for harvest. Villagers were therefore increasingly exposed to urban life, and literacy increased steadily and notably over this period. It is important to note, though, that the overwhelming majority of peasants chose to remain in the villages and therefore had little if any contact with urban culture. Peasants were becoming more assertive as a consequence of their newly acquired literacy (the literacy rate among the peasantry had reached almost 40% by 1914) and this caused a shift in their awareness of nationality and wider society (Moon in Thatcher ed. 2005). Due to the woeful lack of reform in agriculture and attempts by Stolypin to exclude the peasantry in the electoral laws of 1907, most peasants became increasingly indifferent to the new constitutional regime.

Figure 2.4: Dormitory of horse-tram workers in 1898, showing the cramped living conditions of industrial workers.

Social divisions

The position of the nobility in Russia had been getting worse since the 1861 statutes. Noble landowners had seen holdings decrease from 200 million acres in the 1870s to approximately 140 million acres by 1910. Although landowning nobles still occupied two thirds of senior state offices, this proportion was diminishing as newly educated non-landowners tried to make a career in the bureaucracy. The nobility was not a homogenous group; liberal elements were pushing for greater roles in government, as well as industrialists and even some intellectuals. The provincial nobility still maintained a great deal of influence through the *zemstva* and tried to hinder progressive innovations.

By 1914, one can speak of a middle class (approximately 2 million people) that had developed due to the commercial and industrial developments under Witte and Stolypin. But there were divisions even within this small group: Jews, those born outside Russia and those working in commerce were distinctly different to the intellectuals. The number of primary-school teachers and doctors doubled between 1900 and 1914, and these individuals often filled the ranks of the *zemstva* boards. The most famous middle-class capitalists were surely the Morozov family, former serfs who started a dye works and by 1914 employed 54 000 workers. After a strike in 1885, where workers protested against fines as penalties for misdemeanours, the youngest Morozov, Savva, tried to improve conditions for them. In 1905 he proposed sharing profits amongst workers; his mother persuaded the board to dismiss him and he shot himself.

The status of women in Russia was at least as high in 1913 as it was anywhere else in the world. All the radical movements included female liberation among their aims, and these ideas took root amongst the educated classes. In 1905, university co-education began and female doctors, teachers and architects began to filter into *zemstva* and town organisations. In 1908, the first All-Russia Women's Congress was held, where it was decided that, although there was still much to be done, the restrictions encountered by women in Russia were less oppressive than elsewhere in Western Europe.

The proletariat began to act with some solidarity within the period, despite the banning of trade unions until 1905 (even after this they were only allowed with multiple restrictions). The first time that collective industrial action successfully changed working conditions was in 1896 with the St Petersburg textile workers' strike, which achieved an 11-hour working day. However, wages remained low and living conditions were still very poor, and strikes intensified in the more prosperous years from 1911 onwards. The strike at the Lena goldfields in 1912 was perhaps the most notable of these, where around 500 workers were shot by government troops, half of that number fatally. This event became etched into workers' memories as proof that the government was not acting in their interests.

All Russian subjects were required to have internal passports, and in the towns the police had lists of all inhabitants' addresses. Individual rights were almost non-existent: for example on May Day in 1912 the police chased from the streets any men who were not wearing collars (many felt this was merely to try and prevent a workers' demonstration). However, police repression was generally accepted as part of life in Russia, particularly since the shocking assassination of Alexander II in 1881.

Ethnic minorities

The census of 1897 revealed that only 43 per cent of the Russian population could be called ethnically Russian; the regime's overt identification with this group, as well as its commitment to the Orthodox Church, continued to alienate ethnic minorities. Nicholas II continued Alexander III's heavy-handed policy of Russification, which sought to discriminate against minority languages and religions. Nowhere was this discrimination more intense than in Poland: Nicholas even installed a large garrison there to ensure the mass uprising of 1863 was not repeated. This was when mass demonstrations against the loss of 100 000 jobs and terrible working conditions took place in Warsaw in November, which quickly turned violent. Years of imposing the Russian language and the Orthodox Church on communities in Poland and the Baltic states bred bitter resentment, which would become manifest in 1905 in waves of strikes and violent protests against the autocratic regime.

For the Jewish communities in the empire (the Jewish population numbered approximately 5.5 million by 1900) Nicholas II's reign brought dramatic socio-economic change, mostly contributing to their impoverishment. The regime did not attempt to 'Russify' the Jews: they were simply persecuted. As under Alexander III, efforts continued to prevent Jews from acquiring land or accessing higher education, and pogroms were commonplace in times of crisis. The most notable wave of anti-Jewish violence came in 1903, when the *Okhrana* and state police not only turned a blind eye but also seemed to endorse the violence. Such events only helped accelerate massive Jewish migration to the United States and elsewhere, which drained something in the order of a fifth to a quarter of the Jewish population from Russia between 1881 and 1914. Those who stayed were often drawn in disproportionately high numbers to radical socialist groups, which were playing an increasingly important role by 1905 in drumming up proletarian unrest: Trotsky, Martov, Zinoviev and Kamenev are all examples of ethnic Jews who took up the revolutionary cause.

Cultural changes

By 1914, most writers of the 'Golden Age' of Russian literature were dead, and writers such as Maxim Gorki were foretelling a new generation of proletarian writers who would come to dominate literature in the 1930s. Gorki had been influenced by the playwright Anton Chekhov, who had grown up in a middle-class family much like those that later dominated his plays. Gorki, however, was an orphan who achieved success writing about lowly characters, and epitomised the movement of 'critical realism' that began to put down roots in Russia during this period. He had given money to the Bolsheviks in the early days, but from 1906 became an anti-Leninist. A selection of essays by liberal philosophers entitled *Vekhi* ('Landmarks') was published in 1909 and became influential (see the section 'Opposition to radicals after 1905'); these writers tended to reinforce the mystical, even the occult, in contrast to the critical realists. Their writings demonstrated the divide between the old, traditional values and the new, radical values of the proletariat.

With the development of primary schools (there were 120 000 by 1914, with 8 million pupils) and the increase in working-class participation in secondary education, Russian publications began to achieve wider readership after 1900. The illustrated weekly *Niva* was one example of a liberal, family-orientated journal, and had a circulation of 235 000. The novel was attracting popular readership by 1914 and Aleksei Suvorin (publisher of the ultra-conservative newspaper *Novoye Vremiya*) produced cheap editions of novels that were sold at railway stations. Women were influencing publishing for the first time: Anastasia Verbitskaya's *Keys of Happiness* sold 30 000 copies in four months (though it was criticised for lacking depth). The Bolsheviks capitalised on this new female readership, developing a women's section in their publication *Pravda*.

By 1914, St Petersburg had become one of the European capitals of art, and artists such as Repin, Serov and the abstract painter Kandinsky drew large crowds to their exhibitions, despite many traditionalists criticising the newer 'Western' styles. Ballet had flourished throughout the 19th century, heavily influenced by French and Italian styles. By the 1890s, Russian music was becoming popular, composers such as the innovative Igor Stravinsky becoming well known. Stravinsky achieved international acclaim with three ballets that were commissioned by the impresario Sergei Diaghilev and first performed in Paris by Diaghilev's Ballets Russes:

Voices from the past

Pogrom in Kishinev, 1903

Kishinev, the capital of the Tsarist province of Bessarabia, today's Republic of Moldova, was a town of some 125 000 residents, nearly half of them Jewish. Ethnic tensions were running high in the spring of 1903, thanks in part to a campaign of anti-Semitic incitement by local nationalists.

Rumours had spread through the town on Easter Sunday that a Christian had been killed by Jews in a ritual murder. This provoked a two-day pogrom where houses and synagogues were burned to the ground and it was reported that women were raped and killed. It is estimated that, by the end of the pogrom, 49 Jews had been killed and 500 wounded, 1300 homes and businesses had been looted and destroyed and 2000 families were left homeless.

Figure 2.5: Cover for a record created in New York in 1904 to commemorate the Kishinev massacre of 1903.

The Firebird (1910), *Petrushka* (1911) and *The Rite of Spring* (1913). Stravinsky transformed the way in which subsequent composers thought about rhythmic structure and he became known as perhaps the most important composer of the 20th century.

Opposition

Ideas and ideologies: liberalism, socialism and Marxism: individuals and radical groups

Although opposition had been active during both his grandfather's and his father's reigns, under Nicholas II discontent increased across society, from the privileged to the peasantry.

Social Democrats

The failure of the terrorism of groups such as People's Will in the 1870s gave rise to Marxist groups that came to form a distinct group within the intelligentsia, which represented the greatest threat to the regime by 1917. Georgi Plekhanov had fathered the Marxist movement with his Emancipation of Labour group (founded 1883), which was based on the idea that terrorism was futile and political change would only come about through fundamental changes in economic relations. Plekhanov advocated a two-stage revolution in which, initially, socialists would help the emerging bourgeoisie to topple the autocratic regime and adopt Western-style freedoms. Then, in the second stage, they would organise the working class for the inevitable day when the proletariat would rise up against their bourgeois oppressors. Plekhanov's followers became known as the **Social Democrats** (SDs). However, the activists found little support for the idea of revolution from the industrial workers with whom they worked throughout the 1890s. The workers seemed to be more interested in forming illegal trade unions and campaigning for better pay and conditions. However, by banning trade unions the Tsarist regime was politicising industrial relations, and waves of strike action at the end of the 19th century would turn the tide for the popularity of the radical Marxist groups.

It was the strike of 1896 in St Petersburg textile factories that first seemed to suggest Social Democratic ideas were taking a wider hold. By June 1896, about 19 factories were affected and 16 000 workers were involved; Social Democrat activists organised delegate meetings and supported workers because they believed every strike provided agitational material. The strikes were brutally suppressed, with the arrest of over 1000 workers; it became clear that the actions of the SDs needed to be formalised.

The Russian Social Democratic Labour Party (RSDLP) was founded in March 1898 with the merger of over 20 very small Marxist groups, all of which were opposed to *narodnichestvo* (revolutionary populism, i.e. the focus on the peasantry as revolutionary agents). All RSDLP leaders elected at its founding conference were quickly arrested and exiled – not quite the auspicious start they had hoped for. By the time of the RSDLP's Second Congress in August 1903, two young intellectuals had come to dominate the group: Vladimir Ulyanov, who went by the pseudonym 'Lenin', and Julius Martov, who together had set up the newspaper *Iskra* ('The Spark', taken from a poem by Alexander Pushkin that reads 'From a spark a fire will flare up'). Soon they drew older revolutionaries such as Vera Zasulich (see the section 'Judicial reforms') into their orbit, as well as younger Jewish revolutionaries including Leon Trotsky.

The role of Martov and Lenin

Martov and Lenin used their *Iskra* newspaper to engage with the intellectual struggle between worker-leaders who thought strikes were becoming too politicised and the SDs who condemned what Lenin called 'economism' (where unions focused on pay and conditions instead of true revolutionary goals). *Iskra* was used as a vehicle to convince workers that they needed a group of professional revolutionaries to lead them, sticking firmly to Marxist principles. 'Economism' seemed to triumph at first, helped by Lenin's exile in Siberia for political agitation; the question was only really addressed when the Second Congress of the Russian Social Democratic Labour Party (RSDLP) met in London in August 1903. Lenin had outlined his agenda in the treatise *What is to be done?* published in 1902.

Lenin was drawn to Marxism as a result of the famine of 1891. He had been schooled by the father of Alexander Kerensky – ironically, his arch-rival by 1917 – and had a fairly typical liberal background. His older brother had been a member of the People's Will group and was executed in 1887 for his part in a plot to execute Alexander III. Historians have debated the extent to which this event influenced the development of his brand of Marxism thereafter. Figes (2014) suggests that much of Lenin's ideology – his stress on the need for a small, tight-knit revolutionary leadership; his belief that action could alter the course of history; his defence of terror and his contempt for liberals – stemmed not just from Marx but early Russian revolutionaries like Tkachev and People's Will. This is supported by the pamphlet *What is to be done?, the title of* which was taken from a book by one of Lenin's heroes, Chernychevsky (see the section 'Radicals'). Many of the ideas laid out in his pamphlet seemingly have little do to with Marx, and it was clear already that Lenin believed in expediency over doctrine (i.e. he was willing to sacrifice his moral convictions for practical purposes). Later, he would develop his own brand of Marxism to lead the Bolshevik Party.

Speak like a historian

The Social Democrats were a group of Marxists who believed that it was the workers who would become the revolutionaries in Russia. The problem was that they relied on Marxist theories about capitalism and its effect on the proletariat: industrialisation was not yet fully developed in Russia, which meant the country had not yet reached the stages of capitalism described by Marx. This is one reason why the Social Democrats split in 1903: they disagreed on how capitalism would develop in Russia and therefore on how the working classes would be best led towards revolution.

Voice from the past

Trotsky

Leon Bronstein, better known as Trotsky, was a Marxist revolutionary and theorist who was born into a Ukrainian-Jewish farming family in 1879. After schooling in Odessa, he became involved in revolutionary activities in 1896 and, like Lenin, was influenced by the populist movement. He was arrested in 1898 for forming a workers' union in southern Russia. Whilst in prison in Siberia he read Lenin's work and began to identify himself as a Marxist; he escaped in 1902 and fled to

London using a false passport under the name 'Trotsky', which he adopted as his revolutionary pseudonym. He returned to Russia briefly in 1905 to take part in the revolution, during which he was elected vice-chairman of the St Petersburg Soviet. He was arrested and sent to Siberia again, although he once again escaped and spent time in Vienna, Paris and New York. Trotsky returned to Russia in May 1917, where he would play a significant role in organising the seizure of power by the Bolsheviks in October 1917.

The Second Congress of the RSDLP was significant because it caused a rift in the party that was never to be mended. The Congress met in London – it was safer to do so there – and despite quickly agreeing that a centralist organisational structure was needed, the delegates could not agree on what constituted a party member. In *What is to be done?* Lenin had argued for restricting membership to those workers who participated in party cells, because they would need almost permanent tutelage from professional revolutionaries to move beyond trade-union consciousness. Martov disagreed and wanted to include members who were not prepared to attend secret meetings but still distributed leaflets. The Congress took a vote: although Martov received more votes on this issue, his group became known as the Mensheviks (minority) and Lenin's supporters as the Bolsheviks (majority). In the wake of the Congress, Lenin began to focus not only on battling the Mensheviks (an ironic struggle, given Marx's view that historical development was motivated by impersonal forces) but also on the plight of the peasantry. Lenin saw the peasant uprisings of 1902 as evidence of their revolutionary potential as allies of the workers. Martov and the Mensheviks (supported by Plekhanov) believed in a gradualist approach to build a party of workers and intellectuals. These intellectual struggles were one reason why, when revolutionary activity broke out at the beginning of 1905, both factions of the SDs found themselves unable to harness the growing industrial discontent.

Social Revolutionaries

The Social Revolutionary Party, set up by Victor Chernov in 1902, was distinctly different from the RSDLP. The Social Revolutionaries (SRs) saw the 'proletariat' as anyone who was being exploited, not just the industrial workers. The SRs maintained a close affiliation to the peasantry and continued to try to organise the peasants into a revolutionary force. The SRs had largely grown out of the Populist movement and saw Marxism as a callous scheme obsessed with the vision of capitalism as a necessary precursor to the egalitarian revolution; in Russia, they saw this vision resulting in the encouragement of the exploitation of the workers. The SRs launched a Peasant Union in November 1902 with the specific aim of organising rent boycotts and illegal pasturing as well as violence, including arson. They formalised their programme at their First Congress in 1906. The SRs were more successful than the SDs at first: as the historian Perrie (1982) notes, peasant unions were established in Saratov, Kharkov and Ekaterinoslav, and peasant disturbances increased. Peasants were increasingly responsive to the SRs' calls for 'socialisation of the land' and the abolition of all private property. Another distinct difference between the SDs and SRs was that the Social Revolutionaries were committed to terror. Even before the formalisation of the party, members of the movement had assassinated the Tsar's Minister of Education in 1901, followed by the Minister of the Interior in 1902. These acts formed part of a chain of assassinations that would include those of the Governor of Kharkov in 1902 and the Governor of Ufa in 1903. Perhaps the most high-profile killings were those of the new Minister of the Interior, V.K. Plehve – a much hated figure – and the Governor-General of Moscow, Grand Duke Sergei, in July 1904 and February 1905, respectively. The SRs' terrorism was disciplined, however, targeting specific officials on the basis of their policy or their perceived closeness to the Tsar. They might have assassinated more if Yevno Azef, a key member of the SRs, hadn't also been working for Plehve as a double agent. However, after extreme violence had been perpetrated against Jewish communities without police intervention in 1904 (see the section 'Ethnic minorities'), Azef, himself a Jew, took no action to prevent the assassination of his chief.

Liberals

Russian liberals were of the Westernising tradition and were found mostly amongst *zemstvo* officials and other groups of professionals. There was no inevitable drift towards conflict with the regime inherent in this group. The more conservative amongst them (generally the landed gentry of the *zemstva*) only wanted an extension of the *zemstvo* to a national scale, perhaps as a consultative body. In 1896, moved by Nicholas II's 'senseless dreams' speech, the Moscow zemstvo chairman D.N. Shipov lobbied Goremykin, the Minister of the Interior, to extend the *zemstva* to the Western regions of Russia. In Shipov's view, the Russian tradition envisaged a benevolent Tsar guided by the loyal advice of a few representatives. Goremykin agreed but was dismissed from his post and replaced by the ultra-conservative Plehve; thus, in one simple action Nicholas II undermined the credibility of the moderate liberals. The regime increasingly became involved with matters of local government: *zemstvo* activities had flourished since the famine in 1891 and Pobedonostsev and the police believed *zemstvo* meetings were a cover for carrying out subversive activities amongst the peasants. These fears were mostly unjustified. The failure of successive Ministers of the Interior to recognise the liberals as allies of the regime pushed even the most moderate among them to support revolution in 1905.

Other liberal focuses included social reforms such as the extension of primary education and an end to the separate legal status of the peasantry. The more radical elements of the liberal movement – small but significant numbers of doctors, lawyers and teachers – advocated a constitutional monarchy akin to the British model, with an elected parliament. They did not intend open revolution, but thought change was necessary. The former Marxist Pyotr Struve founded the liberal newspaper *Liberation* in 1901. Struve suggested that revolutionaries and Marxists could move together but end at different terminal points, which was an alarming prospect for some close to the Tsar. The appointment of Prince Mirskii to the Ministry of the Interior after the assassination of Plehve convinced Struve to act. Mirskii was very different to his predecessor: his key idea was to win the 'trust' of the Russian people, and he set about eliminating the most hated elements of Plehve's policies. Struve set up the Union of Liberation in January 1904 and a vote was taken on whether to ask Mirskii for a parliament with legislative authority. Struve's supporters won by a ratio of two to one. People at the time compared it to the meeting of the Estates-General in 1789, on the eve of the French Revolution. The Liberationist movement led by Struve and the history lecturer Paul Miliukov had the widest appeal of all the opposition groups active at the beginning of the 20th century; support for it would only increase as the regime became embroiled in its humiliating war with Japan in 1904.

Trade unions

From the mid-1880s there was a marked upsurge in strikes: in 1896 the textile industry was almost completely paralysed for a short period. A famine in 1898–9 in the central Volga region, followed by peasant unrest in the Kharkov and Poltava provinces in 1902, demonstrated the sensitivity of the national economy to international recessions and continuing troubles in the countryside. The growth of trade unions, illegal in Russia until 1901, was evidence of the proletarianisation of the workforce in the towns of Russia, and it frightened the authorities. Fears were nourished by the concentration of large numbers of workers in relatively few factories; for example, in 1895, plants with more than 1000 workers accounted for 31 per cent of those engaged in industry. The larger factories were fertile soil for socialist propaganda, particularly given the fact that male factory hands were more literate than the population as a whole: the census of 1897 showed that 58 per cent could read, compared to only 28 per cent of Russians of both sexes across the rest of the country. May Day strikes in St Petersburg in 1891 saw a departure of the workers' movement from purely economic concerns: banners held up by the strikers demanded the right to strike, political liberty and an end to autocracy. The police treated strikes as breaches of public order, and experience made the workers receptive to socialist arguments that an alliance between factory bosses and the authorities was the inevitable outcome of bourgeois capitalism.

Sergei Zubatov, head of the Moscow *Okhrana*, believed that the threat of striking workers and socialist agitators could be neutralised if their working conditions and wages were improved. Zubatov's scheme aimed to wrest initiative from radical opposition groups and provide the workers with trade unions and education under police sponsorship and supervision. He allowed educational lectures to be given by liberal-minded professors on topics such as labour exchanges and even politics. Zubatov allowed three unions in Moscow, which amalgamated workers in different industries, headed by men he trusted to espouse his views. Perhaps unavoidably, these men became genuine spokesmen for their members and 'Zubatov Unions', as they came to be called, spread to cities across Russia. This alarmed Witte in particular, for he saw them as a threat to the industrial programme as the number of strikes increased and demands for higher wages grew more vocal. It was not until 1903 that the programme of police-approved unions was abruptly terminated after a strike in Odessa became uncontrollable. A prison chaplain named Father Gapon would use Zubatov's ideas to mobilise thousands of workers in St Petersburg to show the regime that workers' discontent could not be ignored (see the section 'Mistakes: Bloody Sunday').

Opposition to radicals after 1905
It has been estimated that, between 1906 and 1907, SR terrorists killed or maimed at least 4500 Tsarist officials; if private persons are counted, the number could have been anything up to 9000. Radical politics was becoming exile politics (either forced or voluntary) as the regime extended the police state and ratcheted up the pressure on revolutionaries. Stolypin attempted to suppress the terrorists by setting up field courts-martial, which were show courts led by military generals that tended to summarily dispense death sentences regardless of the evidence presented (see the section 'The First Duma'). These courts-martial were so efficient that approximately 3000 'terrorists' were convicted and executed by hanging (referred to by contemporaries as 'Stolypin's necktie') between 1906 and 1909; a further 38 000 were sentenced to penal servitude. The policy of intimidation seemed to have some success: peasant uprisings and industrial strikes virtually ceased between 1906 and 1910. The Social Democrats, whose membership figures

had reached an impressive 150 000 in 1905, saw this figure dwindle to just 10 000 by 1910, with no more than five active committees operating within Russia. This was probably due to the repressive government measures and their leaders' exile.

Shocked at the violence that had swept through the countryside in 1905, zemstvo leaders began an effective purge of so-called 'radicals', particularly in the teaching and medical professions, who were accused of having placed the fomenting of political disquiet above their professional responsibilities during the disturbances. Attacks on radicalism accelerated in 1909, led by the Liberationist Struve, who led a literary assault on the radical political intelligentsia, criticising their alienation from popular culture. He and a few others published a series of essays called *Landmarks* (see the section 'Cultural changes'), condemning fellow intellectuals for failing to understand Russian society. The retreat from radicalism served to distance the middle classes from the working-class movements with whom they had united in the turbulence of 1905. However, by 1914 most liberals were dissatisfied with the parliamentary experiment and felt alienated by the regime. The victories of 1905 had not led to greater political participation as they had hoped; Stolypin had thwarted their ability to dominate the Duma with the 1907 '*coup d'etat*', creating rightist majorities that opposed even mild reform.

Educational repression

University students and teachers had particular reason to feel frustrated with the regime. Successive Ministers of Education ignored the temporary rules instituted in 1905, which had restored autonomy to universities regarding intake and academic appointments. Dozens of deans and professors were replaced with pro-government academics. When Leo Tolstoy died in 1910, university students held giant demonstrations for academic freedom. The government responded in a predictably heavy-handed way, provoking further disorder, which spread across almost all universities in Russia. In 1911, the Minister of Education, Leo Kasso, launched a crackdown on student activities and a further purge of professors. The purge backfired in the long term, as it pushed young intellectuals towards the revolutionary parties that had begun to establish themselves as a real political force in Russia by 1914.

Industrial unrest

The celebrations of 1913 that marked the tercentenary of the Romanov dynasty's rule over Russia appeared to show there was widespread support for the regime. However, industrial strife had exploded once more after February 1912 and the Lena goldfields massacre (see the section 'Social divisions'). Following this, 2032 strikes were recorded that year as news of the government's actions spread. Like Bloody Sunday in 1905, the massacre seemed to show the regime's contempt for its own people, and precipitated renewed growth in trade-union membership as well as increased support for the Bolsheviks. The Bolsheviks had been able to infiltrate unions in Moscow and St Petersburg due to increased funding, secured largely through illegal activities such as bank robberies. Their newspaper, *Pravda* ('The Truth'), was selling 40 000 copies a day after 1912, demonstrating the party's growing support.

Trade unions had about 300 000 members in 1907, but in 1913 – even after a year of growth – only 40 000 were recorded. Workers' grievances had not been eradicated by the right to organise, which was granted in 1906, but trade unions continued to be shut down on grounds of sedition until 1912. The industrial boom that swept through Russia in 1909 did not dispel workers' demands, as urban population growth caused living conditions to deteriorate. Nor were workers appeased by accident insurance, which provided sickness benefits from 1912. Intolerable strains were put on public services and the death rate from infectious diseases was the highest in Europe at the time. In the first half of 1914 alone, there were 3000 strikes in which workers demanded a democratic republic, an eight-hour working day and the expropriation of noble landholdings (that is, they wanted the government to seize all privately held land and share it amongst the people). The growth of the cities was still being fuelled by fresh arrivals from rural areas; historian Ian Thatcher (2005) suggests their frustrations at encountering worse conditions than those they had left behind might help explain the anarchic turbulence that broke out after 1912.

Leopold Haimson (1964) convincingly argues that the politicised elements of Russian society were undergoing a dangerous process of polarisation in the major urban centres: on the one hand were the privileged groups that had retreated from revolution after 1905, and on the other were the growing numbers of discontented industrial workers, 'exposed to the pleas of an embittered revolutionary minority'[9]. Polarisation was also occurring between elements of privileged society and the Tsarist regime. Although the nobility seemed to have retained their status and influence over policy, and the *zemstva* had gained responsibilities as Land Captains lost their judicial functions, the high hopes that had characterised 1905 had been unfulfilled largely because of Nicholas's unwillingness to reform. This served to undermine liberal calls for gradualist reform and increased the likelihood of radicalism seizing Russia.

The role of Rasputin

By 1914, it seemed that even educated and privileged Russians were disillusioned with the Tsarist regime. In the Duma, Guchkov had taken his military interests further by waging frequent attacks on the Minister of War, Sukhomlinov, who he accused of associating with a German spy. More serious, however, were widespread rumours regarding the new favourite at court, a Siberian peasant mystic named Gregori Rasputin. The mystic had inexplicably appeared to help stop the Tsar's haemophiliac son's bouts of bleeding, and this had convinced the Tsarina he had been sent from God to protect them; he soon became ensconced in royal circles. His name became synonymous with intrigue and many regarded him as a sinister influence, as he used his position to secure favours for those who paid enough. Rasputin also brought scandal to the court as tales of sordid, alcohol-fuelled orgies circulated St Petersburg. Even the nobility began to castigate the royal court for decadence, bribery and corruption.

Conclusions

Historians have long debated how stable Russia was on the eve of the First World War. To the general observer, on the surface there had been economic prosperity and the regime had regained control after weathering the revolution of 1905. Yet underneath the surface, tensions were simmering, particularly after the Lena goldfields massacre of 1912. Socialist politics had been marginalised after the electoral laws, and left-leaning liberals on the *zemstva* had become disillusioned with the parliamentary monarchy, as by 1914 the Duma had been reduced virtually to an ornamental institution. As Figes (1997) summarises, 'during its political downfall, the old regime chose repression instead of compromise and thus created the political hostility'[10]. Trade unions were legalised in 1905 but the state police recurrently shut down particular unions (estimates suggest 600 had been closed by 1911). Political parties were legal; even the revolutionary parties could stand for elections in the Duma, yet members were still scrutinised by the *Okhrana* and subject to frequent arrest. Many revolutionary activists, such as Lenin, were forced to emigrate to avoid imprisonment or exile. Some peasants had prospered, but after Stolypin's assassination agricultural reform lost direction and pace, and the commune remained at the heart of the agricultural system. Industrial workers enjoyed higher wages and more frequent employment, but they had not forgotten 1905, and living conditions failed to improve. As Hans Rogger (1983) asserts, 'Of the major governments of Europe, none had so little credit with the people it would shortly have to lead in war as that of Nicholas II'[11].

Political authority: opposition and the state of Russia in wartime

The First World War

Whether or not Russia was on the brink of a revolution in 1914 has been vigorously debated amongst historians, though it is clear that even ministers close to the Tsar feared the worst. What is unarguable is that the First World War was a huge contributory factor in making revolution come about. In February 1914, Pyotr Durnovo, the head of the secret police and Minister of the Interior, wrote a chillingly prophetic memorandum to the Tsar, warning him against war with Germany:

The trouble will start with the blaming of the government for all disasters. In the legislative institutions a bitter campaign against the government will begin, followed by revolutionary agitations throughout the country, with Socialist slogans, capable of arousing and rallying the masses, beginning with the division of the land and succeeded by a division of all valuables and property. The defeated army, having lost its most dependable men, and carried away by the tide of primitive peasant desire for land, will find itself too demoralized to serve as a bulwark of law and order. The legislative institutions and the intellectual opposition parties, lacking real authority in the eyes of the people, will be powerless to stem the popular tide, aroused by themselves, and Russia will be flung into hopeless anarchy, the issue of which cannot be foreseen.

Source: (cited in Golder, 2008 (original edition 1927) pages 21–22)

Durnovo was to be proven correct, and by 1917 the ravages of war had done irreparable damage to the 304-year-old Romanov dynasty. It finally collapsed on 15 March 1917.

Summary of key events

- In some ways, Russia could be considered politically stable by 1914; for example, Duma members were co-operating better and could pass legislation.

- In 1913, Tsar Nicholas celebrated the tercentenary of Romanov rule over Russia and thousands of people visited St Petersburg to join the celebrations.

- In many ways, though, Russia could be considered a cauldron of discontent ready to boil over in 1914, as radical groups were gaining popularity through sustained agitation in soviets. More strikes were taking place than in 1905.

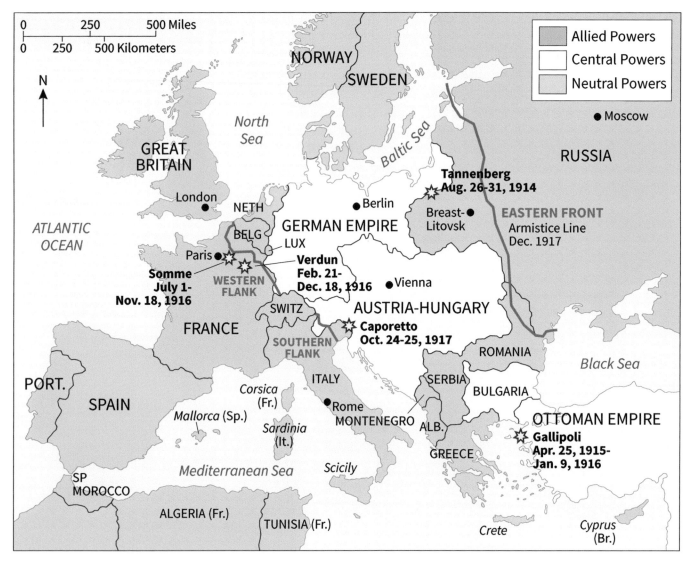

Figure 2.6: European alliances and battlefronts, 1914–17

The political, economic and social problems of wartime

The onset of war took the Tsar's military advisers rather by surprise. After the losses of the Russo-Japanese War, a huge rearmament programme had been launched focusing particularly on the navy (see the section 'Industry 1905–14'); however, few of Nicholas's advisers had expected another conflict before 1916. Fewer still expected that if hostilities broke out they would last any longer than five months. What forced the reluctant Nicholas II to mobilise Russia's army was Austro-Hungary's interest in the Balkans, including the Straits (a narrow sea channel stretching from Russia's only year-round, ice-free port in the Black Sea to the Mediterranean). The assassination of Archduke Franz Ferdinand on 28 June 1914 provoked localised hostilities in the region, inevitably dragging the great empires of Russia and Austro-Hungary – as well as the young, ambitious Germany – into conflict with each other.

The map in Figure 2.6 demonstrates the key territories Russia wanted to protect. It also shows the two opposing blocs of power.

A protracted war, such as the First World War became, provided Russia with insurmountable problems. The first three weeks of the war saw Russia inflict some remarkable victories against the Germans, forcing them to retreat from attacking positions. However, the Battle of Tannenberg (26–30 August 1914), where the veteran German general von Hindenburg prevailed, was a catastrophe for the Russians. Whilst the German high command celebrated 92 000 Russians captured and 78 000 killed, the Russian General Samsonov committed suicide. Tannenberg was followed by swift defeat at the Battle of the Masurian Lakes, where the Russians suffered around another 100 000 casualties. By the end of 1914, long trenches had been dug on both fronts from the mountains to the sea, and unprecedented pressures were being placed on the regime. Russia had 6.5 million soldiers engaged in the conflict but only 4.6 million rifles. Production in artillery shells demonstrated a woeful lack of capacity to fight a lengthy war; factories could only provide 360 000 shells a month, against a demand of 1.5 million; some batteries were unable to return enemy fire by 1915. By the end of 1915 Russia had suffered almost two million casualties and, as Peter Gattrell's (1999) study of the war illustrates, 35 million people – about a third of the total population of European Russia – were under occupation.

Infrastructure also caused critical problems for Russia: she had a mere 1.1 km of railway to every 10.6 km of German track; three-quarters of Russia's railways were only single track, further limiting the transportation of supplies and troops. After German and Turkish successes in blockading Russia's major ports in the Black Sea and the Baltic, Russia was left with only Vladivostok, 5000 km away from the battlefields, and Archangel, which was frozen for six months of the year. This left Russia unable to import vital war materials donated by the allies.

Despite these problems, Russia had not been decisively defeated by 1916, and General Brusilov's offensive against the Austrians in Volynia, Galicia and Bukovina brought spectacular advances. This was in part enabled by the efforts of the Union of Zemstvos, formed in support of the war effort. Popularly known as 'Zemgor', the Union created dressing stations and war hospitals and provided supplies to the front, as well as coping with the 17 million refugees that flooded Russian towns after the losses of 1915. However, facing the Germans in a war of attrition after they sent 15 divisions from France to halt the Russian advances proved a different story, and would prove too much for the faltering autocracy.

Population issues

Russia had by far the largest population of any of the countries at war, and one of the youngest. But many of those who would otherwise have been fighting (approximately 48% of 27 million men) were exempt on grounds of being only sons or the sole male workers in households; Russia was therefore the first country to run into manpower shortages and was forced to rely on poorly trained reserves after a million men were lost during the first year of fighting alone. Yet, as Norman Stone argues in his seminal 1975 study of Russia at war, the military high command was perhaps Russia's greatest weakness. They blamed shell shortages and industrial inadequacy to cover their own incompetence. Drawn from the aristocracy, they often had little professional training and had learnt nothing from the Russo-Japanese War. They continued with 19th-century military tactics, such as building fortresses to stockpile supplies – a serious misjudgement, providing

Speak like a historian

Historians speak of the First World War as being a 'war of attrition': a war in which each side seeks to wear the opponent down through continuous losses of either men or resources. This is because, by 1916, all of the initial fronts of the war had reached stalemates. As both sides 'dug in' (built trenches) to protect ground already won, battles became fruitless exercises in what seemed like a gruesome contest to see which country could afford to lose the most soldiers. Britain, France and Germany relied heavily upon their colonies to bolster their supplies of fighting men, whereas Russia and the United States (who joined in April 1917) relied solely upon their own populations to fight the war.

easy targets for advancing armies. They wasted resources and created discontent by requisitioning 1 million horses from peasant lands in the Pale of Settlement for a cavalry that was obsolete in modern warfare. The army's morale and discipline began to fall apart; some officers resorted to flogging conscript soldiers, evoking memories of serfdom and cementing a gulf between the noble officers and their peasant foot soldiers.

The war had been greeted by jubilant outpourings of nationalist sentiment across Russia. The Duma's Octobrist President Rodzianko had happily relinquished his position saying: 'We shall only hinder you; it is better, therefore, to dismiss us altogether until the end of the hostilities.' Two of Nicholas's daughters, never normally allowed out of the palace, were so desperate to help the war effort they disguised themselves in order to work as volunteer nurses at a local military hospital. Some workers changed their names to sound less German, and the government followed suit, changing the name of the capital from St Petersburg to Petrograd. 'War Industries Committees' were set up to bring together workers and employers to increase factory output, which helped industrial relations. In a wave of patriotism, strikes halted almost completely for a year; in the countryside, peasants hurriedly organised conscription in a way they hadn't during the Russo-Japanese War, and even revolutionaries (with the exception above all of Lenin, who argued the war was an example of imperialist capitalism) closed ranks behind the government. **Zemgor**, which ran the military supply campaign, grew quickly into an unofficial government body, with several hundred thousand employees and a budget of 2 billion rubles provided partly by the state and partly through public donations. Even whilst the people of Russia were galvanised in its support, the regime was thus quietly losing its monopoly on the state administration, and a new Russia was taking shape during the early years of the war.

Figure 2.7: Russian prisoners of war after defeat at the Masurian Lakes in East Prussia, 1915

Nervousness had spread throughout Russia by 1915, generated by extensive defeats and exacerbated by the execution of a close friend of the Minister of War, Sukhomlinov, for being a German spy; following the minister's subsequent dismissal, both the military and the public began to question whether Russia could win the war, and who should take the blame if she didn't. In a desperate attempt to restore morale, against the counsel of his advisers Nicholas II made what many historians agree was the single worst decision of his career: he dismissed his Uncle Nikolai from the Supreme Command of the armed forces, and took over personally. The Tsar loved army life and had assumed that if the soldiers would not fight for Russia, they would at least fight for him. Nicholas II's diary entries from Stavka – the location of the military headquarters – reveals his relief at being at the front and his dislike for political discussion: 'My head is resting here – no ministers, no wearisome questions to trouble one.' Now, Nicholas had to inspire his troops; accounts suggest, however, that he did not know what to say to them and only succeeded in undermining the authority of his officers. He would shoulder the blame personally for each defeat that followed.

Historians often speak of catalysts for change or 'agents' of history. War was an important locomotive of change in Russian history in the period covered by this book: the Crimean War, the Russo-Japanese War, and the First World War all had a huge impact on Russia lasting well beyond the years of conflict.

Opposition and the collapse of autocracy

A crisis in government

The Tsar interpreted his ministers' advice not to go to the front as a demonstration of disloyalty and dismissed almost every one of them, destroying in one blow the civilian government of Russia. He left Tsarina Alexandra in charge in St Petersburg, who was regarded as a German spy by a large proportion of the public; under the influence of Rasputin, a succession of changes in government followed. The Tsarina appointed and dismissed officials according to her wildly fluctuating perceptions of their loyalty: in the course of 1916, there were three Chairmen of the Council, three Ministers of the Interior, three Ministers of Justice and three Foreign Ministers. This confusion only helped undermine the goodwill the autocratic government had enjoyed with the outbreak of war. Provincial governors also came and went with alarming speed, and civilian ministers were reduced to administrators for Russian generals. A majority of Duma deputies (300 of 430 members) formed a **Progressive Bloc** in August 1915 to call for a 'Ministry of National Confidence' through which the centre-right nobility could participate in the business of governing. Beyond that, they called for an end to political imprisonment, equality for all religions, greater press freedoms and a legislative programme agreed by the Duma. Nicholas's response was to suspend the Duma in January 1916 and replace the ageing Prime Minister Goremykin with B.V. Stuermer, an inept leader but a close ally of the Empress and Rasputin. On 1 November 1916, Paul Miliukov, a Kadet, summarised the feeling of the Duma deputies when he gave a speech listing a series of criticisms of the regime, asking after each point 'Is this treason or stupidity?'. This was an ill-judged speech, creating waves of speculation about German influences at court which had previously been mere rumour, but it was perhaps the clearest display yet of the liberal loss of faith in the regime.

Increasing worker militancy

Economic strains were becoming increasingly damaging to the regime too. The government had financed the war primarily by printing money because foreign loans, war gifts from allies and raising taxes had not been enough: this caused rapid inflation. By early 1915, the volatile situation of pre-war towns had returned, with widespread strike activity resuming. Pressure to boost production, spiralling inflation and food shortages led to more intense worker militancy. Between April and June 1915, there were 440 strikes and 181 600 strikers, double the figures for the previous eight months of the war. People were driven to extreme action by desperate need; many of the workers in factories were young women or mothers, drafted in to replace the conscripted male workers. Governors of cities met strikes with brutality, as in the case of the Kostroma flax factory where 10 were killed, including four girls under 17. In September, 150 000 workers from the Putilov armaments factory went on strike after 30 Bolshevik workers were arrested on suspicion of being pro-German. Government action seemed to be provoking crises now rather than solving them and the old radical programme of 1905 was once again heard on the streets. Strikers called for the convening of a constituent assembly, an eight-hour day and expropriation of noble land.

Agricultural unrest

By the end of 1916, discontent had spread to the countryside, as industry was failing to provide the peasants with goods such as tools, boots, nails and cloth. Grain hoarding was aggravated by the government's introduction of fixed prices for grain. There was sufficient grain to feed Russia but it was no longer being supplied to the areas that needed it, not only because of hoarding but because the rail networks were being utilised for armaments and troops. Bread queues became common in larger cities, mostly made up of women who came to stand in line after their factory shift. Figes (2014) compellingly argues that these queues became political forums, where the latest news from the front and rumours about the Empress and Rasputin were circulated. Prices were rising faster than wages; some goods saw price increases of 500 per cent, creating conditions for hunger riots in the major cities.

Chris Read (2013) has suggested that perhaps the first violent act of the revolution was the murder of Rasputin. Three young aristocrats, Prince Felix Yusupov (husband of the Tsar's niece), Vladimir Purishkevich (a Duma delegate) and Grand Duke Dimitrii Pavlovich (the Tsar's cousin), desperate to save the monarchy, conspired to murder the monk by poisoning him with cyanide. When this did not work, Yusupov pulled out a gun and shot Rasputin twice. Yet still Rasputin did not die, so he was shot twice more and beaten with a rubber club, tied in a blanket and dumped in the Neva River. The conspirators had killed their enemy but they also succeeded in antagonising the Empress, who held nearly all the Duma responsible for Rasputin's death. His death also had the effect of drawing Nicholas II and his wife even closer, and the Tsar became steadfast in his conviction to resist reform; he even banned four dissident Grand Dukes from Petrograd. Faced with mass uprisings and a war that it was now clear would be lost, some of the Progressive

Bloc were driven to a desperate strategy. Convinced there was no other way to prevent Russia from anarchy, Guchkov, leader of the War Industries Committee, and two associates began working on plans to convince the Tsar to abdicate.

The impact of food shortages

A bitter winter in December 1916 froze the railway tracks into the cities of Moscow and Petrograd, causing even more critical shortfalls in food and heating materials. As a result, the army's bread rations were cut from three pounds to one, and later replaced with lentils. In the last two weeks of January 1917, food supplies to Moscow fell 60 per cent short of requirements and Petrograd only had a week's supply of grain left, prompting widespread strikes and unrest. In Petrograd, 79 factories were idle, although 39 of these simply didn't have enough fuel to operate. Living conditions were almost unbearably cold for most workers. These conditions alone did not cause the revolution, but certainly fuelled the discontent.

Protests in Petrograd

Matters came to a head in Petrograd during the milder weather on International Women's Day (8 March 1917), when the usual marches turned to protests focused on food shortages. The workers proved determined to take their grievances beyond the workplace to the capital's centre. By the end of the day, women from the Vyborg district had gathered 100 000 workers from the Putilov works to strike with them, though Cossacks and police managed to disperse them by nightfall. The next morning the protestors returned, this time armed with whatever they could lay hands on, and over 200 000 people descended on Znamenskaya Square. Powerless to stop the crowds, the police stood by and watched as banners and red flags saying 'Down with the Tsar!' and 'Down with the war!' were carried aloft, while mobs looted food stores on Nevsky Prospect. Emboldened by the lack of response from the police, the next day even more citizens took to the streets. The handful of revolutionaries tried to give some focus to the movement and Menshevik Duma deputies discussed forming a workers' soviet. Yet at this point even the revolutionaries failed to see how quickly events were spiralling out of control. Even Alexander Shliapnikov, a leading Petrograd Bolshevik, dismissively said, 'Give the workers a pound of bread and the movement will fizzle.'[12]

At Stavka, the military governor kept the Tsar informed of the situation in Petrograd. Although Nicholas seemed to find the news more irritating than threatening, he gave the order to General Khabalov to 'put an end' to the troubles. On 11 March police and soldiers, under orders to fire into the crowds if necessary, surrounded Petrograd; members of the Volynsky Regiment shot 50 demonstrators at Znamenskaya Square. Again, the regime shed the blood of its own people and this proved to be a decisive turning point. The soldiers were now forced to make a moral choice: abide by their oath to the Tsar, or join the people. The Petrograd garrison, in addition to the Pavlovsky and Volynsky Regiments (numbering 160 000 soldiers in total) chose to mutiny, and joined their fellow Russians in protest. The regime had lost control of its own troops and its days were numbered.

Crisis in government

The Tsar received six telegrams from Prime Minister Rodzianko, who sounded increasingly desperate from the first, in which he wrote, 'procrastination is fatal' to the second, 'the final hour has struck' to the final, 'tomorrow may be too late!'.

But to the end, Nicholas failed to grasp the urgency of the situation and refused to reply to the man he referred to as 'that fat Rodzianko [who] has written me lots of nonsense.' Nicholas II merely prorogued the Duma (discontinued it without dissolving it), made it known that he would refuse to make concessions such as creating a constituent assembly, and, assuming he could restore order by force as he had done before, dispatched General Ivanov to Petrograd. Exasperated and frightened that real anarchy would sweep through the capital, the Progressive Bloc and some other liberal elders refused to disband and kept the Duma meetings going, thinking they could re-establish order by forming a 'Provisional Committee of Duma Members for the Restoration of Order in the Capital and Establishment of Relations of Individuals and Institutions'. Headed by Rodzianko, this group declared itself the de facto government of Russia in the Tauride Palace (seat of the Duma) on 13 March.

But a rival centre of authority emerged in the Palace on the same day in the form of the Mensheviks and the newly converted SR leader Kerensky, who announced the founding of the Petrograd Soviet of Workers' and Soldiers' Deputies, headed by an Executive Committee. Over 3000 deputies had been elected (haphazardly) to the Soviet by the end of March. Two thirds of these were soldiers; Richard Pipes (1997) convincingly argues that the February Revolution can be regarded principally as a soldiers' mutiny. The Executive Committee (known as *'Ipsolkom'*) was not made up of factory delegates but socialist agitators – six Mensheviks, two Bolsheviks, two SRs and six soldiers – who sought to deepen the revolution and ensure the 'bourgeois' men of the Duma did not undermine it.

News that the mutiny had spread to Russia's second city, Moscow, with protests degenerating into violence, forced the members of the Provisional Committee and the Executive Committee to work together to restore order throughout the nights of 14–15 March. In this way, 'dual power' was exercised by the legitimately elected Duma members of the Provisional Committee on the one hand, and the influential Committee of the Soviet on the other, claiming to represent soldiers and workers. The Soviet's Order Number One established soldiers' committees and abolished the authority of officers; it also guaranteed the immunity of soldiers participating in the mutiny and sought to persuade them to return to their barracks. With the agreement of the Soviet, the Provisional Committee formed a **Provisional Government** until a constituent assembly could be elected.

the Provisional Government agreed:

- to call an amnesty for all political prisoners
- the immediate granting of freedom of speech, press and assembly
- the dissolution of all police organs (e.g. the *Okhrana* would be disbanded)
- to guarantee that military units taking part in the revolution would neither be sent to the front nor disarmed
- to make immediate preparations for the convocation of a constituent assembly.

General Alekseev, Chief of the General Staff, and five other commanders at the front were persuaded by Rodzianko that nothing less than the Tsar's abdication would solve the revolutionary crisis. They were driven by nationalism and a fear that anarchy would bring defeat if the generals deserted their leader. Instead of forming a counter-revolutionary force to defend Nicholas II, Alekseev and the generals intercepted the Tsar's train at Pskov as he was on his way back to Petrograd on 15 March, in order to persuade him to abdicate. With little fuss, and after his brother had refused the Crown because he did not want to face the raucous crowds, Nicholas II signed away the 304-year-old dynasty in the railway carriage, and so ended Romanov rule in Russia.

Conclusions

The question of why Tsarism collapsed in 1917 has caused much debate among historians. The events that led to the abdication of Nicholas II largely took place in one city – Petrograd. The autocracy had been placed under increased and widespread pressure in 1905–6 and had not succumbed; why, then, did it seem to collapse with such ease in 1917? In many ways, the strains of the First World War had a much greater impact at all levels of society than the Russo-Japanese War in 1905. However, Chris Read (2013) proposes that the military and the elites were the principal driving force of the revolution: motivated by a deep-seated patriotism, they sought to preserve Russia from defeat and saw the removal of Nicholas as the only way to achieve this. All involved in the newly formed Provisional Government assumed that the war must go on.

The political developments of 1917

Anti-monarchical fervour spread quickly through Russia during early March 1917. Statues were defaced, schools closed, and prisoners set free; governors and police were replaced with elected citizen militias, and in a matter of days the old centralised administration had vanished. The speed with which peasants, workers and soldiers organised themselves bears testament to the intensity of the revolutionary storm that had swept through this vast nation. There were 400 workers' soviets by June 1917. Those who joined local soviets won considerable gains almost immediately, such as wage increases and the long sought-after eight-hour day. Russian peasants slowly began the redistribution of land nationwide, sowing crops on untended landowners' fields, refusing to pay rent, or gathering firewood from landowners' forests. Soldiers and sailors were quick to form councils and soviets, rejecting the authority of all officers, executing the unpopular ones, and leaving military discipline and organisation in disarray.

Dual power system

The members of the new Provisional Government were little-known propertied men, drawn from the elite, who were keen to keep Russia in the war. This explains in part the timidity of their actions in redistributing land and postponing elections for the constituent assembly until mid-November (by which time they had succumbed to the Bolshevik *coup d'etat*). Prince Lvov was made Prime Minister and most of the remainder of the delegates were Octobrists (including Guchkov as Minister of War) and Progressists (including Miliukov as Foreign Minister). The only exception was the ambitious Alexander Kerensky, who represented both the Petrograd Soviet and the Provisional Government. The Provisional Government needed the Petrograd Soviet because it controlled the railways, the postal and telegraph services and the food supply to the towns, but also because it was the only body able to restrain political radicalism. Perhaps unexpectedly, the Soviet did not try to assume power from the new government, which had been co-opted from a Duma elected from a narrow franchise. However, many of the socialist

Summary of key events

- The First World War created huge socio-economic problems for Russia and stirred up discontent amongst workers and peasants alike.

- The military suffered humiliating losses in dreadful conditions, and when strikes broke out in St Petersburg soldiers refused to support the Tsar in repressing the people.

- Tsar Nicholas II was forced to abdicate, leaving a collection of liberal intelligentsia and revolutionary groups in charge of a Provisional Government.

Developing concepts

The following concepts have been very important in this section. For each one, write a definition of the concept and give an example of what it means in the context of Russian society 1894–1914.

- Industrialised proletariat
- Social Revolutionaries
- Social Democrats (Bolsheviks)
- Social Democrats (Mensheviks)
- Duma
- Kulaks
- Provisional Government
- Soviets

leaders, such as Chernov and Lenin, didn't return to Russia until April. Those prominent members of the Soviet, such as Kerensky (SR), Chkheidze and Tseretelli (both Mensheviks), who could have opposed the Provisional Government, all acquiesced to the compromise because of doctrinal considerations. They believed they were living through a bourgeois revolution, so their concern lay with working-class interests for the time being. The uneasy symbiosis of the Provisional Government and the Soviet had parallels across the country, and although a fragile co-operation was maintained in the months following the revolution, it was clear the 'bourgeois' settlement would not last.

The return of Lenin

The problems of the 'dual power' system were underlined by the events of April 1917. In exile in Switzerland, Lenin had read the news of the February Revolution with frustration. Luckily for him, the German authorities saw the benefit of getting him back to Petrograd to further destabilise Russia and perhaps bring about her surrender. Lenin, Zinoviev and a few other socialists were given passage on a sealed train through Germany, arriving at Finland Station in Petrograd on 16 April 1917. There, Lenin delivered an uncompromising statement of policy, later called the April Theses. He called upon the Bolsheviks not to co-operate with the Provisional Government in any way; he promised an end to Russia's problems by offering 'Peace, land and bread', 'All power to the Soviets' and an immediate withdrawal from the war. His ideas successfully isolated the 26 000 Bolsheviks from all the other parties, which was to be his greatest political move.

On 3 May, news that the Provisional Government was still pursuing territorial gains in the war provoked outbreaks of violence in the streets of Petrograd. Since only the **Central Executive Committee** of the Petrograd Soviet had the influence to quell the violence, a coalition was formed between the Committee and the Provisional Government. Lvov remained Prime Minister but six socialists joined the government, including Tseretelli, Skobolev and Chernov. Kerensky was promoted to Minister of War and a renewed offensive was planned for June. Entry into the coalition was a fatal move for the socialists: they would now be held jointly responsible for the failures of the Provisional Government during the summer, becoming increasingly discredited in the eyes of the masses. In May, Martov, leader of the Mensheviks, returned to Russia and also spoke out in opposition to the war and the coalition. But this only strengthened the Bolshevik cause, as Richard Pipes (1997) suggests, as they came to be seen as the true custodians of the revolution. This was demonstrated in the first election of the All-Russian Congress of Soviets on 16 June, when the Bolsheviks managed to win 105 seats. Although they were outnumbered by the 248 Mensheviks and 285 SRs, this marked rapid growth. Funded largely by the Germans (figures suggest the German government had donated up to USD 10 million by the end of the year), the Bolsheviks were able to infiltrate factory committees that supervised management within the workplace and the **Red Guards**, formed of armed workers to defend the factories. By July 1917 there were 20 000 workers in the Red Guards in Petrograd alone. Robert Service (1999) suggests that what made the Bolsheviks so dynamic as agents of revolutionary activity was their direct link to the workers in the factories, as well as their belief that the difficulties Russia faced because of the war and the economy were immediately surmountable.

The June Offensive and the July Days

The June Offensive was marked at first by rousing speeches by Kerensky but latterly by war-weary soldiers fleeing from German counterattacks in Galicia. It is estimated that by this point the Russian armies had suffered almost 2 million fatalities, with around double that number captured. The catastrophe was to precipitate the unrest of the so-called 'July Days'. Triggered by the government's decision to dispatch units from the Petrograd garrison to the front, and fuelled by the propaganda campaign orchestrated by the Bolsheviks, thousands of soldiers, primarily from the Machine-Gun Regiment, took to the streets to protest against the Provisional Government. They marched on the Tauride Palace chanting 'All power to the Soviets!'. The government, aided by allegations that Lenin was a German spy, and by Lenin's failure to provide direct orders to the soldiers, managed to put down the disorder, forcing Lenin to flee to Finland in fear of arrest. There, he planned an armed uprising against the government. A short wave of anti-Bolshevik hysteria followed the July Days, although in the longer term it served to ally the party more closely with the soldiers and workers.

Figure 2.8: The July Days: demonstrating soldiers disperse and Cossacks shoot into the crowds.

The end of the Provisional Government

Kerensky replaced Lvov as Prime Minister on 21 July; by 25 July, he had closed public meetings, restored the death penalty at the front and appointed as Commander-in-Chief General Kornilov, who wanted to apply the penalty to reserve units in the rear, as well as militarising the railways and banning workers' organisations. Kornilov appeared to conservative admirers to be the only man capable of stabilising Russia and strengthening the government; they warmly welcomed his appointment. Rumours of a Bolshevik uprising prompted Lvov to mediate plans between the two new premiers, albeit ineptly. Kornilov was led to believe he would be invited into government and Kerenksy, alarmed at the prospect of military dictatorship and his own removal, armed the Soviets of Petrograd to mount a defence of the capital. Kornilov was intercepted by railwaymen, exhorted by Soviet delegates and finally arrested by 1 September.

According to Christopher Read (2013), this event was 'a game-changer' and began the dissolution of the last elements of power held by the Provisional Government as renewed radicalism swept through Russia[13]. The main targets of dissent were Kornilov, who had assured the ascendancy of the left, and Kerensky, who had been discredited for appointing Kornilov. Kerensky frantically tried to re-establish his radical credentials in the following days by releasing Trotsky and other Bolsheviks from prison, but the damage had been done. Kerensky's reputation, built in 1912 defending the victims of the Lena goldfields massacre, was in tatters. Army desertions rocketed during September because soldiers suspected their officers of supporting Kornilov; they returned to their villages armed and organised, prompting a surge in violence against landowners (the military were called to intervene 105 times in September alone). There is no doubt that the Bolsheviks were the ones who mainly profited from the crisis, and upon winning their first majority in the Petrograd Soviet on 12 September they passed their first resolution: the abolition of private ownership of landed estates and establishment of workers' control of production and distribution. Within a week, Moscow and Kiev followed suit. Whilst some Bolsheviks hoped success in the constituent assembly elections would follow, Lenin urged the party from Helsinki that it was now time to take power on behalf of the soviets. He would return in October to convince all but two of the Executive Committee that the spirit of history was on their side.

The Bolshevik takeover

The Bolsheviks are often said to have seized power on 7 November; actually there was no-one to seize it from, as the beleaguered Provisional Government had all but lost control of the country during July and August. Ostensibly to strengthen the defences of Petrograd, Kerensky had decided to remove 'unreliable' troops from the capital to transfer them to the Northern Front. The soldiers refused to move, and either declared their solidarity with the Petrograd Soviet – dominated by Bolsheviks and chaired by Trotsky – or remained neutral, rendering them a redundant force for the government. On 29 October the Petrograd Soviet formed the Military Revolutionary Committee (MRC), under Trotsky's command, for the defence of the city from counter-revolutionary forces, effectively bringing the workers' militias (the Red Guards), as well as the Petrograd garrison under Bolshevik control. The insurrection was planned to coincide with the convocation of the Second Congress of Soviets on 7 November. Kerensky came inadvertently to Lenin's aid on 5 November, ordering loyal troops from the suburbs to requisition Bolshevik premises and ordering the battleship *Aurora* out to sea. Later that day and on the next, MRC members occupied strategic points across the city, claiming that the Provisional Government had been overthrown and that power had passed to the Petrograd Soviet. The final assault on the Winter Palace took place on 8 November 1917; it was taken with startling ease.

Key term

Sovnarkom is the Russian term for 'Council of People's Commissars' and became the governing apparatus in Russia shortly after the October Revolution. Commissars were posted to government institutions, thereby laying the foundations to transform Russia into the Soviet Union. (The term 'ministers' was rejected because it was too reminiscent of the bourgeoisie.)

Opposition and the establishment of the Bolshevik government by December 1917

Against the distant thunder of the battleship *Aurora* still firing blanks at the Winter Palace in support of the revolution, the Congress of Soviets, which met on 9 November, declared overwhelming support for the Bolsheviks. Martov's Mensheviks and the SRs walked out, serving only to strengthen the Bolsheviks' position. Lenin, met by thunderous applause, issued the so-called Peace Decree: negotiations would be sought to secure immediate peace with the Central Powers. He also issued the Land Decree, which confiscated all land belonging to the Church and landlords, to be redistributed when the constituent asssembly met. Although revolution had been carried out in the name of the soviets, Lenin had no intention of ruling through Congress or its executive committee, so he created **Sovnarkom**, or 'Council of People's Commissars', made up exclusively of Bolsheviks. Lenin was Chair of the Council, Trotsky its Commissar for Foreign Affairs and Stalin its Minister for Nationalities. Russia had undergone its second revolution of 1917, but in reality the Bolsheviks had only seized power in Petrograd, not the rest of the country. Although the party had grown to approximately 240 000 members (though this figure included even individuals who contributed little more than to distribute the party newspaper), the peasantry had not necessarily been converted to socialism, and the threat of civil war loomed.

Figure 2.9: A still from Sergei Eisenstein's propaganda masterpiece October 1917. Such images were hung in the USSR's museums of the revolution as if they were photographs of real historical events.

Kerensky tried to mount a counter-revolution using Cossack troops, posing the first military threat to the new regime. He was halted by the Red Guards at Tsarskoe Selo, ex-residence of the former Tsar, forcing the former Prime Minister to flee disguised as a nurse. The second threat to the Bolsheviks seemed to

Speak like a historian

Students commonly question how Lenin managed to garner so much support in 1917 given his lengthy periods of exile up until March 1917. Robert Service (2000 p.272) has explained in his stunning biography of Lenin:

He had an unrivalled ability to set out his arguments and lay out a militant case. His aggressive descriptions of his enemies and their policies gave everyone the feeling that here was a man who could wield governmental power. Provisional Government ministers were tame by comparison. Kadets, Mensheviks and Socialist Revolutionaries had to compromise with each other; but Lenin treated compromise as a dirty word. He wanted dynamic, ruthless, correct measures to be taken, and contended that only a standpoint based upon 'class struggle' would suffice. He wrote a great deal; forty-eight pieces appeared in Pravda in May 1917 alone … he thought, wrote and acted as if he and the party were interchangeable. The country's other newspapers had the same opinion that Lenin embodied the sole alternative to the political status quo.

He made public appearances too, delivering twenty-one speeches in May and June …

come from within its ranks. Within days of coming to power, Sovnarkom, made up of Bolsheviks who had no experience of governance, declared the closure of newspapers of the ideological centre and right, and within weeks the ban was extended to left-wing parties. This caused five members of the Bolshevik Central Committee to resign: Zinoviev, Kamenev, Rykov, Miliutin, and Nogin. The civil service went on strike and food shortages were so acute that most of the Commissars themselves were living on black bread and vegetable soup. The primary threat was the long-awaited election of the constituent assembly, due on 25 November 1917. With the strong support of the peasantry that was enjoyed by the SRs it seemed unlikely the Bolsheviks would win a majority. Indeed, the Bolsheviks polled 24 per cent but were trounced by the SRs, who won 38 per cent. Sovnarkom quickly issued a decree declaring that the assembly had been dissolved because it had been taken over by counter-revolutionaries. Lenin then used the Military Revolutionary Committee (MRC) to arrest Kadet, Menshevik and SR leaders; by 18 December the duties of the MRC were transferred to the **Cheka** – the Extraordinary Commission for the Struggle against Counter-revolution and Sabotage.

A few days later, the Bolshevik action was approved by one third of the All-Russian Congress of Soviets. Within weeks the Russian empire had imploded, as a domino effect of the Bolshevik revolution in Petrograd spread across Russia. Civil war gripped the country, and as Trotsky noted many years later 'It was impossible to tell in advance whether we [Bolsheviks] were to stay in power or be overthrown.' [14]

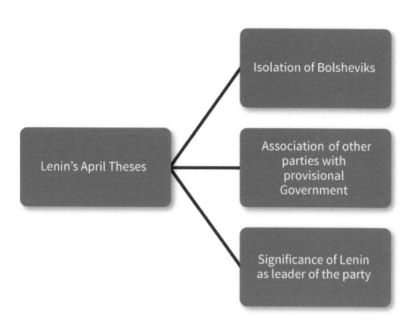

Figure 2.10

Conclusion

With the outcomes of the February Revolution already decaying, the Bolsheviks were able to seize power. It had been likely since the beginning of 1917 that some form of socialist government would emerge from the chaos of war and the collapse of autocracy. The Mensheviks and SRs, in colluding with the Provisional Government, left a vacuum on the left for the Bolsheviks to fill, particularly after the Kornilov affair. But as Robert Service (1999) argues, it was Lenin's initiative that determined the shape of the government that had taken control of Russia by December. Fitzpatrick (2008) argues that in some ways the events of October and November can be seen as the beginning of the Bolshevik revolution rather than the end, because the future of the party's dominance over Russia was uncertain. They had won in the urban centres, but how they would tackle the local soviets, which had successfully asserted their authority in rural areas throughout 1917, was another matter. Judging by how they handled the October coup, Lenin clearly had reservations about his own slogan 'All Power to the Soviets!'.

Key term

Cheka: formed on 2 January 1918, this was the Bolsheviks' secret police force. It was responsible for carrying out the 'Red Terror' (mass oppression) during the Russian Civil War of 1918–22.

ACTIVITY 2.4

Events moved quickly in 1917 from the collapse of Tsarism to the Bolsheviks seizing power; it is therefore useful to note how one event leads to another. Go through your notes and identify the 'turning points', that is, events that had multiple consequences or changed the direction of events considerably. Use the example in Figure 2.10.

91

Practice essay questions

1. 'The economic policies of Witte were a turning point in Russia becoming an industrial power between 1894 and 1914.' Assess the validity of this view. (A Level)
2. Richard Pipes suggests that Russia was dangerously close to revolution in 1914. Explain why you agree or disagree with this view of Russia between 1894 and 1914. (AS Level)
3. 'The collapse of the Tsarist regime in February 1917 was due to successive governments' failure to improve living and working conditions in the towns since 1894.' Explain why you agree or disagree with this view. (AS Level)
4. With reference to these extracts and your understanding of the historical context, which of these extracts provides the more convincing interpretation of the collapse of Tsarist Russia in February 1917?

Extract A

The First World War required the unprecedented mobilization of society behind the war effort. This depended on a civil society with tentacles stretching down to every family and on a state closely allied to this society and capable of coordinating and co-opting its efforts. To do this effectively, the state needed to have common values, confidence, and commitments. The Russian Empire entered the war deficient in all these respects, and this proved a fatal weakness in 1914-17.

…the end of tsarist Russia came in the course of a few days in late February and early March 1917. A dynasty that had ruled for three hundred years departed almost overnight and with a whimper rather than a bang, because very few Russians were willing to defend it.

Lieven, D., Towards the Flame: Empire, War and the End of Tsarist Russia, *Penguin: 2015 Chapter 8*

Extract B

The inability, or perceived unwillingness, of the Kerensky government to protect the gains made by workers after the February Revolution, led to growing disillusionment with the moderate socialists who supported the government. Workers now began to look to their own organisations for protection. It was the movement for workers' control of production which translated growing economic discontent into sympathy for the Bolshevik party. … As economic disorder and class conflict grew, however, the factory committees broadened the scope of control. … [T]hey increasingly intervened in every sphere of management decision-making, demanding the right to attend board meetings and access to financial accounts and order-books. … Whilst the committees rejected Menshevik and SR calls for state control of the economy, they endorsed Bolshevik perspectives for centralised coordination of the economy by a proletarian state power. … It would be wrong, however, to conclude that the Bolsheviks cynically manipulated the factory committees for their own ends. The radicalisation of the movement for workers' control gave the party enormous opportunity to win wide support for its policies, but it did not control the movement: it responded to it, trying to steer it in the direction it believed was proper. It was the organised working class, not the Bolshevik party, which was the great power in society – more powerful than even the capitalist class, as its success in resisting redundancies suggests. The collapse of the system of war capitalism, however, in early 1918 destroyed the strength of the working class, and it was only at that point that the Bolsheviks were in a position to achieve a monopoly of power.

Smith S.A. 1983, *Red Petrograd, Revolution in the Factories, 1917–1918* page 258.

Extract C

The rapid disintegration of Russian unity gave the Bolsheviks the opportunity to loosen the Mensheviks' hold on organized labor. As transport and communications disintegrated, and each region, no longer able to rely on the central government, had to take charge of its own affairs, the network of national trade unions weakened. … This development promoted syndicalism, a form of anarchism that called for the abolition of the state and for worker control of the national economy. One expression of the trend was the emergence of Factory Committees (Fabzavkomy), which embraced workers of diverse trades working in the same enterprises. The Fabzavkomy … soon radicalized, evicting proprietors and their managers and taking charge of factories. … Lenin now identified himself with syndicalism, joining calls for 'worker control' of industry. This gained for his party a strong following amongst industrial workers: at the First Conference of Petrograd Factory Committees at the end of May, the Bolsheviks controlled at least two-thirds of the delegates.

Source: Pipes, Richard 1997, A Concise History of the Russian Revolution p.121

Further reading

John Reed's *Ten Days That Shook the World* (1919) is an American journalist's account of the October Revolution in Russia in 1917, which Reed experienced first-hand.

For an analytical view of both the February and October Revolutions, Christopher Read's *War and Revolution in Russia 1914–22* (2013) is accessible but cleverly synthesises the latest scholarship on the events.

Chapter summary

After studying this period, you should be able to:

- describe the rise of socialism as a political force in Russia
- assess the impact of rapid industrialisation on the workers
- evaluate the weaknesses of Nicholas II as a leader
- explain why Tsarism collapsed during 1917
- explain the changes in agriculture and the impact on the peasantry.

End notes

1. Figes O. *Revolutionary Russia, 1891-1991.* London: Penguin; 2014. p.23
2. Acton E. *Russia: The Tsarist and Soviet Legacy (The Present and The Past).* Pearson; 1995. p.114
3. Thatcher ID. Late imperial urban workers. In Thatcher ID (ed.), *Late Imperial Russia: Problems and Prospects.* Manchester University Press; 2005.
4. Ascher A. *A Short history of the 1905 Revolution. Stanford University Press;* 2004. p.72
5. Pipes R. *A Concise History of the Russian Revolution.* Vintage Books; 1997. p.44
6. Cited in Figes O. *A People's Tragedy: The Russian Revolution, 1891-1924. Pimlico;* 1997.
7. Rogger H. *Russia in the Age of Modernisation and Revolution 1881-1917.* Longman; 1983. p.237
8. Rogger H. *Russia in the Age of Modernisation and Revolution 1881-1917.* Longman; 1983. p.251
9. Haimson L. The Problem of Social Stability in Urban Russia 1905-1917. Slavic Review 1964;23(4): 639
10. Figes O. *A People's Tragedy: The Russian Revolution, 1891-1924.* Pimlico; 1997.
11. Rogger H. *Russia in the Age of Modernisation and Revolution 1881-1917.* Longman; 1983. p.247
12. Pipes R. *A Concise History of the Russian Revolution.* New York; 1997.
13. Read C. *War and Revolution in Russia 1914-22, European History in Perspective.* Palgrave Macmillan; 2013. p.92
14. Cited in Wood A. *The Russian Revolution. Second Edition – Seminar Studies in History;* Routledge; 1986. p.46

3 The emergence of Communist dictatorship, 1917–1941

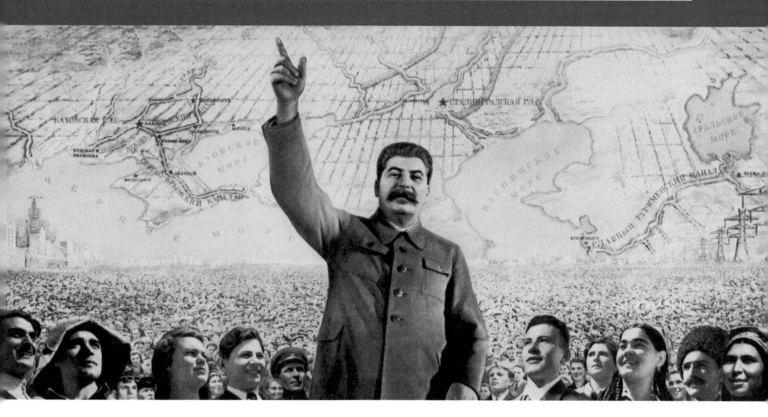

In this section, we will examine the nature of political authority in Russia from 1917 to 1941, consider some of the changes that were taking place and how these changes began to affect the relationship between the people and the Bolsheviks. We will look into:

- Lenin's Russia, Stalin's rise and political ideologies
- the nature of the Bolshevik regime in the Russian Socialist Federal Soviet Republic (RSFSR)
- opposition from within the party and external opposition
- Lenin's and Stalin's impact on social development
- Lenin's and Stalin's economic policies
- the political, economic and social condition of the Soviet Union by 1941.

Introduction

Lenin believed the providence of history had worked to create the Bolshevik-led revolution of October 1917, but he was not so naïve as to assume that his position was secure. In fact, Lenin was prudent in attempting to preserve the successes won in October and liquidating those phenomena in Russia which appeared to him to be oppressive or backward. Lenin's ideological commitment

Speak like a historian

Providence of history refers to Lenin's determinist beliefs, in other words that because all history can be defined by class struggle, that revolution would come to Russia eventually, whether he had acted in October or not.

Key term

Factionalism is often associated with weak government. The Bolshevik party split into factions (groups which tried to outdo each other) as Lenin became more ill.

remains a much debated topic, although there is evidence to suggest that he was often forced to make pragmatic concessions to resolve the considerable political pressures he faced in the years following 1917. There is no doubt about the personal impact Lenin had on the nature of the Bolshevik regime in his time: it was crucial. The abandonment of moral consideration, the use of terror, the one-party state and Comintern were all established under his leadership. Lenin's unshakeable confidence that his ideas were superior led to deep-seated **factionalism** within the Bolshevik party, which was perhaps exacerbated by his ill health after 1921. Joseph Stalin managed to use his position as General Secretary of the party during 1922 to 1924 to rise to the fore as an unrivalled leader of the party, something which even Lenin had not attempted. Under the auspices of 'Leninism', Stalin attempted to build **'Socialism in one country'**, which justified an increased use of terror, party purges and transformative state-led economic policies to crippling effect. The 'Five Year Plan' sought to mobilise the masses towards building a utopian Socialist society, but it had catastrophic consequences in the countryside and many workers in the factories suffered too as a result of the optimal targets set by the state. On the eve of the 'Great Patriotic War' against their ideological enemies (Nazi Germany) in 1941, the **USSR** was a **totalitarian** state with a seemingly unassailable leader – although Stalin was about to face his most severe test yet.

Political authority and government

New leaders and ideologies; Lenin's Russia, ideology and change

Lenin's ideology

The interplay between Lenin's ideology and implementation of policy is a huge area of research and one which has provoked virulent debate between historians. Ideology was central to Bolshevik policy-making and cannot be ignored if one is to understand the pragmatic steps undertaken by the Bolsheviks, from 1917 until Lenin's death in 1924. It is well known that, in their long careers as revolutionary thinkers and activists, Marx and Engels devoted comparatively little attention to the institutional forms and governing principles of the post-revolutionary political order. Therefore the Bolsheviks, who had no experience of governance, had to formulate policies in a reactionary way most of the time. Only Trotsky and Lenin dedicated significant amounts of time to policy consideration as most members of *Sovnarkom* concentrated on their institutional functions. For example, Yuri Larin composed weekly proposals for the fundamental reconstruction of one or other of the People's Commissariats rather than contributing to policy formation. This, as well as the forcefulness of Lenin's personality, can partly account for the dominance his ideas were to have on party policy.

Lenin was a utopian theorist and had spent much of the build-up to the October Revolution writing pamphlets such as, '*Imperialism as the highest stage of capitalism*' (1916) and '*The State and Revolution*' (1917) which indefatigably preached his interpretation of what Marx had called 'the dictatorship of the proletariat'. Lenin used this to initiate a period of severe repression of those who opposed the revolution – namely, the workers and the peasants – as a historical necessity. The age-old tension between proletarian self-determination and the party's vanguard (leading) role was woven into the fabric of Russian Social Democracy and was to remain a contentious issue when the Bolsheviks seized power in October 1917. Lenin took the view that the Paris Commune established during the French Revolution of 1870/71 had been the ideal example of proletariat autonomy, which might explain why he stifled initiative from below time and again during the course of 1918–21.

Development of the Bolshevik dictatorship

How the Bolsheviks survived the first few years following the revolution has been extensively debated. Historians such as Schapiro(1960) have argued that Lenin was a fanatical leader who reinforced the worst traditions of Tsarism. However, this view has been supported more recently by Orlando Figes(1997), who has argued that by 1921, 'the revolution had come full circle, and a new autocracy had been imposed on Russia which in many ways resembled the old one'[1]. Although a persuasive argument, Robert Service(1997) takes a broader view by suggesting that the Bolsheviks, if they wanted to impose order on the country, had to rule firmly. Transport, communications and particularly the economy were in a dreadful condition by the beginning of 1918 and the war with Germany had caused ruin in many of the states bordering Europe. In this context, the dictatorial nature of Lenin's leadership of the party and the highly centralised one-party state that developed, was perhaps not completely unexpected.

The first signs of difference between Bolshevik objectives and those of the masses (the workers of major towns and cities) became apparent very early on. The masses had a programme which included 'All Power to the Soviets' as one of its main elements (evident in the slogans chanted through the streets in 1917), and the programme took precedence over parties, largely because most people were not so politically engaged that they bothered with comparing party manifestos. Parties had only received support insofar as they adhered to and publicised the popular programme. The Bolsheviks set up a Soviet-based government, peasants were encouraged to seize land and workers increasingly took over factories, all of which was in line with the calls made for revolution in February and July. As Christopher Read (2013) argues, for the masses these actions were the core of the revolution, for the Bolsheviks they were just the first step. Lenin's party had a longer-term agenda which sought to transform society completely.

Early after their seizure of power (as discussed in Chapter 2) the Bolsheviks sought to exclude members of other socialist groups to preserve control of the rapidly changing situation in Russia. By November 1917, the Bolsheviks had already established Sovnarkom and the **Central Executive Committee**, which was supposed to act as a restraining force on Sovnarkom (made up entirely of Bolsheviks) and drew its legitimacy from the Congress of Soviets. Very early on, Lenin claimed that Sovnarkom must be able to pass decrees independent of the Central Executive Committee. Lenin justified this on the grounds of urgent necessity and doing away with 'bourgeois formalism' (to rid the country of unnecessary bureaucracy which slowed the promotion of moral socialist values), but it effectively gave Lenin the power once enjoyed by the Tsar. The Constituent Assembly, which had gained sovereignty since its conception in February 1917, was dismantled within a few days with little bloodshed and secured Bolshevik

Speak like a historian

The Social Democratic party split in 1903 due to a disagreement over the leadership of the party, which would prove fundamental to the future of the organisation. Lenin favoured a small elite 'vanguard' of the working classes (or proletariat) to lead the revolution whereas Martov wanted a broad base of support and democratically elected leadership. The tension between Lenin's rhetoric on the dictatorship of the proletariat and the reality of the Bolshevik dictatorship became manifest very quickly after the October Revolution. Lenin spoke of the working classes assuming power after the removal of the bourgeoisie, but in truth this never materialised. Some historians have accused Lenin of using the concept of a vanguard party to justify their suppression of other parties and maintain his own power. They took the line that since they were the vanguard of the proletariat, their right to rule could not be legitimately questioned.

Key term

The **Central Executive Committee** (sometimes referred to as VTsIK) was the highest legislative, administrative body of the Russian Socialist Republic and directed the local Soviets about implementing the new constitution.

supremacy in central government. Following this, policy would become the reserve of a small number of those on the party's Central Committee, which was formalised in early 1919 into the **Politburo**, which Lenin also dominated. Lenin now in effect reversed his former theories that the state would gradually 'wither away', arguing that the greatest concentration of power in the hands of the state was necessary to radically transform the economic and social base, and that the road to a stateless society ran through the temporary strengthening of the dictatorship of the proletariat.

However, the historian Siegelbaum (1992) convincingly argues that the Soviet state that evolved after 1917 was not a monolithic bloc, but a constellation of four functionally distinct sub-systems or networks:

- a military and police state
- a civilian state focused on the Soviets
- an economic state revolving around the commissariats and the trade unions
- a political state residing within the Communist Party.

Voices from the past

Extending reading: Discussion of links to French Revolution

The Paris Commune was a socialist government that briefly ruled Paris from 18 March until 28 May 1871 during the French Revolution. The killing of two French army generals by soldiers of the Commune's National Guard and the refusal of the Commune to accept the authority of the French government led to its harsh suppression by the regular French Army.

Lenin, along with Marx, judged the Commune a living example of the 'dictatorship of the proletariat', though Lenin criticised the Communards:

'But two mistakes destroyed the fruits of the splendid victory. The proletariat stopped half-way: instead of setting about "expropriating the expropriators", it allowed itself to be led astray by dreams of establishing a higher justice in the country united by a common national task; such institutions as the banks, for example, were not taken over, and Proudhonist theories about a "just exchange", etc., still prevailed among the socialists. The second mistake was excessive magnanimity on the part of the proletariat: instead of destroying its enemies it sought to exert moral influence on them; it underestimated the significance of direct military operations in civil war; and instead of launching

a resolute offensive against Versailles that would have crowned its victory in Paris, it tarried and gave the Versailles government time to gather the dark forces and prepare for the blood-soaked week of May.'

V.I. Lenin, 'Lessons of the Commune', Marxists Internet Archive. Originally published: *Zagranichnaya Gazeta*, No. March 2, 23, 1908. Translated by Bernard Isaacs. Accessed February 2015.

Lenin and the Bolsheviks interpreted the Paris Commune to suit their political strategy for Russia. Lenin presented the Commune as a working model of a broad people's revolution and used this to justify his assertion that an alliance between the peasants and the workers was necessary to bring about Socialism. He believed the Commune failed because the members had been led astray by dreams of justice and patriotism, not because they had taken power too early (as some commentators suggested at the time). Lenin used this to justify the liquidation of the bourgeoisie in the first few years of Bolshevik rule and for strong party rule to instil discipline in those who might be distracted by class enemies. The Penguin Classics edition of *The Communist Manifesto* has a fantastic introduction written by Professor of Political Science, Gareth Stedman Jones.

How the networks would operate were (like everything else) not worked out in advance, and this provoked considerable debate within the party. All developed in a similar way however, that is, towards a centralised bureaucratic system. The ministries, which became commissariats, and many of the regional and branch institutions governing the economy as well as the Provisional Government's state militia, which was renamed the Workers' and Peasants' Militia, were largely inherited from the Tsarist regime and staffed by the same people. Others, such as the Soviets, the trade unions and the co-operatives, had formed non-governmental bodies before the October Revolution but were 'statised' after 1917 (brought under the control of the government). The Cheka (secret police) had equivalents in the Tsarist period (the gendarmerie or *Okhrana*), but little if any continuity in personnel. Finally, certain institutions, including the court system, much of the educational system and almost the entire party apparatus, were newly created during the civil war period 1918–21.

ACTIVITY 3.1

Figure 3.1 illustrates the various government organs during 1921–24 – can you draw links between them to show how they related to each other?

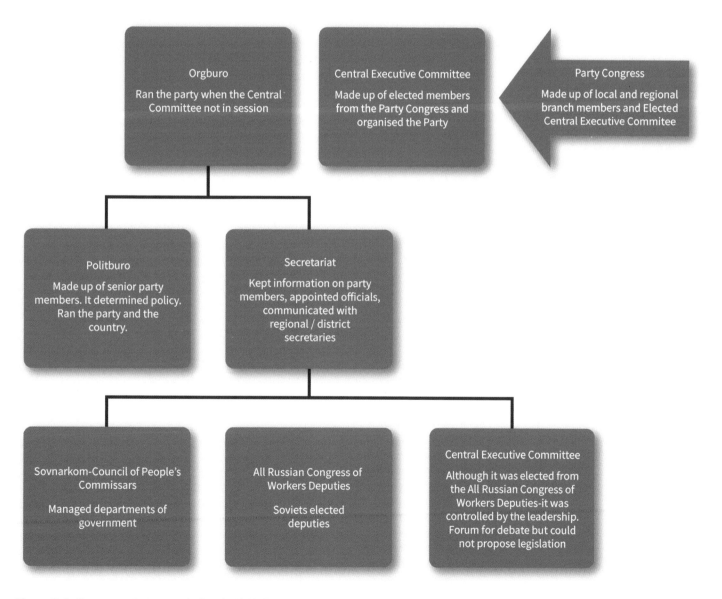

Figure 3.1: Government structure in Russia 1918–24

All of the revolutionary institutions created in 1917 were housed in one building, the Smolny Institute. The Bolshevik, Central Committee, the Military Revolutionary Committee, Sovnarkom, the Petrograd Soviet and the Central Executive Committee of the Congress of Soviets were all housed there. This meant that Lenin could exercise a direct and steady influence over all of them as he could literally walk between departments. It also meant he was continually hounded by committee members and so, in December 1917, he escaped briefly to Finland (ironically, where he had just granted independence and was therefore illegally crossing a state border without permission). Incidentally, there are accounts that in Finland Lenin started to talk in a low voice so the political agents of the Ministry of the Interior would not hear him; he had forgotten it was he that was now in control of the secret police. Whilst in the tuberculosis sanitorium of Halila, Lenin instituted a number of rules to enhance the operational procedure of the new government institutions in order that they could respond to the growing turbulence outside Petrograd. He gave commissars a maximum of ten minutes to deliver reports, interrupting them if he felt their words were too doctrinal in nature. He personally reprimanded anyone who was late to meetings and he banned smoking in Sovnarkom meetings, which upset the chain-smoking Felix Dzerzhinsky (Head of the Cheka). Policy formation was a matter of urgency to Lenin but seemingly no one else in the party. This encouraged Lenin's authoritarian tendencies, as political consolidation seemed an elusive prospect by December 1917.

Ideology and the Treaty of Brest–Litovsk

The American journalist John Reed gave an emotive account of the Decree on Peace delivered by Lenin to the Second Congress of Soviets on 26 October 1917 which was welcomed with thunderous applause. However, the reality of withdrawing from the First World War provided Lenin with what historian Robert Service (1997) suggests was the fiercest struggle of Lenin's career. Persuading the other Bolsheviks and SRs to accept the terms of peace thrust upon them by the Central Powers in December 1918 was a costly undertaking. Millions of soldiers had demobilised themselves upon hearing the Decree on Peace, allowing the Germans to press their advantage as the Russian front melted away. Trotsky (as People's Commissar for External Affairs) had believed that if negotiations with the Germans were strung out, he could facilitate the spread of revolution when Russian and German soldiers mixed. After all, most Bolsheviks had assumed that without the revolution spreading to Germany, the Russian revolution would ultimately fail. However, Trotsky's weak policy of 'neither war, nor peace' was exposed in February 1918 when the Central Powers offered an ultimatum at **Brest–Litovsk**: either the Soviets signed a peace treaty or the German advance would resume in two days. By 18 February, the Germans were within 400 miles of Petrograd and Lenin threatened to resign from Sovnarkom if members did not agree to peace. Lenin eventually won against significant opposition, and the Treaty of Brest–Litovsk was signed on 3 March 1918. Sovnarkom members were still unconvinced that the Germans would retreat and so the seat of government was hurriedly (and reluctantly) moved from Petrograd, the heart of the October Revolution, to Moscow. Following this, on 8 March 1918, the Bolsheviks changed their name to the Communist Party, in honour of Marx's *Communist Manifesto*, which they claimed to be putting into practice.

Historians have often been highly critical of Soviet leaders' willingness to use Marxism to justify political decisions, even when they appear to be misinterpreting Marx's texts. It is true that much of what Lenin and later Stalin called Marxist is at best an interpretation and at worst a perversion of his original ideas. However, Marx was a theoretician and deviation from his theories was likely to happen.

There seems to be no doubt amongst historians such as Lieven (2015) that if Russia had not withdrawn from the First World War in March, the Central Powers would almost certainly have conquered Petrograd and the October Revolution would have been lost. The Treaty of Brest–Litovsk was, to many, a shameful peace according to which the Bolsheviks were forced to relinquish most of the states in European Russia. Poland, Finland, Estonia, Lithuania were all granted autonomy and with them 89% of Russia's coalmining and 54% of Russia's industrial regions were lost, not to mention the breadbasket of the Ukraine (which, along with the North Caucasus, provided approximately 60% of all grain procurement in 1916). The Treaty of Brest–Litovsk also foreclosed any possibility of testing Lenin's Decree on Nationalities which had been formalised at the Third Congress of Soviets, January 1918, when he announced the formation of the **Russian Socialist Federal Soviet Republic (RSFSR)**. The Russian in the title was deliberately *Rossiiskaya* (not *Russkaya* which had an ethnic dimension); this emphasised his belief that Russians should not enjoy any privileges as they had under the old Tsarist system. The signing of the Treaty was significant for the future direction of the Soviet State. This signaled that future action would be determined by establishing domestic concerns, or 'Socialism in Russia' rather than the spread of international revolution. These actions provided Stalin with an intellectual basis on which to base his 'Socialism in One Country.' By March 1918 however, the Bolsheviks were contained in a country which reflected the amount of territory Russia had occupied in the 16th century, with very few ethnic minorities now part of the state, and mounting opposition in the south threatened even this.

Ideology and preserving the Soviet State: Civil War 1918–21

There is much evidence to suggest that Lenin and Trotsky viewed war against the opponents of the revolutionary regime as part and parcel of the revolutionary process. As Sheila Fitzpatrick (2008) reasons, such conflict was inevitable and even sought after. However, Lenin had assumed that once the Brest–Litovsk conflict had subsided, the real job of ruling could begin. He vastly underestimated the level of discontent amongst nearly all groups in society or the threat of complete annihilation that his party was under from the allied forces and old Tsarist supporters. The Civil War, which began in earnest in May 1918, was a most complicated affair. Christopher Read (2013) helpfully describes the frequent changes in advantage between 'the **Reds**' (the Communists) and 'the **Whites**' (anti-Bolshevik forces ranging from proto-fascists to Kadet Liberals to Tsarists) as 'a political patchwork quilt'; he writes, 'Over the next four years or so the colours on the quilt changed but never reverted to a single colour.'

At the peak of the conflict in 1919 at least 23 groups claimed to be governments of all or part of the former Russian Empire … Politically the next four years were marked by confusion and conflict …'.[2]

Speak like a historian

Lenin's Decree on Nationalities (carried out by Commissar for Nationalities Stalin) suggested that the Bolsheviks promulgated self-determination for ethnic minorities who had a right to decide how they wanted to participate in the federal Soviet institutions. Lenin did this in the belief that ethnic minorities were too closely integrated into the Russian economy to withdraw. He never expected the Ukraine, Finland, Lithuania, Latvia, Estonia and Transcaucasia to leave Russian control. Lenin was forced to renege on self-determination pledges during the Civil War as the territorial land of Russia shrunk. Instead, he reverted to a pseudo-federalism which gave all legislative and executive power to the Communist Party, but the state would be divided along ethnic lines – providing little satisfaction to anyone.

Key terms

The **Reds** were a paramilitary organisation within the Bolshevik party, made up of factory workers, peasants and ex-soldiers. They were reorganised into the Red Army during the Civil War beginning in 1918.

The **Whites** formed as a loose confederation of anti-Bolshevik forces who fought the Bolsheviks for control of Russia, 1917–22. Some wore the white uniforms of imperialist Russia but some chose white to be distinct from the Reds.

The map in Figure 3.2 illustrates the main 'fronts' of the Civil War and which White General led them. As you can see, the Bolsheviks faced attack from every direction at one time or another during the war.

The Whites

Threats to the Communists had been building since November, but the beginning of the Civil War beginning was marked by a bizarre, and in some ways, unnecessary incident in March 1918. Approximately 30 000 Czechoslovakian soldiers had been fighting with Russia hoping to gain independence from the Austro–Hungarian Empire and were attempting to return to the fight after Brest–Litovsk had dissolved the Eastern Front. The Communists were allowing them to leave the only way they safely could, via the Trans-Siberian railway eastwards. Local Communists spread rumours that the Czechs were going to join with the Social Revolutionaries against the new government and so Trotsky (now Commissar for War) told them to disarm. This was a disastrous order and only encouraged the Czechs to join some Social Revolutionaries ejected from the Constituent Assembly in January and who they had a good deal of support in this region. Together they proclaimed a new government based in Samara (the Volga region), known as *Komuch*.

By June 1918 Komuch had control of the whole of the Trans-Siberian railway from the Urals to Vladivostock. In July, the Czechs took Simbirsk and advanced on Ekaterinburg, where Tsar Nicholas II and his family had been kept in custody. The Bolsheviks ordered the immediate execution of the Romanovs to remove the threat of Nicholas becoming a figurehead for anti-revolutionary activity. In fact, Nicholas was largely unaware of the events that were unfolding outside of his compound and had spent most of his days shovelling snow. By November 1918, however, the Czech resistance had fallen apart as their reason to fight had been negated by the end of the First World War.

Trotsky saw the need for a new army but volunteers were not forthcoming from the war-weary population. In June 1918 he introduced mass conscription; 275 000 enlisted but on the day of enrolment only 40 000 men attended. Trotsky abandoned earlier assumptions he had promoted after the February revolution in 'Order Number One' and reorganised the 'Red Army' along Tsarist lines. The election of officers was abolished and he set up his own mobile headquarters in a train carriage so he could visit the front lines speedily. The Red Army grew extremely quickly, with 48 000 former Tsarist officers drafted in to lead a defence against the Whites. This caused deep fracture lines within the Communist Party itself (none more so than between Trotsky and Stalin – Stalin disliked the practice of employing 'bourgeois officers'), but Trotsky was not going to allow doctrine to stand in the way of utilising expertise. However, he did take precautionary measures by employing 180 000 loyal commissars to ensure the strict supervision of every military unit. The descent into all-out war caused chaos in political terms too, and Lenin saw this as an opportunity to tighten the hierarchical authority he already wielded. Power at the party's apex was devolved from the Central Committee to two inner sub-committees in January 1919. The *Politburo* was to decide strategy and policy and the *Orgburo* to oversee internal party administration. Robert Service (1997) contends that the ascendancy of the *Politburo* was a turning point in Communist supremacy because the party's

functions had expanded so much it had become the supreme agency of state by
1919.

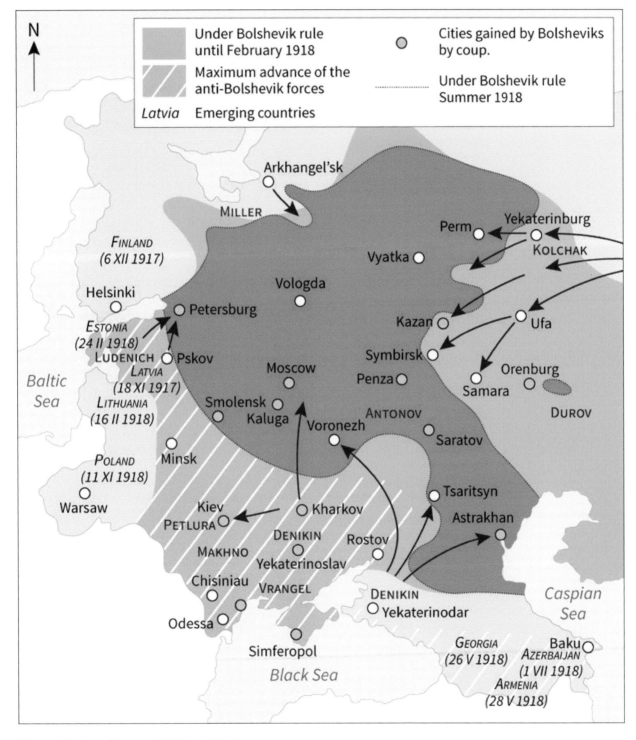

Figure 3.2: Map of Russian Civil War, 1918–21

Figure 3.3: Trotsky leading the Red Army. Trotsky was an inspirational speaker and a ruthless commander of the Red Army, despite having little military experience.

Meanwhile, during April 1918, a number of Tsarist generals including Deniken (who replaced Kornilov after his death in April) and Krasnov had amassed 9000 soldiers from Cossack regiments in the south and south east. Trotsky arrived in his command-train and encouraged the Red forces there. Although Deniken's troops made terrific advances in May to August 1918, reaching 400 miles from Moscow, his forces were worn down by continuous counter-attacks from the Red Army, and the Whites rapidly retreated thereafter. A third, rather modest army, led by General Yudenich, would also threaten the Bolshevik regime by attacking Petrograd from Estonia. Co-operation between these forces, though theoretically possible, was difficult and unlikely. Trotsky masterfully saw off Yudenich's threats within a week.

The SRs had fled to Omsk in September 1918. There, a brief Directory Government was set up but later overthrown by officers who wanted to establish Admiral Kolchak as a military dictator. The historian, Jonathan Smele (1996), suggests that the White army in Siberia experienced only short-lived success under Kolchak because he was a poor leader. Kolchak's fragile nerves seem to have cracked altogether under the strain of a Red Army counter-attack in June 1919. Eyewitnesses invariably talk of his 'appearing to be in a state of extreme nervous tension' in July and his looking 'really and truly worn out', and speak of 'gloomy, mistrustful and suspicious moods' alternating with 'uncontrollable fits of anger' as Kolchak snapped pencils or paced manically about his office, railing against everyone from the Allies to the Masons for sabotaging the White cause. By 1920, the final blow to the White armies came when Kolchak was handed over (by his own troops) to the Communists and shot.

The year 1919 saw large-scale offensives by the White armies on all three fronts and they posed a severe threat to the Communist regime, gaining large tracts of land (although not necessarily heavily populated) as they attempted their respective advances on Moscow. In the south, Baron Wrangel, who had taken over from Deniken, was unable to repel the Communist invasion of the Crimea and was defeated. In April 1920, the Poles came to the defence of the Ukraine but were soon repulsed, allowing the Red Army to advance to within 480 miles of Warsaw. The Communists signed a peace accord in March 1921 which gave the valuable Ukraine back to the Russians: they had won the Civil War.

Civil War: an analysis

Christopher Read (2013) argues that a primary reason for the Whites' failure was that its only secure territory was that on which its armies stood. As the Whites moved forward they left political vacuums, or worse - opponents - to take over. In contrast, Orlando Figes (2014) believes it was the Whites' failure to accept the peasant revolution on the land that led to their failure: they simply didn't frame policies that won mass support. It is widely agreed amongst historians that the Whites were politically divided and got little co-operation from the peasant population who, although treated atrociously by both sides, still felt some loyalty to the Communists who had nationalised the land. The Allies were too occupied with fighting Germany in the first instance, and too weary thereafter to provide much support to the Whites. The Reds used the railways to excellent effect, had an organised and inspirational leader in Trotsky, and above all possessed a fanatical unity of purpose in defeating anti-revolutionary forces.

The Greens

The desire to evade military conscription, which had been introduced in June 1918, eventually gave way to a more militant form of neutralism that saw hundreds of thousands of young men take up arms in or near their native villages, shifting major confrontation to that between the Reds and the 'Greens'. The Greens were irregular bands of peasant insurgents, most of whom had seen service in the Tsarist army and/or deserted from the Red or White camps. The Greens' primary aim was to rid their districts of all officials, both *zolotopogonniki* (gold-epaulettes, meaning White officers), and 'commissars' (a generic term for representatives of Soviet power that included local Communists, food collectors and Cheka). Their characteristic military action was raiding railway depots, local military training units, and state farms. Their punishment of captives took such ancient and brutal forms as live burial and disembowelment. The historian Erik C. Landis (2008) suggests that former officers of the Tsarist army and other individuals with service-experience played a prominent role in the organisation of these groups of 'Greens', both because of their own status as deserters and, presumably, their willingness to assume a leadership role among local men in a similar position.

The disturbances associated with the Greens were in areas encroached upon by the shifting front lines of the Civil War. The uncertainty regarding the approach of Denikin's armies from the south, or of the fortunes of the other White forces in the east and north, heightened anxieties in the villages and towns alike. Mobilisations to the Red Army, in some areas, were combined with declarations of martial law and even evacuations of Soviet personnel. The Greens cannot be understood

Summary of key events

- Lenin created a government which concentrated decision-making power in the hands of a few Bolsheviks, but set up complex administrative systems which increased bureaucracy.

- Almost as soon as Lenin and the Bolsheviks had signed the crippling Treaty of Brest–Litovsk to end war with Germany, Russia descended into Civil War.

- The 'Whites', led by Yudenich, Deniken and Kolchak attacked from the south-west and east.

- The Bolshevik army, 'The Reds', reinstated conscription and used the Cheka to spread terror in the countryside to enforce support, and eventually won in 1924.

exclusively in terms of widespread unwillingness to serve in the Red Army. It was the strategic context, with all the risk and uncertainty that it entailed in the summer of 1919, that made something like the 'Green army' possible.

Perhaps the most well-known example of 'green resistance' came from Nestor Makhno, a Ukrainian peasant. Makhno and his anarchist army increased after the defection of 40 000 Red Army troops in Crimea to the Black Army in July 1918, pitting them against the Communists. By late 1920, Makhno had successfully halted General Wrangel's White Army advance into Ukraine from the south-west, capturing 4000 prisoners and stores of munitions, and preventing the White Army from gaining control of the all-important Ukrainian grain harvest. Even though this helped the Red Army, Makhno and the anarchists maintained their main political structures, refusing demands to join the Red Army, to hold Bolshevik-supervised elections or accept Bolshevik-appointed political commissars.

When General Wrangel's White Army forces were decisively defeated in November 1920, the Communists immediately turned on Makhno and the anarchists once again. On 26 November 1920, less than two weeks after assisting Red Army forces to defeat Wrangel, Makhno's headquarters staff and many of his subordinate commanders were arrested and later executed. Makhno escaped, but was soon forced into retreat as the full weight of the Red Army and the Cheka's 'Special Punitive Brigades' was brought to bear against not only the Makhnovists, but all anarchists, even their admirers and sympathisers.

The second major Green force took shape in the late summer of 1919, where full-scale insurrection erupted in Tambov province where as many as 50 000 insurgents were led by a former left-SR peasant, A.S. Antonov. By January 1921, much of Omsk province in western Siberia was in the hands of peasant insurrectionaries. These and many other widely scattered rebellions lasted well into 1921, but were ruthlessly crushed by units led by Red Army Commander Tukhachevskii, who shot hundreds without trial and deported thousands to newly created labour camps.

Stalin's rise, ideology and change

Finding Lenin's successor

Lenin's illness became apparent in February 1921 when his bouts of insomnia and headaches stopped him from writing. At the Eleventh Party Congress he made two rambling speeches which attacked anyone who disagreed with him and it was clear to all of his closer associates that the search for a successor should begin. Given his masterful leadership of the Red Army during the Civil War and his mesmerising oratory skills, Trotsky seemed the natural heir. When Trotsky had returned from America to find the Mensheviks co-operating with the Provisional Government, he had joined the Bolsheviks (relatively late) in 1917; the old guard never forgave him for this late enthusiasm for the Party. He also never held an executive post in the Party, unlike his main rivals Zinoviev (member of the Politburo), Stalin (General Secretary of the Central Committee) and Kamenev (full member of the Politburo but also acting Council of People's Commissars and Politburo chairman during Lenin's illness). Trotsky was arrogant and ambitious and gained few friends in the Party as a result; even Lenin had a low opinion of him, stating that when it came to politics Trotsky 'didn't have a clue'.

In April 1922, the amiable, seemingly moderate, quiet Georgian, Josif Stalin was appointed General Secretary by Lenin. At the time, this did not seem of great importance but it was to give Stalin a unique power base as from here he could use his authority to appoint executive positions within the Party to those who were loyal to him. During 1922 alone, more than 10 000 provincial officials were appointed by the Orgburo and Secretariat. At the end of May 1922 Lenin suffered his first stroke, resulting in the temporary paralysis of his right leg and arm and loss of speech. During this period his responsibilities would be taken over by a *troika*, or triumvirate, of Kamenev, Zinoviev and Stalin. Stalin would visit Lenin to solicit his counsel and then submit matters to the Politburo who would routinely approve his ideas as, by now, other members of the Politburo – Rykov, Tomsky and Bukharin – had come to support the triumvirate. Stalin seemingly deceived everyone by taking a moderate line on every issue. In September 1922, Lenin sent a note to Stalin asking the Politburo to appoint Trotsky deputy chairman of the Council of People's Commissars and Kamenev as deputy chairman of the Council of Labour and Defence. The minutes of the Politburo meeting show that Trotsky 'categorically refused' the position, which was an unprecedented move and served to further undermine his position in the Party.

Figure 3.4: The Troika. From left to right: Stalin, Rykov, Zinoviev, Kamenev.

Stalin was afraid of a Lenin–Trotsky alliance towards the end of his life when it had become clear that he and Lenin fundamentally disagreed on the nationalities question and the spread of the revolution. Stalin headed the Commissariat for Nationalities that wished to deprive Soviet republics of their formal independence by turning them into autonomous republics within the RSFSR; this was a form of federalism which would bring the Ukraine, Belorussia, Armenia, Georgia and Azerbaijan into an enlarged RSFSR. Lenin thought this smacked of imperialism and discussions on the matter became acrimonious. In Lenin's testament, dictated in January 1923, he criticised all of the members of the Politburo, although described Trotsky as the most capable. It was clear that Lenin advocated a collective leadership for the future of the Party, although this was perhaps because he inflated his abilities to lead. In a postscript he added, 'Stalin is too coarse, and this shortcoming … becomes intolerable in a General Secretary.' Following this, Stalin announced the delay of the Twelfth Party Congress for one month, hoping that this would stifle Lenin's opportunity to denounce him. His gamble paid off as Lenin suffered a massive stroke that prevented him from speaking again. He died on 21 January 1924.

The consolidation of Bolshevik authority and the development of the Stalinist dictatorship

Just after Lenin's death, Trotsky was accused of the terrible crime of 'factionalism' by the triumvirate: the charge against him was that, supported by 46 Party members, he criticised the 'police regime' the Party had become. Trotsky, once thought to be the natural successor to Lenin, had become hopelessly alienated. Stalin had more Party support as demonstrated at the Thirteenth Party Congress held a few months after Lenin's death when the dead leader's testament was read out – including his negative comments about Stalin (which Zinoviev and Kamenev persuaded the meeting to ignore). This Congress had come after Trotsky had denounced the 'old guard' for stifling debate. Bukharin accused Trotsky of factionalism and Zinoviev had branded 'Trotskyism' as a particular tendency within the Russian workers' movement. By the time the Congress met, the triumvirate had become the 'semerka' (the seven) and completely isolated Trotsky. Stalin's position was enhanced by the launch of the 'Lenin enrolment', which sought to increase the membership of industrial workers in the party. Over 500 000 workers were recruited between 1923 and 1925, supervised by Stalin. The new recruits to the party were mostly politically naïve due to their lack of education. This probably strengthened Stalin's position further as many joined the party to obtain better living quarters or promotions at work. It has also been suggested that Stalin's humble Georgian background and 'proletarian look' gave him an advantage over the intellectuals, such as Trotsky and Bukharin. Trotsky defended his position in a series of seven letters, which were collected as '*The New Course*' in January 1924, but it was too late: he was removed from office in 1925 and expelled from the party altogether by November 1927.

Cult of personality

Following Lenin's death, the party sought to create a 'cult of personality' around the leader of the revolution and increasingly depended upon it for a source of legitimacy. Monuments to Lenin were erected everywhere. Stalin even forbade Lenin to be buried next to his mother (as he had wished) and instead embalmed him to be displayed like a saint in a church in Moscow, where he still is today. Petrograd was renamed Leningrad and schools set up 'Lenin corners', elevating him to idol status. Zinoviev introduced the term 'Leninism' at his funeral and the triumvirate sought to present themselves as true defenders of his beliefs, marking out anyone (mainly Trotsky) as 'anti-Leninist' if they contradicted their ideas. This marked a change in the ideology of the Party away from Marxism and traditional Socialist beliefs, as had been the case under Lenin's leadership. In fact, Lenin's ideas had always evolved and changed to suit the circumstances and Stalin took full advantage of this by assembling a doctrine, drawn selectively from the dead leader's writings, which he published as *'The Foundations of Leninism'*. Stalin also set up two special institutes, which collected the works of the founding fathers of Communism, allowing Stalin to attack the ideas of opponents as illegitimate. One theme Stalin invoked without exception at almost every congress was 'Party Unity', which had been established at the Tenth Party Congress. This enabled him to build upon his dictatorship in the 1930s, but for the time being, meant that the Party line would hold against Trotsky.

Figure 3.5: Lenin's body lying in state in the Kremlin. The onlookers include his wife Krupskia and his sister Mary Illichna.

'Socialism in One Country'

By 1923, it was evident that revolutions were unlikely to occur in Europe. The Spartacist Uprising failed in Germany in 1919 and the fascist dictator, Mussolini, had assumed power in Italy in 1922. Stalin began to advance the idea of 'Socialism in One Country' from 1924 as a form of protection for the USSR, which was encircled by hostile capitalists. 'Socialism in One Country' would be a dramatic departure from the Party's Marxist revolutionary strategy, and was another area where he could undermine Trotsky and the Left Opposition as 'anti-Leninist' if they disagreed with him. Historians have debated whether Lenin would have approved of this policy or not; there is evidence to suggest he was less convinced that spread of revolution was needed for the Bolsheviks to succeed. The policy became Party doctrine when the Fourteenth Party Congress, in April 1925, resolved that 'in general the victory of socialism is unconditionally possible in one country'. It was obvious that Stalin was successfully developing his own brand of Communism, which would have dramatic consequences for the people of the Soviet Union.

It is difficult to pinpoint when Stalin became absolute dictator of the USSR as he was obliged to operate in a collective leadership in the years following Lenin's death. It was not until the 1930s when it was clear he was absolute premier. However, there is much evidence to suggest that the point when the Party agreed to build 'Socialism in One Country' in 1925 was when Stalin asserted his dominance over the Party. It was assumed by most Party members that building socialism meant increasing the USSR's industrial base. Trotsky and the Left Opposition (including economist Evgeny Preobrazhensky) contended that New Economic Policy (**NEP** – described in a later section) created money-grabbing peasant markets and reversed the effects of the revolution. Trotsky suggested that rapid industrialisation was necessary, enabling agriculture to be mechanised and thereby facilitating the creation of collective farms. Bukharin and Stalin argued that Lenin had explicitly sought an alliance between the proletariat and peasantry therefore consolidation of the NEP was needed.

Moves and counter-moves

Having sided with Trotsky against NEP, and with the Left Communists and Workers' Opposition in 1925 to form a United Opposition, Zinoviev and Kamenev faced a similar fate to the once hailed leader of the Red Army. Stalin exploited their weaknesses and potential divisions well. Defeated at a Central Committee meeting in April 1926, the Opposition then tried to present their case to the Fifteenth Party Conference in October, but they were denied the right to speak. Party militants then broke up meetings they had tried to hold with factory workers; this marked the first time the Party had used violence against its own members. The Opposition began working in secret on a statement to give to Party members; however, the State Political Administration or GPU (the secret police 1922–34) discovered their clandestine printing press, and determined that this constituted criminal activity. Zinoviev and Kamenev were subsequently expelled from the Party (although only for a short time – they were allowed to return in 1928 as long as they publicly denounced 'Trotskyism' and repudiated any oppositional activity they had been involved with). Trotsky was later deported from the Soviet Union in 1929 and was famously found with a mountaineer's ice axe in his back on 20 August 1940, reportedly murdered by undercover Stalinist agents.

After 1927, Stalin turned against Bukharin and the NEP, mobilising his supporters in the Party for a return to Civil War methods to fight the *'kulaks'* in the 'battle for bread' and force through the rapid industrialisation strategy called the Five Year Plan to industrialise the Soviet Union. It was through this struggle against Bukharin and the other members of the Politburo who would form the 'Right Opposition', namely Aleksei Rykov (Lenin's successor as the Head of Government) and Mikhail Tomsky (Head of the Trade Unions), that Stalin consolidated his leadership of the Party.

A grain crisis in 1927 provoked Stalin and his supporters to maintain that the peasantry, *kulaks* in particular, was holding the proletarian state to ransom in an attempt to raise grain prices. Stalin's response was to revert to grain requisitioning,

Key term

The **Five-Year Plans** were a series of nationwide economic plans, developed by the Communist Party and carried out by the state planning committee who acted under strict guidelines.

as had taken place during the Civil War. Bukharin and his allies, Rykov and Tomsky, baulked at the violence used in the villages, which Stalin successfully managed to turn against them as 'right-wing deviations' from Leninism. Bukharin and his supporters did little to rally support as war scares from Britain, France, and China in 1928 persuaded them that any in-fighting could damage the country as a whole. This combined with the 'Shakhty Affair', when 55 engineers from the Donbass mines were convicted of 'sabotage', and many bourgeois specialists were arrested, convincing most Central Committee members that NEP should be abandoned. In Comintern too, Bukharinists were defeated in 1929 when Stalin identified 'social democrats' with 'social fascists' who were responsible for repressing the proletariat. Stalin's ultra-leftist tactics again forced Bukharin to the right, and he was finally excluded from Comintern's Executive Committee in July 1929.

Stalin's rise to power was not just about consolidating his own supremacy, but about the direction the revolution should take. All of the inner-party factionalism was couched in ideological and policy-making terms. Factionalism occurred because of fundamental questions about the spread of revolution and the best way to achieve socialism in the USSR. However, the effect of Stalin's victory was to severely curtail scope for inner-party discussion or disagreement over policy. Stalin was now free to initiate his utopian vision for socialism, which would completely transform the social structure and economy, and ultimately the political system of the USSR.

Consolidation of Bolshevik Authority and the Development of the Stalinist dictatorship

Consolidation Bolshevik Authority: Constitutions

The Bolsheviks undoubtedly survived the first months in power by a mixture of concession to pragmatism and ruthless action. Other left wing groups were swiftly excluded from sharing power, following the dissolution of the Constituent Assembly and eruption of Civil War. Under Lenin's leadership, the Bolsheviks successfully bypassed the Soviets to establish a Bolshevik dominated government, headed by Sovnarkom. This was entrenched under the Constitution of July 1918, which established the RSFSR. Although the Constitution stated that supreme power rested with the All-Russian Congress of Soviets, it was the Central Executive Committee, which would be the supreme organ of power, in effect making decisions as a President might. The Soviets would be relegated to electing Sovnarkom, which would carry out the administration of the State. Although the constitution appeared to mark a move away from the autocratic nature of Tsarism, it was much less democratic than it appeared. Only the workers and peasants received a vote. That meant the 'bourgeoisie' of the former regime, including businessmen, tsarist officials, clergy and nobility were excluding from voting or holding public office. Even then, during elections to the Congress the workers votes were weighted more heavily than the peasants, at a ratio of five to one. Sovnarkom was in fact appointed by the party's Central Committee in practice, this limited even further the role of the Soviets and therefore the constitution created a centralised form of government that focused real power in the hands of the party.

The Constitution was redrafted in December 1922 and created the USSR (Union of Soviet Socialist Republics). In reality there was little change from the previous document. Although Lenin prevailed in creating a federation of republics with equal status, the states, which made up the Union were kept under strict control. The governments of the republics were considered as no more than branches of Sovnarkom, which would provide the necessary coercion to ensure parity across the republics.

Impact of the Russian Civil War

The Russian Civil War (1918-21) bought even greater centralisation and Party control, due to the reliance on the Central Committee to formulate policies and decisions quickly in the midst of war. In 1919, another sub-committee was created – the Politburo - because fewer than half the members of the Central Committee could attend meetings, due to practical reasons. The 8th Party Congress in 1919 therefore formalised the creation of the Poitburo, which became the real centre for Party policy from then on.

Many historians (such as Richard Pipes, (1997) have criticised the highly centralised nature of the Communist regime that developed during the Civil War. Robert Service (1979) has suggested that 'Centralisation' can mean a host of different organisational methods, and the party exhibited several of them during its first years in power. The serious splits which had occurred at central committee level in November 1917 and again over Peace in March 1918 demonstrates the inexperience and experimental nature of Bolshevik rule and can explain the regime's faltering stance on centralisation. Provincial committees became increasingly important and within local committees, individual secretaries progressively assumed more responsibility for day-to-day affairs. Service (1979) also argues there was an increasing reliance on "appointmentism" as officials nominated those below them along lines of loyalty rather than specialism or talent. All these measures were justified by civil war conditions, which, as a resolution of the Eighth All Russian Congress (December 1920) defined at length the division of power between central and provincial organs. The Congress agreed the division on the basis of the "dual subordination" of commissariat officials. They were supposed to carry out their tasks in accordance with resolutions of the provincial executive committees to which they were assigned and the commissariats from which they received instructions at the same time. This was not an easy task during peacetime let alone in the midst of a bitter Civil War. However, centralism, although borne out of civil war, certainly outlived it and was to become a key feature of the Soviet Union under Joseph Stalin in the late 1920s.

In addition to the ban on factions, instituted by Lenin in 1921, which severely restricted criticism of the Central Committee decisions, was the introduction of the nomenklatura system. Intended to ensure that officials in key positions were loyal, lists of approximately 5500 key Party and government posts were drawn up and reviewed by the Central Committee. Becoming a party official bought particular privileges such as superior housing, in return for ensuring that central directives were administered as the party intended. This development increased the control Lenin and the Party had over the state.

Development of the Stalinist Dictatorship

Stalin can be said to have extended and personalised some of the structures already established - for example, the rule by one party dominating state institutions and centralised control created through the nomenklatura and Politburo – were all established under Lenin's rule by 1924. However, Stalin called Party congresses less frequently – none at all were summoned between 1939 and 1952 – and began to assert a personal dictatorship in the way Lenin had never attempted.

Stalin used his position as General Secretary of the party to control appointments to the Party 'apparat' (the party's administrative system). This meant Stalin acquired patronage over the most important positions in Soviet society and he used his power of appointment to develop both an elaborate bureaucracy, and legions of loyal servants. The 'Lenin Enrolment' only aided the development of a more personal form of government, when party membership was extended to commemorate Lenin's death. The number of members increased to 1,677,910 by 1930. Most of the new members were drawn from the younger and less well-educated workers who were less interested in ideology and saw enrolment as an opportunity to further their own careers. At this time Stalin began to use more nationalistic language, which seemed to energise newer members of the party. Despite Stalin's increasingly brutal policies following 1928, many party members saw that loyalty to the regime could bring opportunity to alleviate the harsh realities of living in RSFSR. Historians argue that the 'Lenin Enrolment' entrenched inequality that had already developed under the nomenklatura system.

Development of Stalinism: 1936 Constitution

It was left to one of the few remaining members of the old guard, Nikolai Bukharin, to draft the Constitution of 1936 which Stalin claimed was the 'most democratic in the world'. It created a new USSR, a federation of eleven Soviet Republics, replacing the previous seven. For the first time, the leading role of the Communist Part was recognised as 'the vanguard of the working people'. The Congress of Soviets was replaced with the new 'Supreme Soviet,' which comprised the Soviet of the Union and Soviet of the Nationalities. Each republic was also granted its own soviet. The new constitution promised autonomy to ethnic groups and support for national cultures. It also promised to enfranchise everyone over eighteen, even those who had been deprived before, such as the old elites. The constitution promulgated civil rights such as freedom from arbitrary arrest and the right to free speech, although these were never intended to be implemented. Party leaders in Georgia planned to leave the Union in 1951, but were purged, demonstrating clearly that promised rights were largely ignored and the status quo was maintained. In this respect, many historians have suggested the constitution was not much more than a propaganda exercise designed to feed into the cult of Stalin, which had been manufactured on Stalin's fiftieth birthday in 1929.

Economic developments

Lenin's decrees

State capitalism

In May 1918 Lenin wrote the pamphlet '*Left Infantilism and the Petty Bourgeois Spirit*,' which advised fellow Russian socialists to 'study the state capitalism of the Germans, [and] to adopt it with all possible strength'. In Lenin's view, this meant co-operation with employers whilst asserting the power of the state and was completely necessary if the Bolsheviks were to survive the first few months in power, roughly from October 1917 to June 1918. A flood of decrees issued from Sovnarkom created this 'mixed economy' and began by initiating the seizure of the State Bank and subsequent nationalisation and amalgamation of all private banks into the People's Bank of the Russian Republic in November 1917. In January 1918, all Tsarist domestic and foreign debts were annulled. The bourgeoisie were attacked as personal ownership of large houses was declared illegal, just as large landowners had had their estates taken over by peasants.

Lenin imagined factory committees would assume managerial roles within the general framework laid down by the central executive committee of the Soviets. However, control of industry was incredibly difficult as, since October, production had slumped and even ground to a halt in some factories, and radical local Soviets sprung up throughout towns and cities. 'Nationalisation', which had already occurred in agriculture, spread to industry as workers took control of factories throughout the early months of 1918. Lenin acted to ban further 'nationalisation from below' without permission in January 1918 and again in April, but such decrees went ignored until June. The decree of June 1918 began a process of imposing greater discipline on the workers, introducing 'bourgeois specialists' and one-man management. SRs and Left Communists deplored this aspect of Lenin's industrial policy, as they predicted his encouragement of State Capitalism would lead to bureaucratic centralisation, in which commissars might destroy the independence of local Soviets. Lenin's imperative was survival and a restoration of order.

War Communism

The onset of Civil War created massive problems of supply; until 1920 the Communists were cut off from coal in the area of the Don and from the oil of Baku. War Communism, a term coined by Lenin to refer retrospectively to the Party's civil war-induced economic policies, was his first attempt at a command economy to deal with the disastrous economic situation.

However, as several Marxist commentators have argued, these priorities were always latent in the Bolshevik schema and became manifest even before the onset of full-scale civil war. As early as December 1917, Lenin established a Supreme Council of the National Economy (Vesenkha) to organise a general economic plan, and financial administration for the state, although it did so on a small scale. Headed by A. Rykov from April 1918, Vesenkha took its place in Sovnarkom and developed an elaborate infrastructure of sections and departments to handle its enormous but ill-defined responsibilities.

> ### 🔑 Key term
>
> **War Communism** was the economic system introduced by Lenin that existed during the Civil War. It was a combination of Marxist ideas and emergency measures and involved nationalising the land and banks.

Grain requisitioning

Lenin's economic policies can be seen to have an ideological underpinning in more ways than one. War Communism, it has been argued, was Lenin's way of dealing with the bourgeois influences in the countryside. Since Stolypin's agricultural reforms in 1906 (see Chapter 2) that allowed consolidation of farms, there had been a low but marked growth in richer peasants or *'kulaks'*. Lenin voiced his abhorrence of this perceived class of peasant who, in his mind, were responsible for hoarding and withholding grain in order to get the highest price, as rationing had been in place under Tsar Nicholas II from 1916. Therefore, the party introduced grain requisitioning (*prodrazverstka)* in June 1918. This involved sending 'food detachments', squads from the cities under the control of the *Cheka*, who would seize what they defined as 'surplus' grain. Lenin intended to promote class war between the poorer peasants and their better-off neighbours. Lenin issued further decrees in June tasking 'committees of the poor' with achieving the expropriation of the *kulaks*. The consequences of this process were calamitous because they created antagonism between the peasants, but also because they failed to improve food distribution. Peasants, knowing their surplus would be seized, sowed smaller acreages and more actively hoarded and hid their grain. The food detachments confiscated any grain they could, including seed grain which was required to sow the following harvest. This created a vicious cycle of lower grain production and ever more punitive requisitioning. As an economic policy and a way of feeding the cities, grain requisitioning was a failure.

A crisis in industrial production

Critical food shortages caused by grain hoarding by angry peasants, and rapid inflation caused by the printing of paper money, meant food was so scarce that workers in the cities were forced to return to the countryside to look for food. Between 1918 and 1920, Moscow experienced a loss of approximately 100 000 workers and, over the same period, the number of factory and mine workers in the Urals dropped from 340 000 to 155 000. Among the major branches of industry, textiles experienced the greatest reduction, declining in terms of its workforce by nearly 72% between 1917 and 1920. Large enterprises, where the Bolsheviks had concentrated their agitational and recruitment efforts, suffered disproportionately, partly owing to the shutting down of entire shops (*tsekhy*) and partly due to heavy mobilisation for the Red Army and food procurement detachments. Petrograd, whose population had swelled to 2.5 million by 1917, had only 722 000 inhabitants by 1920, or approximately the same number as in 1870. Moscow's population, which had stood at slightly more than 2 million in February 1917, shrank to just over 1 million by late 1920, or less than the number recorded in the 1897 census. Shliapnikov (a leading Bolshevik) said the party were 'the vanguard of a non-existent class'. It is estimated by historian Donald Raleigh (2004) that epidemics of typhus and cholera killed up to 5 million and the famine of 1921–2 killed approximately 5 million people too; this is set alongside battle-dead figures of approximately 350 000.

The famine of 1921–2 affected primarily the Volga and Ural river regions. Historians have suggested that although problems with grain production began during the First World War, it was War Communism (and grain seizures) that really disturbed these areas because the rail systems could not distribute food effectively. This problem was compounded by intermittent droughts during 1921, leading to catastrophe. Writer Maxim Gorky issued appeals to the Western powers for aid, resulting in Britain sending over 600 tons of supplies to the Soviet Union. The US Hoover administration sent aid too.

Extending state control

The extension of the state was an obvious response to these desperate circumstances. From the autumn of 1918, the level of rations distributed was tied to the 'class principle'. This meant that manual workers (and among them, those engaged in the most physically demanding work) were permitted more than clerical personnel, who received a higher ration than 'the bourgeoisie'. The system proved unwieldy and, as E.H. Carr (1952) notes, led to 'widespread anomalies, jealousies and discontents'[3]. This exacerbated already critical problems: by linking

 Voices from the past

Eyewitness account

Yevgeny Zamyatin was a Russian author. He is most famous for his 1921 novel '*We*', a story set in a dystopian future police state. Despite having been a prominent Old Bolshevik, Zamyatin was deeply disturbed by the policies pursued by the CPSU (Communist Party of the Soviet Union) following the October Revolution. In 1921, '*We*' became the first work to be banned by the Soviet censorship board. Sombre sentiments began to appear ever more palpably in Zamyatin's writing. In 1921 he published the article 'I Am Afraid', which addressed the suppression of freedom of thought, and the short story 'The Cave', which juxtaposed communism with prehistoric primitivism. On several occasions over the next few years, his fearless calls 'to defend the human being and humanity' saw Zamyatin put in prison. The following extract is taken from 'The Cave'.

GLACIERS, mammoths, wildernesses. Pitch-dark, black rocks, somehow reminding one of houses; in the rocks-caves. And one cannot tell who trumpets of a night along the stony path amid the rocks and, sniffing his way, drives the white snow dust before him. It may be the grey-trunked mammoth; it may be the wind; and it may be that the wind is only the icy roar of some super-mammothish mammoth. One thing is clear: it is winter. And one must clench one's teeth as tight as possible, to prevent them from chattering; and cut wood with a stone axe; and each night move one's fire from cave to cave, always deeper; and muffle oneself up in an always increasing number of shaggy hides.

Of a night, among the rocks where ages ago stood Petersburg, roamed the grey-trunked mammoth. And muffled up in hides, in coats, in blankets, in rags, the cave-dwellers were constantly retreating from cave to cave. On the lst October Martin Martinych and Masha barred up the study; on the 22nd they abandoned the dining-room and entrenched themselves in the bedroom. They had nowhere to retreat now; here they must holdout, or die.

In this cave-bedroom of Petersburg things were like in Noah's ark: clean and unclean creatures in ark-like promiscuity; Martin Martinych's writing-desk books; cakes of the stone age looking like pottery; a flat-iron; five lovingly white-washed potatoes; nickelled bed-frames; an axe; a chest of drawers; a stack of wood. And in the middle of all this universe was its god: a short-legged rusty-red squatting greedy cave-god: the iron stove.

Discussion Points

1. Why is he referencing pre-historic phenomena in this passage? What effect is it meant to have on the reader?
2. Zamyatin is writing from experience – what is he criticising in this passage?

Research Zamyatin and find out what happened to him under Stalin's regime.

rations to livelihood rather than individual performance, it provided little or no incentive for improved productivity. The inability of the state to accrue adequate measures of rations meant that, even for workers in the highest category, the amount of food remained well below the caloric minimum – evidence suggests that workers in this category received one quarter pound of bread and a bowl of meat soup per day at some points during the war.

Urban contraction was essentially the result of the catastrophic decline in supplies of food and fuel. This decline was itself the product of a combination of factors:

- The breakdown of the rail transport system owing to wartime overstrain and the inadequacy of repairs.
- Foreign and/or White occupation of some of the former empire's richest food- and fuel-producing regions.
- Peasants' reduction of crop-sown area and resistance to grain requisitions.
- Priority given to the Red Army in the field.

Lacking adequate nourishment, shelter, warmth and medicines, many urban residents found themselves engaged in what Isaac Deutscher (1965) called 'an almost zoological struggle for survival'[4]. Epidemics of typhus, cholera, influenza and diphtheria wiped out tens of thousands of urban residents, many already weakened by deficiency diseases. In Moscow, the death rate soared from 23.7 (per thousand) in 1917 to 45.4 in 1919.

In such circumstances, workers had to resort to other sources for food. Illegal private markets flourished outside railway stations. The biggest was perhaps at Orel station where up to 3000 traders (called 'bagmen') would pass through every day, exchanging household goods for food. According to one estimate, such illegal channels accounted for 60% of the urban consumption of bread grain in 1918–19. But as the state increasingly resorted to raising funds by printing more paper money, the value of currency plummeted. Eventually, the government acceded to the demands of trade unions for payment in kind, that is, in 'natural' goods. These rose as a proportion of the average Moscow worker's wage from 48% in late 1918 to 93% two years later. This suited those on the left of the party like Bukharin, who saw money as a symbol of capitalism; therefore bartering in goods was a sign of revolutionary progress. Lenin seems to have abandoned strict Marxism as he pursued his policy of one-man management, nationalising industry in 1919 so he could threaten workers with dismissal if they showed intentions to strike. Trotsky, having established the Red Army, began to advocate the militarisation of labour, particularly in 1920 as the army was demobilised.

New Economic Policy (NEP)

By the autumn of 1920, when Wrangel had been defeated and a treaty signed with the Poles, the Communists had survived civil war, but their country lay in ruin. The end of the war arguably allowed internal opposition to resurface in the form of ferocious peasant revolts in the Tambov province, and this convinced Lenin that something other than force was needed to quell them. The Party had promised the masses so much but delivered crippling hardships not even experienced during the First World War. Historian Isaac Deutscher (1965) suggests the 'vicious circle of war communism'[5] had reached its fullest extent. Unable to supply enough

 Key term

NEP: The New Economic Policy was introduced by Lenin in 1921 after it had become obvious that War Communism had failed. NEP was controversial because it allowed the peasants to sell some of their produce for profit and allowed small independent businesses to flourish once more.

goods to the peasants or food to the cities, the state had to tolerate and even rely on private trade. Initially, Lenin focused the **New Economic Policy** (NEP) on the peasantry. There was to be a reduction in the amount of grain requisitioned by imposing a tax-in-kind and peasants would be allowed to trade some of their surplus again; this would cause a rise in prices in the towns. The monopoly on industry exercised by *Vesenkha* would also have to be relaxed so that peasants would agree to sell their crops as they would have goods to buy; within a year, 3800 nationalised industries had been leased out. Lenin even signed a trade treaty with the British to encourage foreign investment in the Soviet Republic once more. This created a new class of private trader called the *'Nepman'*. By 1923, these traders had captured almost half the market, taking full advantage of what was a resurgence in capitalism.

While Lenin, of course, claimed that this was an improvised response to economic circumstances and that war communism had to be abandoned wholesale to save the revolution, in fact it was a tactical retreat. It could be argued that Lenin was trying to stifle internal opposition against Trotsky's efforts to militarise labour in 1920. Bourgeois experts were brought in to stabilise the currency and introduced limits on public spending, which meant that schools and medical care ceased to be free at the point of use and pensions and sick pay became contributory. Large industries were broken up into trusts, which had to compete with each other and with the private sector (although *Vesenkha* still supervised their activities). Wages were reintroduced and rationing was abolished in November. Inflation, however, continued and trusts were unable to pay their workers, resulting in rising unemployment. In July 1922, a new currency, the *chernovet*, was introduced but the previous currency, the *rouble,* remained in circulation until February 1924. The government maintained command of heavy industry and banking, but it was clear Lenin was allowing a bourgeois class of shopkeepers and farmers to re-emerge. William Rosenburg (1991) argues that NEP was a period in which the Communist Party 'were forced to come to terms with the complex cultural residues of pre-revolutionary Russia, implicitly at odds with ongoing goals of building a Socialist or Communist order'.[6]

ACTIVITY 3.2

It is a good idea to consider how far Lenin had departed from Marxist principles and which of the economic systems that existed under Lenin was the most Marxist.

	State Capitalism Nov 1917–May 1918	War Communism June 1918–March 1921	New Economic Policy (NEP) March 1921–1928
Key features			
Marxist features?			
Successes			
Failures			

The Stalinist economy

The departure from NEP

Although the departure from NEP seems inextricably tied to Stalin's quest to broker his own dictatorship of the Party and eliminate opposition to him, there were clear economic and ideological imperatives for abandoning NEP too. Lenin had presented NEP as a 'strategic retreat' in order to revive the economy after the Civil War, but he argued that it would still advance the state towards socialism through a mixed economy because the state would maintain control of the 'commanding heights' of heavy industry. The slow pace of NEP raised concerns within the Party, however, as it threatened to restore old enemies (*kulaks* and petty capitalists) to Russia.

A particular source of grievance for the workers was that wages had failed to increase after the revolution. In fact, it took until 1926 for wages to be raised to the average amount paid before 1914. Unemployment reached 1.74 million by 1929 – a massive increase from the 160 000 unemployed in 1922. This was wholly unimpressive given the promises the Bolsheviks had made to be the vanguard of the working classes. Strikes were therefore frequent under NEP. Urban opposition was also galvanised when food shortages occurred due to a lack of consumer goods to trade with the peasants for their grain. The result was the widening gap (which Trotsky referred to as the 'scissors crisis') of deflated agricultural prices against steeply rising prices for consumer goods in 1927.

In 1927, the official government statisticians claimed there were 20 100 strikes in that year alone (or approximately 77 per day given a five-day working week), although the figure was undoubtedly more. However, strikes were short-lived and the GPU advised management about who to sack after the event, preventing any protracted action. By 1928, it was clear that although the NEP had saved the Communist regime from destruction, the principle of private profit clashed in important economic sectors with central planning objectives. It was clear to Stalin that radical change was needed to avoid the anarchic boom and bust of NEP and the social inequalities it had reinforced. The state planning authority, **GOSPLAN**, set up in 1921 to collect economic data, could by 1925 produce economic projections and began to develop longer term growth plans for the state, providing evidence that change was needed. Stalin decided to embark on building a utopian vision of mass industrialisation, borrowed from the Left Opposition, which would see a 'great break' from everything that had gone before.

Collectivisation and the Five Year Plans

Collectivisation

Stalin's words to the masses, 'there are no fortresses which the Bolsheviks cannot capt*ure*', reveal his understanding that resolve and determination were going to be needed if modernisation were to occur. The ominous signs of what Stalin might unleash on the peasantry were already evident by 1928 after the grain crisis threatened mass food shortages. Stalin combated this with more grain requisitioning, which only temporarily solved the problem. After a trip he took to Siberia in January 1928, he became convinced that coercion, forced

Key term

GOSPLAN is an abbreviation for 'State Planning Committee'. It was established in February 1921, originally to advise the government on decision-making regarding the economy. It quickly began to advocate central government planning for the economy and eventually was made into the agency that was responsible for planning and administering the Five Year Plans, which began in 1928.

Key terms

Dekulakisation: a policy which developed as part of collectivisation, it involved liquidating the richer peasants or those who fought against collectivisation. Under it, at least 1.8 million peasants were deported and up to 5 million more shot. (Figures from the time are unreliable and historians still debate the numbers involved.)

Kolkhozy were collective farms where all the land was held in common and run by an elected committee. They consisted of between 50 to 100 families pooling their land, tools and livestock.

Key term

Cadres was a term used by Lenin to refer to those members of the intelligentsia who were loyal to the Bolshevik regime. It came be used as a term which meant 'dedicated revolutionaries' or committed communists.

collectivisation and **dekulakisation** was needed to finally bring the peasantry under full state control.

Requisitioning was backed up by a series of emergency measures, including Article 107, which allowed brigades to arrest any peasants and confiscate their property if they were suspected of withholding grain; it became known as the 'Urals-Siberian method' of grain extraction. As Moshe Lewin (1994) and Orlando Figes (2014) have argued, this paved the way for Stalin to implement all-out war against those peasants who would refuse to conform to the Soviet ideal or collective productivity by 1929.

Collectivisation, which meant the pooling of land, equipment, tools and livestock into collective farms (**Kolkhozy**), began in December 1929. At the time there were 1.9 million peasants in collectives (although they were really loose producer co-operatives), which had increased since a recorded 1 million in June of that year. Stalin used these figures as a basis for arguing that peasants were joining collectives of their own free will and so the process needed to speed up. However, it is unlikely this was occurring spontaneously. The drive for collectivisation was carried out by squads of party activists, secret police detachments and approximately 25 000 volunteers who swept through the countryside persuading, cajoling and if necessary coercing peasants into the collectives. Stalin refused to urge caution, supported by the Head of Propaganda, Kamisky, who declared, 'If in some matters you commit excesses and you are arrested, remember that you have been arrested for your revolutionary deeds.' Fearful of accusations of right-wing deviation, local activists responded enthusiastically to the call, perhaps accounting for the confusion which followed. The regime publicised one incident where a 15-year-old boy from a village in the Urals, Pavlik Morozov, denounced his father as a *kulak*. The boy was named a model Young Pioneer (see Section 'The effect of Leninist/Stalinist rule on young people') and statues of him were erected.

Collectivisation went hand in hand with the policy of dekulakisation, at first deliberately giving the 'middle peasants' high procurement quotas so that they could be expropriated for failing to deliver, but moving towards (in Stalin's own words) 'a determined offensive against the kulaks, eliminate them as a class'. *Kulaks* were to be divided into three categories: the first were 'actively hostile' and handed over to the **OGPU** (name given to the secret police in 1922) and sent to labour camps or inhospitable areas of Siberia; the second, 'the most economically potent', were to be deported outside the region of residence; and the third, 'the least noxious', given the worst land in their region. This involved confiscating property and deportation for approximately 1.5 million people by July 1930, a further 400 000 households uprooted, 390 000 sent to labour camps and 21 000 peasants shot.

Local activists used the threat of being labelled a *kulak* to encourage peasants to join the collective farms; it was reported that, by February 1920, over 50% of peasants had transferred, although of course these government figures must be treated with caution. The speed at which collectivisation was carried out seems to have worried even Stalin about the prospect of grain shortage, therefore he bizarrely called a halt to the policy in a famous article of March 1930, titled 'Dizzy with Success'. In the article, he condemned feverish **cadres** or coercing peasants and suggested that small-holdings would still be allowed to exist. Within weeks, the proportion of peasantry collectivised fell from 55% to 23%, and Table 3.1 (taken from historian Alec Nove's (1993) masterly account of the economic history of the USSR) demonstrates the dramatic instability that the people of Russia endured and the extent to which many remained in collectives in certain areas.

The peasants, particularly women, responded with fierce and sometimes armed resistance to collectivisation. In 1930, it was reported that 13 754 outbreaks of mass demonstrations occurred involving over 2.5 million peasants and killing of 3155 Soviet officials. There is evidence to suggest that peasants were more perturbed by the attack on the traditional way of life and culture rather than the imposition of collective methods per se. The abolition of the village commune (*mir*), closing down of Orthodox Churches, and fears of state requisitioning of livestock led to the mass slaughter and consumption of cattle, sheep and pigs, from which the USSR did not recover until the 1950s. The most common response to collectivisation was to migrate to the towns and cities: approximately 19 million peasants followed this course between 1926 and 1939, an unprecedented demographic shift.

The Great Famine

The 'Great Famine' of 1932 and 1933 was the result of the catastrophic policy of forced collectivisation. It is estimated that 5.7 million people died of hunger in those years, an enormous figure primarily caused by Stalin's procurement policies. In 1931 there were already grain shortages due to poor harvests, demoralised peasants, inefficient collective farms and too few mechanised tractors for sowing fields. This was compounded by very high exports in 1931 which depleted reserves, and a rapid growth in the urban population which lead to a sharp increase in food requirements and higher procurement quotas,

	1 March	10 March	1 April	1 May	1 June
USSR Total	55.0	57.6	37.3	—	23.6
North Caucasus	76.8	79.3	64.0	61.2	58.1
Middle Volga	56.4	57.2	41.0	25.2	25.2
Ukraine	62.8	64.4	46.2	41.3	38.2
Central black-earth region	81.8	81.5	38.0	18.5	15.7
Urals	68.8	70.6	52.6	29.0	26.6
Siberia	46.8	50.8	42.1	25.4	19.8
Kazakhstan	37.1	47.9	56.6	44.4	28.5
Uzbekistan	27.9	45.5	30.8	—	27.5
Moscow province	73.0	58.1	12.3	7.5	7.2
Western region	39.4	37.4	15.0	7.7	6.7
Belorussia	57.9	55.8	44.7	—	11.5

Source: Bogdenko (citing archive and other materials), page 31.
Table 3.1: Percentage of peasant households collectivised, 1930.

leaving the peasants and their surviving animals very little to eat. The Ukraine and North Caucasus suffered severely, so much so that requisitions had to be returned so that there would be some seeds for food and fodder. Stalin relaxed the procurement quotas in 1932, from the impossibly high 29.5 million tons to 18.1 million. However, persistent poor harvests, combined with high free market prices, meant grain was hoarded by the peasants or sold privately – discipline collapsed altogether in some areas.

Stalin implemented state counter-measures for which historians such as Robert Conquest (2002) have vilified him because collections and exports of grain were maintained despite widespread starvation. More recent historians, Robert Davies and Stephen Wheatcroft (1994), have concluded that Stalin was undeniably responsible for the deaths of many Russians. Stalin implemented a new law in April 1932 which introduced the death penalty for anyone found pilfering foodstuffs from the Kolkhozy, but it was used to purge any groups of peasants or local party leaders who could not meet the procurement demands. Mass arrests were carried out in the North Caucasus and the Ukraine and all grain was removed without exception, creating grave shortages. The wave of liquidation against *kulaks* carried out in 1930 was also repeated in 1931 and 1932, causing many 'middle peasants' to starve in the inhospitable areas of northern Siberia or be left with unfarmable land.

During collectivisation, the Party sent out 25 000 urban activists to supervise the transferral process through MTS (Machine Tractor Stations). Peasants had to use one of the 2500 MTS to gain access to tractors and other machinery, and payments were taken in kind (20% of the harvest that year). This meant they became both a service agency but also supervisors of production too by February 1933 (as the Party introduced 'political departments' to MTS, staffed by OGPU representatives). MTS were meant to increase tractor production but also ensure that the 'silent war' against the Soviet Union (grain hoarding) was destroyed, which of course involved rooting out the enemy. However, many political departments came to support the peasants they were meant to supervise as the famine deepened; some officers even condemned procurement quotas, leading the Party to abolish the departments by November 1934. This also coincided with a relaxation on private food-growing after the immediate push for collectivisation, which allowed peasants to sell surpluses of their own produce. However, from August 1932, speculators, dealers or middle-men selling foodstuffs on behalf of peasants were decreed to spend five to ten years in a labour camp, thereby putting the final nail in the coffin of NEP.

The First Five Year Plan: industrialisation

Some historians, such as Geoffrey Hosking (1992), have referred to the First Five Year Plan (1928–32) as a special type of 'revolution from above' – the accelerated conversion of the Soviet Union into a socialist industrial society by means of the state's coercive power to mobilise the masses for its goals. Kevin McDermott (2006) argues that Stalin had inherited a state-led model from Tsarist Russia (for example, Witte's industrialisation policy) and this was bolstered by collectivist 'statism' embedded in Leninism, therefore it was perhaps a natural development that the period of industrialisation would be lead by the Party. Yet Stalin was not the only decisive motor pressing for change; anti-NEP sentiment was strong amongst party activists, militant young workers and Civil War veterans alike, providing pressure from below for change too. On 7 November 1929, the 12th anniversary of the Bolshevik Revolution, Stalin wrote an article in *Pravda* named, 'The Year of the Great Break', in which he heralded the Five Year Plan as the start of the last great revolutionary struggle against 'capitalist elements' in the USSR, leading to the foundation of a socialist industrial society not only able to defend itself against the capitalist states but eventually overtaking them.

Gosplan (see 'Key terms') was put under huge pressure to plan the future of the economy to match Stalin's utopian vision, which was primarily focused on heavy industry. Some former Mensheviks (including Groman) were publicly tried in 1931 for trying to retard the country's industrial development for suggesting equilibrium planning instead. People's Commissariats were set up to take over from Vesenkha the task of administering burgeoning sectors of industry. Once projects had been established, 'over-fulfilment' of the targets became the priority for these secretaries, sacrificing health and safety and other sectors of the economy. In 1929, industry was seen to be expanding so successfully that the Five Year Plan was reduced to four years, which Nove describes as an 'upward revision' where targets were altered.

As Table 3.2 shows, the new targets were impossibly high, causing rush, strain, shortages and disorganisation across industry. Pernicious strategies were also used by local secretaries in competition with others, such as pilfering, lack of attention to quality and repression of the workforce. However, Gosplan did create a centralised, planned economy with detailed quarterly and annual production targets, allocation of capital to certain parts of the economy, centrally organised wages and the distribution and pricing of goods.

The leap made in only four years was remarkable (however dubious some of the figures were – see Table 3.3). Examples of great success were found in Magnitogorsk, which was a great new metallurgical centre created in the wilderness, and exemplified the focus on heavy industry Stalin had envisaged when he first implemented the Five Year Plan. The Dnieper Dam and Volga-White Sea Canal (although largely built using forced labour) also represented speedily built infrastructure that supported the growth in heavy industry. The focus and success of heavy industry was costly for other sectors of the economy; for example, the chemical, housing and consumer industries were seriously neglected. Some of the most ambitious projects, however, did not come online until the Second Five Year Plan (1933–7), which might account for some of the disappointing growth areas up until 1932. It is also important to note that the

	1927–8	1932-3 ('Optimal')	1932 (amended)	1932 (actual)
Coal (million tons)	35.0	75.0	95–105	(64.0)
Oil (million tons)	11.7	21.7	40–55	(21.4)
Iron ore (million tons)	6.7	20.2	24–32	(12.1)
Pig iron (million tons)	3.2	10.0	15–16	(6.2)

Sources: Bessonov, S. 1929 Problemy ekonomiki, No. 10–11, page 27 and plan-fulfilment report.
Table 3.2: Figures for industrial growth, 1927–1932.

Soviet Union was experiencing growth when the rest of the world was suffering the effects of the Great Depression. However this led to reduced imports of cotton (explaining the falling levels of textile production) and machinery which the USSR needed. Combined with collectivisation, grave railway inefficiencies and excessive investment in heavy industry led to severe living conditions for workers during the early 1930s.

The Five Year Plans – a review

Overall, historian Robert Davies (1994) concludes that significant advances were made throughout the first three Five Year Plans (1928–41). Steady growth was maintained, although the Second Five Year Plan had to be revised and delayed by two years as dangerous strains on the economy were evident, targets were recognised as being wildly unrealistic, costs were running far in excess of Gosplan's predictions and bottlenecks in production appeared everywhere. The second Five Year Plan was meant to focus on housing and consumer goods – as cities had grown by up to 50 000 people a week as numbers employed in industry and bureaucracy mushroomed. However, the reality was very different and as the years went by plans were altered to shift towards heavy industry again. The Second Five Year Plan saw the worst excesses of collectivisation come to an end, therefore boosting productivity across the economy. The metallurgical projects begun in the first plan in Tula and Ural-Kuznetsk were able to deliver returns on investment in the second and the USSR became virtually self-sufficient in this area. It was during the second plan that industries were being relocated away from strategically vulnerable European borders too, which slowed the growth rate in certain industries. The three good years of 1934–6 gave way to stagnation in 1937, primarily due to the Great Purges (discussed in next section) and a redirection of investment towards the defence industries, which caused fuel shortages, crisis on the railways and enterprises starved of the materials needed to meet their targets. It is likely that industrial output trebled between 1928 and 1940 overall, an annual growth rate of 10%. The total number of industrial enterprises rose from 9000 in 1929 to 64 000 in 1938. Crucially, armaments and the defence sector (for example, aircraft and tanks) grew 28-fold between 1930 and 1940 which was initiated, no doubt, by the threat of war in Europe and probably accounts for the emphasis on heavy industry throughout the Second and Third Five Year Plans. The Third Five Year Plan was halted after only three years (running from 1938 to 1941) due to the invasion of the USSR by Germany.

Workers

In 1929, the Party introduced the seven-hour day, which in theory provided workers with the best conditions in Russian history. This was complicated by the introduction of the 'uninterrupted five-day week'. The rationale was that factories would run every day but staff would complete four days of work with one day free. In November 1931, the working week was lengthened, increasing to five days working then one day off (it had the benefit of eliminating Sunday as a day of rest and therefore provided a profitable attack on religion too). This, combined with the hasty expansion of the labour force, caused huge disruption to secondary schooling and training of workers as well as disillusioned peasants leaving work to find better opportunities; in these circumstances, outside of the metal industries, production levels did not improve as Gosplan had hoped.

	1927-8 (actual)	1932-3 (plan)	1932 (actual)
National income (1926–7 roubles in 100 m.)	24.4	49.7	45.5
Gross industrial production (1926–7 roubles in 100 m.)	18.3	43.2	43.3
Producers' goods (1926–7 roubles in milliards)	6.0	18.1	23.1
Consumers' goods (1926– roubles in milliards)	12.3	25.1	20.2
Gross agricultural production (1926–7 roubles in milliards)	13.1	25.8	16.6
Electricity (100 m. Kwhs)	1.05	22.0	13.4
Hard coal (million tons)	35.4	75	64.3
Oil (million tons)	11.7	22	21.4
Iron ore (million tons)	5.7	19	12.1
Pig iron (million tons)	3.3	10	6.2
Steel (million tons)	4.0	10.4	5.9
Machinery (million 1926–7 roubles)	1822	4688	7392
Superphosphates (million tons)	0.15	3.4	0.61
Wool cloth (millionmetres)	97	270	93.3
Total employed labour force (millions)	11.3	15.8	22.8

Source: 1932 figures from Sotsialisticheskoe stroitel'stvo (1934) and the fulfilment report of first five year plan.
Table 3.3: Achievements of the first Five Year Plan (Nove, 1993, p.191).

The great influx of labour to the towns as a result of collectivisation put unbearable pressure on housing, amenities and clean water provision and there is overwhelming evidence to suggest that living standards declined considerably throughout the 1930s. However, there were more opportunities than ever before for young workers to become Stalinist *cadres*, or managers in factories, as the war against the 'bourgeois specialists' under NEP was waged. Interestingly, women were employed more than ever before under the Second Five Year Plan and, notably, medicine and teaching became almost wholly the preserve of women. By 1935, almost 8 million women were employed, compared to 3.3 million in 1929.

Historians are in agreement that unemployment had disappeared altogether by 1930, which ended the misery of thousands who had suffered in the 1920s, but the problems of unemployment were replaced by other concerns. The erosion of the power of trade unions had been instilled under Lenin, though between 1932 and 1949 the all-union Trade Union Congress did not meet at all and the People's Commissariat for Labour was abolished in 1934. Real wages also increased for workers during this period; however they had less leisure time and consumer goods to spend it on. This, combined with the chronic food shortages during 1932, made workers turn to the black market where prices rose dramatically for basic goods. Inflation hit workers very hard. During the second plan, more food was made available as new bakeries and meat-packing plants were built in many areas,

Figure 3.6: Propaganda advertising the first Five Year Plan: N.V. Tsivchinskii, 'The Victory of the Five Year Plan is a Strike Against Capitalism', 1931.

ACTIVITY 3.4

Split into pairs or small groups – one person must find evidence to support the view that the Five Year Plans were a success; the other must find evidence to support the view that they were unsuccessful in achieving their aims. Then come together and debate the overall success of the Five Year Plans.

Some historians have suggested that Stalin's Five Year Plans are only successful in light of the state of the economy under Lenin. Do you agree with this? Compare the achievements of the Five Year Plans with the NEP.

but historian Chris Ward (1999) suggests that in 1935 workers were consuming less meat and dairy products than they had ten years previously.

Pressure was applied in ruthless ways to ensure workers met their targets. This was easy in the early 1930s when it seemed as if Socialism was winning against the capitalist West, which was undergoing economic depression. However, motivation to continue the relentless pace of work waned, and so the regime had to look for new ways to motivate workers. In 1935, a coal miner called Alexei Stakhanov was reported to have dug 102 tons of coal in a single six-hour shift (14 times greater than the norm). Stakhanov was rewarded and praised as an example to all other workers. As the propaganda machine sought to draw their own conclusions from his achievements, the authorities neglected to inform the public that Stakhanov had two co-workers, plus machinery in perfect working order, to help him achieve so much. Russians were told to model themselves on Stakhanov and joined what became known as the Stakhanovite Movement. **Stakhanovites** tried to perform feats of great productivity, through working harder and also through reorganising the way things were done in their place of work. They were rewarded with better pay and publicity. This, combined with other incentives such as recasting wage scales as well as implementing new training schemes at all levels, led to increased productivity until 1937. After 1937 there was a great industrial downturn which Alec Nove (1993) suggests was not only due to a shift in resources to the arms industry, but was primarily due to the purges (discussed in a later section).

ACTIVITY 3.3

Use this table to organise your notes on the Five Year Plans – consider economic output against the human cost of the plans.

	First Five Year Plan 1928–32	**Second Five Year Plan 1933–7**	**Third Five Year Plan 1938–41**
Key successes			
Key failures or limitations			
Human cost			

Gulags

The first corrective labour camps (**Gulags** – an acronym for 'Main Administration of Corrective Labour Camps and Settlements') after the revolution were established in 1918 after the attempted assassination of Lenin and a rapidly growing internment system during the Civil War. The *Gulag,* famously written about by Aleksandr Solzhenitsyn in '*The Gulag Archipelago*', was formally and legally created and recognised much later, on 25 April 1930. In March 1940, there were 53 separate camps and 423 labour colonies in the USSR and the utilisation of deportees and prisoners was fundamental to the realisation of some of the greatest achievements in industrialisation during the 1930s. For example, the

Belomor Canal, which connects the White Sea with the Baltic, was almost entirely constructed by hand, using 250 000 prisoners between 1931 and 1933. It is estimated that almost 25 000 prisoners died in the first winter building the canal, their bodies thrown into the ditch they had been digging. Prisoners also worked in mines or cut timber without pay. The increase in prisoner numbers coincided with collectivisation; even political prisoners would now be forced to carry out hard labour, and prisoners were underfed, housed in poor conditions and worked long hours in a difficult climate. Prisoners could be executed if they refused to work. It is possible that around 10% of prisoners in the *Gulag* died each year, although official figures obscure accuracy. The *Gulags* were situated all over Russia – some of the most hostile in Siberia, Kazakhstan and arctic Russia – and by 1939 it is estimated there were approximately 2.9 million people in the labour camp system forced to maintain the state's industrial output.

In 1935 Stalin announced: 'Life has improved, comrades. Life has become more joyous.' The intense human suffering caused by collectivisation and forced industrialisation would suggest otherwise, but for Stalin the price was clearly worth paying as, by 1941, he ruled over a country with a modern industrialised economy and an efficient, well-equipped army.

Figure 3.7: The location of the Gulag camps, which existed between 1923 and 1961. Note that some of these camps operated only for a part of the Gulag's existence.

Social developments

Effect of Leninist/Stalinist rule on class, women, young people and national minorities

Class

Marxist class analysis, which the Bolsheviks had clung to leading up to the revolution, had proven inappropriate to Russian reality in 1917. Fitzpatrick (2008) argues that Russia's weak class structure crumbled under the impact of war, revolution and civil war. The old upper classes (land-owning and service nobility, capitalist bourgeoisie) were destroyed by peasant land seizures and emigration. The middle classes (merchants, shopkeepers and small manufacturers) were put out of business because of war communism. The peasantry, reasserting the traditional communal organisation, dragged Stolypin's independent farmers back into the village, redistributed the land, and, for the time being, eliminated the differences between peasants of the late imperial period. This meant the Bolsheviks had to find rhetorical class enemies, as the collapse of the old upper classes had been so thorough.

However, the historian Lewis Siegelbaum (1992) argues convincingly that 'if, by 1920–1, Soviet Russia was essentially a one-party state, it certainly was not a one-class society'[7]. The Soviet state was far from the classless society envisaged by early Marxists, in fact the Bolsheviks themselves had created some new groups during the civil war – the intelligentsia, technical and cultural; the army of clerical, technical and military employees within the state apparatus itself; and last but not least, the village-based small property-holding peasantry that comprised the vast majority of Soviet citizens. Therefore, what it meant for the 'proletarian dictatorship' to preside over a society in which the proletariat was a tiny and, to use Lenin's term, 'unhinged' element – and, indeed, to what extent it did preside – is a fundamental question still debated today.

The October Revolution and civil war bequeathed to the Soviet state in the 1920s a society that in many ways resembled that under the old Tsarist regime. For example, Sovnarkom's members were drawn entirely from the Communist Party – after the withdrawal of the **Left SRs** in March 1918 – in which they all enjoyed prominence, and with the early exception of A.M. Kollontai who served briefly as People's Commissar for Welfare, were entirely male. In other respects – age, social background, ethnicity, pre-revolutionary occupations, educational levels and convictions – they were a diverse group, though one dominated by the offspring of

 Voices from the past

Alexander Solzhenitsyn fought for the Soviet Union in the Second World War. However, he was arrested in 1945 for writing a letter that criticised Stalin. Solzhenitsyn was sentenced to eight years in various prisons and labour camps. These institutions were similar to the ones he describes in *One Day in the Life of Ivan Denisovich* (1962) and in his groundbreaking novel about the Soviet labour camp system, *The Gulag Archipelago* (published 1973 but probably written in 1958).

ethnically or assimilated Russian families from the middle and upper echelons of Tsarist society, who chose the precarious career of professional revolutionary.

Under Stalin it was the administrative elites who were handsomely rewarded in a society which had undergone dramatic change after the abandonment of NEP. Grain traders, shopkeepers and workshop owners were eliminated in the same way the aristocracy had been following the revolution of 1917 and a new class of *nomenklatura* had been created as state bureaucracy ballooned fourfold between 1926 and the end of the 1930s. Yet at the same time, Stalin continued to wage a war on 'class' as the purges (discussed in the next section) illustrate.

Village-based small property-holding peasantry

Lenin had become convinced since the summer of 1917 that to defy the peasants on the land question would be tantamount to political suicide. Therefore, the initial policy of the Soviet state was to legitimise the seizure of landlords' property and promote the equal distribution of land among those who worked on it. This policy, announced in the Decree on Land of 26 October 1917, was elaborated in the law 'On the Socialisation of the Land' of 19 February 1918. Both acts were loosely based on the agrarian programme of the Socialist Revolutionary Party. 'Socialisation' basically left the peasants to implement the law as they saw fit.

As a result of the redivision of land, the number of landless peasant households dropped from 15.9% of all households in 1917 to 8.1% by 1920. Perhaps ironically, Lenin's decrees actually strengthened the village commune, and in many areas revived its repartitional functions (deciding which families were allocated to specific strips of land). Historians have described a process of 'traditionalisation' that occurred in peasant life, a process that was integral to what Moshe Lewin (1994) has called the 'archaisation' of the socio-economic system. Reverting to a form of self-government that was as old as serfdom and relying on methods of production that were similarly centuries old, the peasantry retreated from urban society and was able to survive the degradations of the civil war better than any other social class. Indeed, it survived not merely as a class but as a social system with its own specific culture. It was this that made the peasantry so awkward, so impenetrable to the designs of 'intruders' (and for most peasants, both Reds and Whites were intruders). The peasantry had ceased to be merely awkward for the state and instead, as was to be the case again during forced collectivisation under Stalin, had become its main antagonist.

There was no pretence about equality before the law, particularly in the area of voting rights. Certain categories of people – large property owners, clerics, White officers and many Tsarist officials – were completely deprived of voting rights. To stress the privileged place of urban workers in the new political order, the Constitution of the Russian Soviet Federated Socialist Republic (RSFSR), which was approved in July 1918 by the Fifth All-Russian Congress of Soviets, stipulated that in elections to all-Russian Soviet congresses, one urban voter was to be the equivalent of five rural inhabitants.

Under Stalin, the peasantry were brought to their knees due to forced collectivisation (see Sections The Stalinist economy; Collectivisation and the Five Year Plans; Collectivisation). Collectivisation had to occur if socialism was to be built in the Soviet Union as the Party could not allow private landholders to exist in a socialist state. The impact of collectivisation was devastating as over half of the most enterprising peasants who resisted were deported or shot. Peasant women led the most vociferous protests against collectivisation but with limited success, as they had specific goals of retrieving collectivised horses or refusing to give over grain that was requisitioned. Although Stalin seemed to backtrack in 1930, the campaign was resumed in 1931, and by 1934 over 70% of peasants were in collectives. Now the peasants had little to work for, passive resistance in the form of apathy took hold, and production slumped. Many peasants referred to collectivisation as a second serfdom. They were broken, but not defeated.

The intelligentsia

When the Bolsheviks swept to power in October 1917 they were forced to make use of the Tsarist-trained intellectuals who possessed the enviable skills and experience of administering the state. Lenin and Trotsky referred to them as *cadres* or 'technical intelligentsia' to signify their allegiance to the party and the revolution. The Bolshevik Party actually contained a strong contingent of genuine intellectuals. However, this involvement of the Bolsheviks with the intelligentsia proved to be a chronic source of discord. As Robert Daniels: 2008 asserts, it was this antagonism, between the literary intellectuals adhering to Communist principles (Bukharin, Zinoviev) and the quasi-intellectuals attracted to the Communist organisation (Stalin), which was to be a major factor in the factionalism that threated to permanently divide the party between 1918 and 1925.

The technical intelligentsia appeared in Russia from the later 19th century as job opportunities (such as government service during the reforms or in factories during industrialisation) created trained experts and professionals whose income was based on their specialisation or skills. Lenin wrote in '*Will the Bolsheviks retain State Power?*' in 1917:

'*We need good organisers in banking and the work of enterprises; we need more and more engineers, agronomists, technicians, scientific experts of every kind. We shall give all such workers work which they are able and are accustomed to do; probably as we shall ... leave a temporary higher rate of pay for such specialists during the transition period.*'

(cited in Daniels, Robert (2008), p.57)

Lenin never seemed to turn his back on this view. Perhaps because there was no practical alternative, this group of bourgeoisie simply grew under Lenin's rule.

The cultural intelligentsia were an awkward set for the Bolsheviks because they always contained intellectuals seeking new theories and challenging old ideas. Christopher Read (2013) argues that where the cultural intelligentsia were concerned, the broad trajectory across the decade was in the direction of tighter restrictions, and most were under routine surveillance by the *Cheka* (later the GPU). In the summer of 1922, most writers who hadn't already fled during the civil war for fear of facing the Red Terror, were deported. This included world-renowned philosopher Nikolai Berdyaev, who wasn't socialist enough for Dzerzinskii's liking. The deportations coincided with the re-introduction of censorship through the agency of a Main Administration for Affairs of Literature and Publishing Houses (it became known as *Glavlit*); the aim was to insulate Russian society from capitalist ideas or those that sought to undermine socialism, and remained in place until the 1980s. Musicians and artists also suffered the same fate as, for example, Shostakovich (a world- renowned composer even today) who was denounced twice (under Lenin and Stalin) for failing to conform to the Socialist conventions and was lucky to avoid arrest.

The Cultural Revolution

The so-called 'Cultural Revolution' began in 1928 after the Shakhty Affair (see Section 'Five Year Plans') –a far flung revolutionary plot to overthrow the economy – caused accelerating tensions among the cultural and technical intelligentsia. Widespread cries to root out 'bourgeois' traitors actually came, in part, from below, as activists sought to 'unmask' non-Marxists through denunciations. The moderate Commissariat for Enlightenment, Lunarcharsky, was dropped in 1929 and waves of academics at universities were subject to dismissals for being 'ideologically suspect', bringing higher education to the point of collapse in 1930. This revolution also saw the 'Association of Proletarian Writers' (RAPP) exhorted to engage fully in the construction of socialism, and pressure was intensified after the show trials of 1930–1. However, as the economy neared the point of collapse during the Great Famine of 1932, the regime realised that stability was needed amongst those with skill to lead the economy. A strategic retreat was enacted and in 1934 Zhadnov (who had a special responsibility for ideology and political education) created the Union of Soviet Writers whose task was to educate the masses about Socialism.

In Article One of the Soviet Constitution (1936), the Soviet Union is defined as a 'socialist state of workers and peasants'. Stalin even reported in 1936 that 80% of the intelligentsia came to be offspring of 'the working class, the peasantry, and other strata of labourers'. Official party congresses later suggested there had been a completely new intelligentsia rooted in the working class and the peasantry; this was merely the regime wielding propaganda to gain support. Soviet trainees in government, industry and propaganda began to replace the old intelligentsia borrowed from the Tsarist regime during the 1930s. By 1939, they accounted for approximately 14% of the Soviet population but seemed to be restricted to functions such as conveying the party line to the masses rather than formulating policy, which was left to the inner circles of the Communist Party.

The effect of Leninist/Stalinist rule on young people

The Communist Youth League

It is difficult to distil the effects Leninist rule had on young people given the short amount of time he was in power. The Communist Youth League (**Komsomol**) was founded in 1917–18 for young people aged 14 to 26; similar organisations – the Young Pioneers for ages 9–15 and Little Octobrists for ages 7–9 – were also established in urban centres.

These were training grounds for future party members and their organisations corresponded to that of the Communist Party (i.e. highly bureaucratic). The

Key term

Komsomol: 'The All-Union Leninist Young Communist League' was established in 1918 and was a youth division (14–28 year olds) of the Communist Party. Although membership was voluntary it was almost impossible to pursue higher education without being a member. Younger children could join the Young Pioneers.

organisations set out to instil discipline, inspire a love for work, to limit the influence of the church, to strengthen Soviet-approved arts and cultural activities and generally aid the party in developing staunch defenders of socialism.

However, during NEP, Komsomol struggled to attract youth workers or convince them to follow the moral, righteous path Marx had expounded. Komsomol Central Committee concluded in 1927 that the Soviet youth organisation 'still does not answer completely the needs, demands and interests which youth have'. This might have been due to poor living conditions. For example, a youth worker health survey was carried out in Petrograd in 1924; 52% were found to be ill and 25% were suffering from tuberculosis (due to shared beds the disease spread quickly among workers).

The Komsomol's perception of the peasantry, and its quest to maintain a respectable proportion of workers in the membership, impeded expansion in rural areas in the early years of Bolshevik rule. Historian Isabel A. Tirado (1993) explains that demographic realities made the Komsomol's outreach to young peasants imperative: peasants made up 80% of the Russian population; their children 19 years of age or younger accounted for half of the rural population in the mid-1920s. Perhaps more importantly, the party had seen a reduction in personnel at the end of the civil war due to demobilisation, and the Komsomol found itself pressured to fill the gap.

The youth organisations became instrumental in assisting the regime to carry out the industrialisation project of the Five Year Plans. In 1929, over 7000 young people from Komsomol were sent to build the tractor factory in Stalingrad, 66 000 to build new factories in the Urals and 36 000 to work underground in the Donets coal mines. In collectivisation the *komsomolites* also played a role in joining the *kolkhozy* – over 15 000 had done so by June 1929 – but more importantly through denunciations of the *nomenklatura* and *kulaks*. This was practised through games such as 'Search and Requisition' when children would role-play as grain requisitioning brigades and *kulaks*. By 1925, one in five children were members of Young Pioneers and Komsomol had one million members (although these figures are low, it can be explained by the difficult physical and IQ tests members had to pass as membership led to a career in the party). Whether the young did all of these activities willingly is impossible to assert, but it would seem that Soviet policies aimed at the young were on the whole successful by the mid-1930s.

Education
Education was seen as a battlefront to the Bolsheviks and education was perhaps the party's greatest achievement. The Komsomol succeeded in becoming a major political educator in villages, so that by the end of NEP more than a million young peasants had joined its ranks. By 1921, the villages of European Russia contained some 70 00 primary schools, 30 000 *likpunkty* (schools and courses set up by the Bolsheviks to eradicate illiteracy), 13 532 libraries and nearly 20 000 reading rooms. Historians have suggested that youths were less resistant than their elders to the propaganda efforts of the Communists and many responded positively it, particularly when Stalin introduced the plans to construct new towns, dams and mines; they felt it was they who were building the new society. Stalin extended the drive for literacy begun under Lenin so that by 1939 over 94% of males between

the ages of 9 and 49 could read and write. This was partly because education was made compulsory, while reading materials such as the party newspapers *Pravda* and *Isvestia* were sold very cheaply at ten kopeks daily, increasing circulation from 9.4 million copies in 1927 to 38 million by 1940.

The effect of Leninist/Stalinist rule on women

Historian Barbara Evans Clements (1997) carried out research into the lives of six women (Stasova, Zemliachka, Samilova, Bosh, Nikolaeva and Artiukhina) who had joined the Bolshevik party around the 1905 Revolution and noted that the revolutionaries tended to come from noble or middle-class backgrounds and tended to be ethnically Russian. She argues that the Bolsheviks gave women opportunities to take positions within the Party they wouldn't have had under the Tsarist regime and suggests the Civil War saw a new generation of women join the Party, although figures are unreliable given poor census data. However, Clements points to the 'masculinist' culture of the movement itself – and to the militarisation of the 'party culture' during the Civil War. She sees this as a turning point for women. The process of consolidating power and transforming the revolutionary party into a 'governing regime' produced a patriarchal and 'tyrannical' regime in which any serious rethinking of gender relations became impossible.

Some women in rural districts certainly did venture across the formidable cultural chasm that had always existed in Russia. Defying male mockery and prohibitions, they attended literacy classes, voted in Soviet elections, served in rural Soviet administration, and participated in meetings and excursions to the towns sponsored by Zhenotdel, the Women's Section of the Party. Who these women were is not entirely clear, but Red Army wives and widows, often single householders, appear to have been the most venturesome. During the Five Year Plans, millions of women went to work as teachers but also in factories, particularly during the Second Plan when wage levels were recast more equally. Statistics suggest however that, in 1936, women were still spending five times longer than men on household chores, so fundamental perceptions of women's role in society had not significantly changed. As the horrors of forced industrialisation and collectivisation were realised, the regime focused a huge amount of attention on the role of family life and the role of the parent was supported as a figure of authority to reinforce Soviet rule at home.

Effect of Leninist/Stalinist rule on religion and national minorities

Religion

The Orthodox Church alarmed Lenin, as a survey in the mid-1920s had suggested that over 50% of peasants considered themselves to be active Christian worshippers. Following his founding of the 'League of the Militant Godless' in December 1922, Lenin arranged the execution of several bishops on the pretext that they were refusing to help famine relief in the Volga region. Anti-religious persecution was certainly a feature of the Leninist era, as priests were denied any civic rights. Many bishops and priests fled Russia as a result; interestingly, even those who remained rarely joined the Whites during the Civil War. During the mid-1920s, the focus of the Party shifted to the demoralisation of the Church by promoting the 'living church' movement, which opposed official ecclesiastical hierarchy. This served to drive a wedge in the Russian Orthodox Church.

The limited tolerance shown to organised religion under NEP was thrown aside during the late 1920s. De-clericalisation was not an official policy as such under Stalin, but the authorities turned a blind eye to physical attacks on religious leaders and during the First Five Year Plan mass killings did take place. In the Russian Orthodox Church alone, the number of active priests plummeted from around 60 000 in the 1920s to only 5665 by 1941. Other religious leaders, such as rabbis and mullahs, were also butchered at this time. Only one in 40 churches was functioning by 1940 and the others had been recommissioned for secular purposes; some, like the Cathedral of Christ the Saviour in Moscow, were blown up (albeit secretly in the dead of night).

National minorities

National minorities were given greater freedom than at any other time in Russian history under Lenin. Under the 'Affirmative action Empire' policy a process of 'indigenisation' took place so that minorities would not feel that Russia was imperialist. Instead they sought to create unity along socialist lines instead of nationalist ones. For example, the Laz people (numbering 635 and native to the Black Sea coastal regions of Georgia) were given their own school-building. The Party was not so concerned with language or culture but ideology, so steps were taken to train *cadres* of the local nationality to promote party ideals. On 31 December 1922, central government declared a new constitution for all of the Soviet republics and renamed the country once more to the Union of Soviet Socialist Republics (USSR). This meant that Russia (RSFSR) was, for the first time, given boundaries within the larger state it belonged to. The central government newspaper hailed it as a 'New Years' gift to the workers and peasants of the world'. However well this was accepted in the regions, it might only have been so because Lenin had sanctioned 'National deportations' in 1921: hundreds of Cossacks were rounded up from the southern regions and sent to other Soviet territory in the north to avoid any backlash.

One of the reasons Stalin had wanted to abandon NEP was to allay the assertiveness of the national minorities. Nationalism was to be fought ruthlessly as imaginary anti-Soviet organisations were 'discovered' in Ukraine (1929) and later in Belorussia, Georgia, Armenia and Azerbaijan. Anti-Semitism persisted throughout the Stalinist era and to it added a resentment towards those from

 Hidden voices

Stalin had already asserted his view on the national minorities during the Georgian affair of 1922; when Georgian nationalists had tried to assert their independence. The Red Army and Cheka troops, under orders from Stalin and Ordzhonikidze, suppressed the insurrection and instigated a wave of mass repressions that killed several thousand Georgian citizens. This can be seen as part of the leadership struggle that developed with Lenin's illness. Stalin wanted Georgia to be Sovietised; otherwise, his claim to becoming leader of the Soviet Union would be severely weakened. For this reason, he advocated Azerbaijan, Georgia and Armenia become republics within the Soviet Union.

the Transcaucasus nations. Most deaths, however, were suffered by the less urbanised nationalities during collectivisation. The Kazakh nomads suffered disproportionately during 1931–3 when up to 1.8 million of them died because of the punitive policies implemented against peasants. The Ukraine was subject to particular forms of persecution under Stalin: borders were sealed in 1932 by Red Army units, and the majority of the Ukraine's peasantry were labelled *kulaks*, forcing them to acquiesce to state requirements. The regime did respond to reports of widespread famine in 1932 by cutting grain collection quotas, but this was nowhere near enough to stop widespread suffering in the Ukraine. It should be noted, though, that the famine was also grievous in parts of Russia too.

Minorities and the Great Terror

Figure 3.9: The Soviet Union's national minorities

Recently unearthed archives have resulted in research being carried out on the national or ethnic components of the Great Terror. Eastern Europeans, Koreans, Chinese, Afghans were all subject to 'national sweeps' of 'ethnic cleansing' during 1937. The 'Polish operation' resulted in the arrest of 140 000 people of which a staggering 111 000 were shot dead – all perceived to be real or potential 'spies' of hostile states and agents of anti-Soviet foreign intelligence services. Jews were also repressed in large numbers, although this may have been due to the proliferation of Jews at the higher levels of organisations, rather than it being an attempt to persecute this minority above any other. Such was the scale of 'national operations' that they became the prime function of **NKVD** activity after February 1938.

The reasons for the abolition of nationalism and, therefore, nationalities were ideological. Stalin had read in Marx that the antidote to national conflict was to

Speak like a historian

Population figures taken from the censuses are extremely unreliable, particularly around 1937, after collectivisation and during the purges. It is reported that figures were much lower than the leadership expected and so were massaged to represent what the Communist Party considered to be a fair representation. Many deaths were not recorded during the famine of 1931 as people died on the streets (for example, it is said that Kiev street cleaners picked up 9472 bodies in 1933 but only 3991 were registered). In 1937 Stalin expected a population of around 170 million. The figures returned were much lower (approximately 162 million). Saboteurs and *kulaks* were blamed for the figures and in 1939 a new census was taken, this time matching almost exactly Stalin's predictions.

create unifying principles behind which all could unite. Stalin knew that as only 52% of the USSR's population were Russian in 1932, a new way of inspiring unity and pride was needed. This coincided with growing concerns about the strength of the Third Reich under Adolf Hitler. Therefore, during the 1930s the privileges of Russian nationhood were expounded. This also coincided with the purges which replaced almost the entire leadership of the party in non-Russian republics with Russian *cadres*. The Russian language was given heightened status from 1938, becoming one of the compulsory subjects in all schools. (Over 130 languages were recognised by the authorities, but in practice there was a strict hierarchy with Russian at the peak.) There were also moves to alter non-Russian languages to a Cyrillic-style alphabet; from 1940 the Uzbek tongue was no longer allowed to be written in Arabic characters. Russian patriotism did not extend to village traditions, however, which continued to exist. So-called 'former people' such as the aristocracy and gentry had to be denounced in any literature or histories as Marxism-Leninism remained at the core of state ideology.

Propaganda and cultural change

Among the arts, the cinema probably suffered more than any other form under Lenin. This was ironic, given Lenin's well-known assessment of it being the most important art form. None of the 143 theatres operating in Moscow before the First World War showed films by the autumn of 1921. Literature suffered too, if only because of the acute shortage of paper and the appropriation of many resources by the party press. In 1913, 392 000 tons of paper and cardboard were produced within the empire; by 1920, Soviet Russia produced only 34 700 tons. Compared to 1913, when 20 000 book titles were published, only 3260 appeared in 1920. Figures for 1914 show that of 4130 titles, over half were in the social sciences.

Under NEP the ethnic Russians were most harshly restricted in their cultural expression. Successful Russian writers such as Fyodor Dostoyevsky, whose major works include '*Crime and Punishment*' (1866), were banned. However, art forms flourished particularly after the Civil War, most notably poster art, film, and theatre, which all fed the workers with stories of heroism from the revolution. Commissar of Enlightenment, Anatoly Lunacharsky, encouraged hundreds of films about the revolution and by the end of the 1930s the USSR had 28 000 cinemas. Radio, too, was harnessed as a medium of mass communication, and performers and broadcasters became celebrities across the country.

The USSR began to look different too: under Stalin, vast apartment blocks were built at Magnitogorsk and other areas to replace wooden huts, although housing was not built as fast as factories. By 1940 significant change had occurred in almost every town and village. Stalin claimed this as a triumph of modernity, although it was a distinctly Stalinist view of it. Typical apartment blocks contained flats called *kommulnaki* which were shared by several families, using the same kitchen and bathroom. Cafeterias were provided at most factories so that workers need not return home to eat. This collectivist approach was extended to consumer goods too, as competition between similar products was seen as a capitalist mentality. Therefore clothes, shoes, tins of food, lightbulbs would be the same wherever you bought them in the USSR. This had the effect of creating a drab uniform which most people wore, and local dress disappeared.

The cults of Lenin and Stalin

The cult of Lenin really began after his death in 1924. The cult of Stalin was simultaneously created alongside that of Lenin to underscore the legitimacy of the regime and to affirm that the state possessed a strong, determined leader. Even though there had been a revolution, the Communists recognised the importance of continuity as well as disruption. Some of the regal pomp associated with Tsarism was kept by Stalin – he had an official birthday and Tsaritsyn was renamed Stalingrad. Crucial to the cult of Stalin was his preservation of the heritage of Marxism-Leninism. The heroism, justice and inevitability of the October Revolution were repeatedly proclaimed, as were the glorifications of the successes of the Five Year Plans. After 1935, the regime consciously sought out artists who could raise workers' awareness of the need for a radical attempt to build socialism. Most propaganda posters reflect the '**Socialist Realism**' that was born in the USSR – a mix of the realist traditions of the 19th century with the romanticism of the Bolshevik tradition.

ЛЮБИМЫЙ СТАЛИН-СЧАСТЬЕ НАРОДНОЕ!

Figure 3.10: This poster says 'Great Stalin is a Flag of the USSR's Friendship' and epitomises the type of propaganda that created the Cult of Stalin.

Robert Service (1997) argues, however, that Soviet propaganda was not so effective; despite the proliferation of films, radio programmes and newsreels demonstrating adulation for the Georgian leader. There remained a paucity of spectators. For example, by 1937 there were only 3.7 million radios in the country (for a population of 162 million) and communication in rural areas was patchy at best. Several weeks at a time passed between official visits to villages, and mass indoctrination was not achieved due to insufficient infrastructure. This view is supported by the historian Sarah Davies: 1997 p. 183 who suggests that Soviet propaganda 'failed to extinguish an autonomous current of popular opinion'. Perhaps the main reason for the failures of Soviet propaganda was the relentless hardship caused by state measures as well as a lack of ability to access the cinema or radio for the majority of the population.

ACTIVITY 3.5

Look back through your notes on the social changes that took place under Lenin and Stalin and complete the table below. This should help you form some conclusions about whether life got better or worse for people under Lenin or Stalin.

You could even stretch yourself and compare life for peasants under the Tsarist regime in 1914 with life in 1941. Had peasants' lives changed much?

Some historians have referred to the policies of the government as 'zig-zag' in approach, which makes the topic a complex one.

	Tsar Nicholas II 1894–1917	Lenin 1917–24	Stalin 1924–41
Peasants			
Workers			
Intelligentsia			
Women			
Young people			
Religious people			
National minorities			
Opposition			

Opposition from the Left

Perhaps the most serious threat to the Bolsheviks in the early years of the revolution were the Left Social Revolutionaries and the Mensheviks. Although there were some disagreements over Brest–Litovsk (as there were within the Bolshevik Party), major disagreements arose over domestic politics. Bolshevik agricultural policy (in the form of grain requisitioning) as well as government-appointed commissariats being given unlimited authority to dissolve soviets that failed to implement the policy from May 1918, forced the Left SRs into opposition. In June 1918, they were expelled from the Central Executive Committee and subsequently formed several provincial soviets. In retaliation, two of their members – Bliumkin and Andreev – assassinated Count Mirbach (a German envoy) in the hope of inciting a renewal of the conflict between Russia and Germany. Although parts of Moscow sympathised with the Left SRs, the Bolsheviks had enough forces to crush the rebellion within hours of it starting. They arrested 260 SRs and forced the rest to reject their central committee or be expelled from the

Petrograd Soviet. The leaders were imprisoned and many others implicated in the plot, therebyending any threat from the Left SRs.

The Kadets

The fate of the non-Bolshevik political intelligentsia was intrinsically bound up with that of the political parties. The Kadets (**Constitutional Democrats**), who had enjoyed the largest following of intelligentsia, constituted the thin political infrastructure of the White governments. As such, P.N. Miliukov and other leading Kadet politicians hoped to gain international support for a counter-revolution against the Bolsheviks. However, neither the Germans in 1918 nor the allied powers thereafter were willing to commit themselves to full-scale armed intervention. Beset by internal wrangling as well as conflict with the White generals, the Kadet politicians eventually removed themselves from Russian soil and took up residence in Paris and other European centres. The Right SRs followed a similar trajectory; the problem was they were supported by Czechs and peasant worker armies and the agendas of these forces differed from that of the civilian politicians, as well as from each other. In November 1918, the SR-dominated Directory based at Omsk was overthrown by Kolchak and, for all intents and purposes, the Right SRs were finished as a political movement. Forced into emigration, such leading SR politicians as N.D. Avksentiev and V. Zenzinov urged the allies to step up the interventionary campaign, but to no avail.

Popular resistance

Resistance to Soviet authorities took increasingly active forms throughout the cataclysmic Civil War. There were paralysing strikes among workers in Moscow and Petrograd, and 344 peasant insurrections in 1919. This discontent intensified after the Tambov uprising in 1920 provided ample evidence of popular disenchantment with Bolshevik governance. Peasants and workers did not co-ordinate their activity but their demands were similar. Both groups called for the abolition of grain requisitioning, better food supplies, a return to democracy and an end to the Communist monopoly of power.

Perhaps the most iconic and threatening of the rebellions was the Kronstadt uprising of February 1921, which took place on the naval base situated approximately 12 miles from Petrograd. The Kronstadt sailors had been at the forefront of the revolution in 1917, though many were not Bolshevik but anarchists. This was not so much a problem in the first year when the sailors were encouraged to assist in land redistribution in the countryside and many fought valiantly in the Red Army during the Civil War. However, as the party expanded its influence and Soviet power was reduced at the hands of party Commissars, hostilities erupted. The Kronstadters tried to support the strikers in Petrograd and joined their calls for freedom for all left-wing, soviet-oriented parties and for a reduction in Communist influence over elections. Lenin and Trotsky ordered a ruthless repression of the Kronstadters. In dramatic fashion, Trotsky sent 50 000 infantry across the ice to reach Kronstadt and capture the city. Cheka execution squads followed closely behind, killing over 2500 men. Just as the Bolsheviks were celebrating the 50th anniversary of the Paris Commune of 1871, they were suppressing Kronstadt. Revolutionary Victor Serge, who witnessed the atrocities, called it 'ghastly fratricide'.

Figure 3.11: The Red Army unit crossing the ice to crush the Kronstadt Rebellion, 17 March 1921.

Suppressing the opposition

The opposition was largely thwarted after 1921 when it was clear the Reds had been victorious during the Civil War. Both Mensheviks and Left SRs continued to participate in the Soviets, had a persistent following in the trade unions and sent delegates to the next all-Russian Soviet congress. However, Lenin was fearful about their influence and as material conditions worsened, it became all too easy to construe opposition as treason and to make Menshevism a convenient scapegoat for unrest among workers. Lenin associated Martov's calls for democracy at the Seventh Congress of Soviets (December 1919) as 'bourgeois' and linked his ideas to the foreign intervention that had come from Kolchak. Without any formal decree, the Soviet government rounded up the leading figures of the opposition parties and imprisoned them in early 1921. Some, including leading Socialist Revolutionaries, were eventually put on trial and convicted of 'terroristic' acts for which they received (commuted) death sentences and long terms of imprisonment. Some were permitted to emigrate; others were released after promising to abandon all political activities, while still others were sent into internal exile. In some senses, this represented the annihilation of the political intelligentsia outside the Communist Party.

During the days of the Tsarist regime, the 'dark masses' (peasants and workers) caused the most anxiety for those who governed Russia. However, even under the Communist regime, set up in the name of the workers, it was still the working classes who posed the greatest threat.

The Red Terror

Perhaps the institutions that grew the most quickly under Bolshevik rule were the coercive organs of the state; specifically, the army and the main security apparatus, the Cheka. From its founding in February 1918, the Red Army was staffed largely by former Tsarist officers who were euphemistically referred to as 'military specialists'. To ensure their loyalty, political commissars, usually Communists, exercised supervisory power and were held jointly responsible for all orders. But the appointment of officers by the Revolutionary Military Council, the allocation to them of special rations and other privileges, rankled with many party members and frontline soldiers.

The Cheka

The Cheka (short for All-Russian Extraordinary Commission for the Suppression of Counter-Revolution, Sabotage and Speculation) was the 'sword of the Revolution', explicitly conceived as an organ of 'mass red terror against the bourgeoisie and its agents'. Headed by the Polish-born revolutionary, Felix Dzerzhinski, it possessed unrestrained powers of arrest, interrogation, intimidation and execution, all of which it applied liberally, though probably no more so than its White counterparts. At the peak of its strength in mid-1921, the Cheka of the Russian Republic is estimated to have contained 250 000 members including 100 000 Frontier Troops and a civilian staff of 30 000. The list of enemies expanded rapidly in 1918 from 'bourgeois opposition' to many Mensheviks, SRs and anarchists, particularly after 30 August 1918 when party member Uritsky was killed in Petrograd and Lenin was seriously wounded when he was shot down in the street in Moscow. The executive committee of the Soviets responded with an uncompromising policy of terror, carried out by the Cheka. During the early months of 1919 it is said to have suppressed 245 uprisings or, more likely, resistance to grain requisitioning, where 3057 people were killed. In terms of executions, there had reportedly been 6300 by the end of 1918 and a further 3456 in 1919, although unofficial figures tend to be much higher. By 1922 the Cheka was no longer 'extraordinary' and so was renamed the GPU (State Political Administration).

Civil war

In December 1918, following excessive desertions from the front, combined with mounting threats to the Bolshevik hold on power, the All-Russian Soviet Executive Committee (VTsIK) ordered the creation of a separate bureaucracy – the Central Anti-Desertion Commission – to round up those who refused to enlist. This followed Lenin's decree on the *kulaks* (or wealthier peasants) in the Penza region for those who refused to hand over their grain. Lenin referred to them as 'kulaks, rich men, bloodsuckers' who had to be hanged in full view of the villagers. The terror was moving into rural districts, towards ordinary people rather than just political opposition.

By April 1919, several provincial commissions had managed to organise their own armed patrols that combed the countryside, and they were also given formal powers to confiscate movable property from the families of known deserters and those suspected of assisting them. In Kostroma, the work of the anti-desertion squads – a low-prestige assignment that frequently enlisted the participation of one-time deserters themselves – inspired revulsion amongst peasants.

Justice

The Constitution of the new Soviet republic was promulgated (declared) on 10 July 1918; it left the implementation of everyday law to judges. Wherever there were gaps, judges were ordered to carry out justice according to the 'revolutionary conscience' of people's courts. Most courts consisted of two lay assessors and a full-time judge, and for more serious cases, revolutionary tribunals (inspired by the French Revolutionary precedents) on which sat six assessors and a judge; their task was to judge cases brought by the Cheka. In 1920 alone, the people's courts tried 881 933 people, of whom nearly 300 000 were found innocent. Among those convicted, 34% were sentenced to confinement, 30% were fined and 23% had to perform compulsory labour. The revolutionary tribunals handled only 26 738 cases, but the rate of conviction was higher (85%) and among those convicted, 16 107 (70.7%) were sentenced to confinement and 766 (3.4%) were shot. Examples of tribunals found in the archives demonstrate that sentencing was very much affected by the class one belonged to, rather than the crime committed. For example in Lugansk, archives show that the two individuals it had convicted of gambling were proletarians, therefore reduced their sentence from five to two years of forced labour. Then again, it was primarily workers who were subjected to another form of revolutionary justice, namely, the comrades' disciplinary courts. These courts, administered by the trade unions, had the power to reprimand, dismiss and sentence to forced labour those guilty of absenteeism and other violations of labour discipline.

Faction

Marx had expounded the view that governments were created for the interests of those that held economic power, and the exploited classes would seek to oust those in power to create institutions of their own. Under NEP, instated in 1921, this had worrying consequences for the Communists as they had effectively reinstated bourgeois supremacy. Lenin had to buttress the regime against those who threatened revolution (standing Marxism on its head), and he centred the basis of power in political structures not economic orders. The political crisis that followed was due to factionalism and dissent within the Party. In the words of Trotsky, 'our party is now the only one in the country; all discontent goes exclusively through our party.'

Factionalism violated the central tenet of Bolshevism as developed under Lenin: that disciplined unity required complete compliance with decisions made by the directing organs of state. In some ways, the growth of factionalism was not unexpected given the radical departures the Bolsheviks had made from their Marxist ideology and the sheer growth of the party. Between 1917 and June 1921, the number of government employees grew nearly five times – from 576 000 to 2.4 million (to put that in context, that was nearly twice as many government employees as factory workers – not quite a dictatorship of the proletariat).

Alexander Shliapnikov, an old reliable Bolshevik, formed the 'Workers' Opposition' during the Ninth Party Congress (March 1920) which ended any form of workers' control in the factories, retuning to a managerial system akin to that under the Tsarist regime. Although Shliapnikov and the Metallurgical Union he led had supported the party in suppressing the Kronstadt rebellion, he began to question what the workers had actually won since 1917, given the hardship of civil war and limited power of the soviets. At the Tenth Party Congress the Workers' Opposition introduced two motions: increased worker participation in the party apparatus and a gradual transferral of control over the economy to trade unions. Lenin took the extraordinary measure of banning factions at the Congress in March 1921 and so the toleration of dissentient minorities outside the party became all the stranger. Just as the party was embarking on a policy designed to loosen the reins of economic control (under NEP, also discussed at the Congress), it was tightening the political reins. Historians such as Richard Pipes (1997) have suggested, convincingly, that it was this measure undertaken by Lenin which not only played a decisive role in Stalin's ascent to power, but also paved the way for the kind of state Stalin would run in the future – a dictatorship.

The purges

Repressive policies had been a key feature of Stalin's rule from at least the late 1920s because of his belief and fear of the 'enemy within', be they *kulaks*, White Guard, priests or disloyal party members. As we have already seen, Stalin was willing even from 1924 to purge the party of unwanted comrades, and many foreign members of the Communist party were cast out because of their perceived Trotskyist or Bukharinite beliefs (see Section 'Development of Stalinist Dictatorship'). By 1928, Stalin had personally overseen the trial of 53 'bourgeois specialists' accused of sabotage of mines in Shakhty (Southern Russia) and five of these were executed. Stalin played on the idea of class struggle and capitalist encirclement from 1928, particularly during forced industrialisation, to account for the increasing resistance he faced and to justify greater state coercion against its own people. The First Five Year Plan also saw 'saboteurs' and 'wreckers' become key accusations levelled at ordinary citizens who were not seen to be fulfilling their targets enthusiastically enough and, as a result, many qualified personnel were deported to the labour camps. The attack was levelled at economists in Gosplan and included the superb chronicler of 1917, N. Sukhanov and prominent economist V. Bazarov, as well as the liberal professor of the old regime L. Ramzin – drawing no distinction between the revolutionary socialists and the former Kadet sympathiser.

Stalin also encouraged denunciations of the ***nomenklatura*** (a category of people within the Soviet Union who held various key administrative positions in government, industry, agriculture and education) by ordinary workers. These were obviously open to abuse but helpfully kept the local politicians in a state of permanent trepidation. Collectivisation led Stalin to pursue pernicious policies against *kulaks*, who were allegedly seeking to destroy the new social order, and deportations and executions were commonplace in 1932. Stalin also sought tirelessly to control the *nomenklatura*, as he believed they were frequently accused of incompetence and 'yawning' on the job. In 1933 there was a purge of the party when up to 854 300 people identified as careerists or drunkards were expelled. In fact, nearly a million Soviet citizens languished in prisons and labour camps of the OGPU by 1933 and further millions had been deported and placed in resettlement areas. In all these attacks a pattern of scapegoating emerges; Stalin used this tactic to deflect popular discontent from himself and the regime and create warnings for any potential opposition in the future. The slave labour created in the camps also supported the drive for industrialisation that he needed.

Speak like a historian

In 1934 the OGPU (secret police) was brought under the control of the NKVD (the regular police and fire brigades). When the two agencies merged, the NKVD became the Main Directorate for State Security, meaning the NKVD was now responsible for all detention facilities, including the Gulags.

Silencing political opponents

Violence had been carried out against the people of Russia under Lenin too. However, from 1937 Stalin used it against his own party members. The turning point seems to have been 1 December 1934 when Sergei Kirov was assassinated by a young ex-Zinovievite (Leonid Nikolaev). Stalin had lost the title of General Secretary of the Central Committee and Kirov had been given the same title in the spring of 1934 – how this happened is still clouded by the fragmentary evidence that has survived. However, Stalin seemed to accept this situation and even made concessions during the summer, transferring the activities of the OGPU to the control of the People's Commissariat of Internal Affairs (NKVD), weakening the mechanisms for repression. Yet this only produced an even larger centralised organ for policing and security. Kirov's death at the end of the year was highly suspicious given the rapid way the killer was dealt with and the mysterious disappearance of the van drivers who transported him. There were widespread rumours that Stalin himself connived the assassination, although this remains unproven.

The first high profile victims of the purges were Zinoviev and Kamenev, who were accused of conspiring in Kirov's death. The filmed trial that followed in January 1935 saw them admit to political and moral responsibility for the death of their adherent. They were asssigned ten- and five-years imprisonment respectively, and 663 former supporters followed them into custody. A further 30 000 deportations of local groups 'hostile' to communism were deported from Leningrad as repression intensified, and by May 1935 approximately 281 872 persons had their party membership cards removed. This had been calculated by Stalin but carried out enthusiastically by Andrei Zhdanov who had become a Central Committee Secretary by 1934. Zhdanov wanted to restore the authority of the party and so thought 'cleansing' it would help bring the commissariats into line. Stalin

Voices from the past

Kirov was a rising star in the Party before his assassination, and although a loyal supporter of Stalin, was not afraid to speak against him.

When a group of older Bolsheviks and known supporters of Bukarin (led by Martemyan Ryutin) were found to be writing a manifesto called *Stalin and the crisis of the Proletarian Dictatorship* in 1932, Stalin demanded the death penalty. He felt betrayed by their denunciation of him as a mediocre politician. Stalin's wife, who committed suicide on 8 November 1932, had read the manifesto and seemed to suggest in her suicide note that she supported it. Sergei Kirov pleaded that Ryutin and his followers should not be executed because it would oppose Lenin's dictum against spilling Bolshevik blood. Kirov's card was surely marked when he became extremely close to the

leader following the death of Stalin's wife, but he was seen as a moderate in the party and received more votes than Stalin at the Party Congress in January 1934. Kirov was assassinated on 1 December 1934 and complicity in Kirov's assassination was a common charge to which the accused confessed in the show trials of the period. The cities of Kirov, Kirovohrad, Kirovakan and Kirovabad, as well as a few Kirovsks, were renamed in Kirov's honour after his assassination.

Discussion Points

1. If Stalin did order the murder of Kirov, what motives did he have?
2. Why is Stalin's reaction to the death controversial amongst historians?

had ulterior motives to settle old political scores and resolve any outstanding political tensions within the central organs of state. On 20 May 1935 the Politburo ordered that every former Trotskyist be directed to a labour camp for a minimum of three years. When evidence was found that Trotsky had been maintaining contact with groups from abroad in August 1936, Stalin frantically set the NKVD to work – Zinoviev and Kamenev faced a public show trial this time, with the added accusation of plotting to assassinate Stalin as well as Kirov. Again they were found guilty but this time condemned to death and shot the following morning.

The Great Terror

The Great Terror began in earnest in 1937 and as historian Robert Tucker (1979) asserts, there is no doubt that Stalin was the Director General of the systematic extermination of Communist oppositionists[8]. Following the show trials of unreliable members of the Politburo (namely, Karl Radek and Pyatakov) the last remaining oppositionist (Ordzhonikidze) shot himself. Rumours again circulated that he was murdered on Stalin's orders. Stalin was able to create a commission who could take decisions on behalf of the Politburo, which empowered him to extend the terror further. The next group that incurred suspicion was the Red Army leaders, especially Marshal Tukhachevski who had argued for a more adventurous military strategy than the one Stalin proposed. He, along with several other high-ranking commanders, were arrested in May 1937 and beaten into confessing to plotting a *coup d'état*; they were shot in June. On the same occasion, Bukharin, Tomsky and Rykov (once leaders of the Right Opposition) were found guilty of espionage, again on highly spurious evidence collected by the NKVD. Bukharin was slightly luckier as he was not physically beaten, as the others had been; he was put on show trial in March 1938 and he 'confessed' to terrorist activity in a deal to save the lives of his wife and child. Bukharin's last message to Stalin was, 'Koba, why do you need me to die?', sent just before his execution. ('*Koba*' was Stalin's revolutionary pseudonym and Bukharin's use of it was a sign of how close the two had once been.) Stalin kept this letter in his desk until his own death in 1953 – perhaps illustrating the personal importance of this particular comrade's slaying.

The role of Nikolai Yezhov

The Great Purges of 1937–8 are sometimes referred to as the *'Yezhovshchina'* (the Yezhov era). Nikolai Yezhov started his career as a secret police official under Stalin and became head of the NKVD from 1936 to 1938, during the most severe period of the Great Purge. The historian Robert Service: 1997 has described him as gleefully fanatical in his administering of repression. After presiding over the arrest of 259 450 persons in the spring, he implemented torture as a form of interrogation in Soviet prisons, which was sanctioned by Stalin in August 1937. Victims were tried by trios, typically an NKVD chief, party secretary and procurator, and trials were extremely brief and afforded the accused no right of appeal.

According to official records, Yezhov presided over the execution of 681 692 persons in 1937–8 – although this figure is probably an underestimate; the figures do not account for the 1.5 million who are likely to have perished from the inhumane conditions of the *Gulags* or killed by firing squad. Yezhov ironically became a victim of the instruments he had helped to foster after unexpectedly resigning from his post at the NKVD. He was arrested, confessed under torture to anti-Soviet activity, and executed in February 1940. This reveals somewhat the chaos of the era and the vast punitive industry that must have ballooned at this time to keep the executions concealed from the public. The ritual of denunciations, confessions, trials, sentencing, imprisonment and executions created thousands of jobs for willing torturers, jailers and grave-diggers, amongst others.

The resolution on anti-Soviet elements was extended to include anyone who had been active or sympathetic to oppositionist factions and virtually no institution was left unscathed. Only one in 30 delegates to the Seventeenth Party Congress in 1934 returned to the Eighteenth Congress in 1939; the Central Committee also haemorrhaged 55 members (out of 71); the Red Army was devastated by the loss of thousands of highly-trained military officers, and the arrest of People's Commissariats impeded industrial output. On the eve of the Second World War (which, by 1938, seemed fairly inevitable) this seemed a baffling policy, but perhaps demonstrates the hysteria that had swept through government organs to root out 'spies, wreckers and saboteurs' under Stalin's direction.

In the days of Tsarism and under the new Communist regime, terror was widely used as a tool for repression. In fact, the use of a secret police organisation to root out internal enemies was established under Nicholas I in 1825 and, if anything, was used to an even greater extent under the Communist regime.

The political, economic and social condition of the Soviet Union by 1941

Stalin continued to use terror fairly liberally throughout the rest of his premiership, but the floodgates of the Great Terror closed behind Yezhov in 1940. Five years had passed between the party congresses, and Stalin only met with certain members of the Politburo when it suited him and he needed to foster tension between the Red Army and NKVD, Commissariats and Council of Trade Unions, for example so that he could maintain his position. Therefore, by 1940, Stalin had elevated himself above the party, people's commissariats, army, trade unions and police – formalising his dictatorship.

Stalin's totalitarian state

It is agreed by most historians that, by 1939, Stalin had transformed Russia into a totalitarian state, the principal characteristics Hosking (1992) describes as: 'the central direction of the economy, a single mass party mobilising the population to build "Socialism in One Country", an official monopoly on mass communications, ubiquitous and terroristic security police force, adulation of a single leader and a single official ideology projecting the final state of mankind'.[9] However apt this description seems, it belies the active role the peasants and workers had in shaping this system; they were not always simply passive victims. Of course, the power of the 'Police State' should not be underplayed by suggesting that the peasants and workers would have been free to oppose the dictatorship – many would have feared execution or exile for exhibiting discontent.

There was a whole new raft of upwardly mobile technical graduates – of which the later leaders of the party, for example Khrushchev and Brezhnev, would derive their early success. The social and educational background of the party had changed dramatically since Lenin's day and leading *cadres* now worked their way up through the youth organisations, such as *Komsomol* and other organs of the party, or held technological posts. A similar process had taken place in the military, education, health, law and the diplomatic service: as long as they were loyal to the party they could enjoy thorough professional training. This developing ruling class enjoyed privileges most ordinary workers could only dream of, yet this *nomenklatura* were subject to scrutiny by the NKVD and could lose everything from a denunciation.

The First Five Year Plan saw changes to Soviet tastes in architecture, the arts and social attitudes. In 1934, 37 divorces were reported for every 100 marriages and Moscow hospitals witnessed 57 000 births but 154 000 abortions in the same year. In the face of these unwelcome developments, the regime's propaganda began to reinforce traditional family values in the hope of increasing the birth rate and stabilising society once more. In education, too, the state sought to reverse the effects of the initial cultural revolution that had occurred after October 1917. Knowledge was put back on the curriculum with the addition of instruction in Marxism–Leninism. By 1939, the entire education system had been remodelled on pre-revolutionary lines for a society which had largely returned to the hierarchical, imperial and conservative one under Tsarism.

Yet for all his successes in developing a cult around his personal leadership and eliminating enemies from within, Stalin was extremely vulnerable when, on 22 June 1941, despite his military advisors' warnings, the Nazi invasion of the USSR took the supposedly infallible leader by surprise. Stalin had declined to mobilise the Soviet armed forces on the Western Fronts and had even signed a non-aggression pact with Hitler in 1939, who had now humiliated Stalin in his betrayal. Stalin was about to lead his people into the most severe of tests – named 'The Great Patriotic War' because it was an ideological war for survival.

ACTIVITY 3.6

These concepts have been important throughout this chapter – go back through your notes and create a 'concept web' around these words. An example is given below.

Words: *centralisation, totalitarian, police state, cult of personality*.

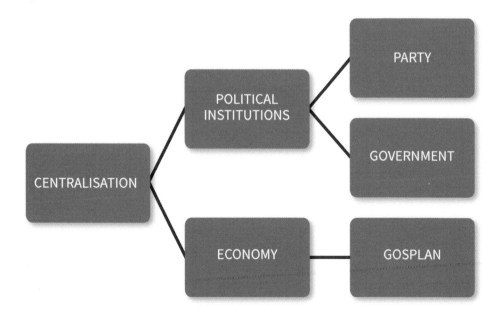

Putting events into chronological order is an excellent revision activity. Go back through your notes and create a timeline (you can use the one below but please observe there are plenty of events missing to encourage you to check back over your own records).

Once your timeline is complete, shade events in different colours to highlight political, economic and social developments.

Do you notice any turning points? Are there links between economic developments and social ones?

Conclusion

Historians such as Pipes: 1997 and Figes: 2014 have claimed that the basic elements of the Stalinist dictatorship were already in place by 1924. The Party apparatus had already become an obedient tool under Lenin during the Civil War and the regime's reliance on terror as a form of political control was instigated almost as soon as the October Revolution of 1917 had taken place. However, the development of the Stalinist dictatorship saw him break away from Leninism in marked ways. Although Lenin had no problem liquidating opposition to the revolution, he took a much more respectful approach to political comrades who disagreed with him, unlike Stalin who carried out purges in 1937–8 against those who contradicted him. Lenin had practised mass terror during the Civil War and continued to demand its application under NEP. However it was unlikely that Lenin would have approved of the torturous and degrading methods used against those arrested. Lenin would probably never have undertaken collectivisation in the violent manner Stalin did, as NEP showed Lenin was willing to win the peasantry over through persuasion. What mattered to ordinary Russians was not whether Stalin continued Lenin's ideology but whether they could earn a decent living, and despite Stalin's brutal dictatorship, by 1941 they could. The extent to which the population had bought into the Stalinist cult would be tested in unimaginable ways during the 'Great Patriotic War' of 1941–5, but if they proved disloyal, Stalin had the apparatus of terror ready to enforce his brand of patriotism.

Timeline

1928	Stalin uses coercion in the grain shortage crisis
	Shakhty affair
1929	Trotsky is deported from the USSR
	Bukharin is defeated and removed from the Politburo
	Full scale collectivisation is announced
	Cult of Stalin is launched
1930	'Revolution from above' begins
	Stalin's 'Dizzy with success' article calls a temporary halt to collectivisation
1932	Stalin's wife commits suicide
	Ryutin platform discovered
	First Five Year Plan considered complete in 4.5 years
	Famine begins in grain-producing areas
1933	Official party purge
1934	Seventeenth Party Congress – some opposition to Stalin
	Assassination of Kirov
1936	Trial of Zinoviev and Kamenev
	Yezhov appointed head of the NKVD – terror intensifies
	Adoption of Stalin's constitution
1937	Yezhovschina – climax of the purges – leading military figures purged
1938	'Right Opposition' purged Bukharin, Rykov, Tomsky
	Yezhov replaced by Beria as head of NKVD
1939	Nazi-Soviet pact signed
1941	Stalin becomes Chairman of the Council of People's Commissars
	Nazi Germany attacks Russia

Practice essay questions

1. 'The Bolshevik state under Lenin, between 1918 and 1924, was just as ruthless as the Communist state under Stalin, between 1928 and 1941.' Assess the validity of this view.
2. 'The Bolsheviks eradicated class between 1917 and 1941.' Assess the validity of this view.
3. With reference to these extracts and your understanding of the historical context, which of these extracts provides the more convincing interpretation of the successes of the Five Year Plans under Stalin?

Extract A

At the end of the 1920s, Stalin launched the Great Leap Forward, an economic revolution of unprecedented speed and magnitude. Although crash industrialisation brought workers certain benefits, such as virtually full employment, it also created enormous hardship. Despite a modest improvement in their living standards during the second five-year plan, the immediate priority for most workers in the 1930s was sheer survival. Unsurprisingly, economic questions featured more prominently that any other issue in popular opinion…

Workers were acutely aware of fluctuations in their standard of living, frequently comparing prices with wages. It was patently obvious to them whether their own economic situation was improving or deteriorating, and they were not deceived by official rhetoric about rising standards.

Davies, S., *'Popular Opinion in Stalin's Russia: Terror, Propaganda and Dissent, 1934-41'*: Cambridge University Press: 1997 p23.

Extract B

The party as known to its first members, and to those who had joined its ranks during the Civil War, was fast disappearing [in 1924]. Henceforth everyone other than rank-and-file members was a 'cadre' – in other words, worked in an apparatus where each person held a precise post in a hierarchy of disciplined functionaries. Some appearances were still preserved, as in the case of the Central Committee, which for a few more years continued to be elected, to deliberate, and to vote on resolutions. But the selection of its members was completely outside the control of party members.

In this way, Stalin accomplished his 'master plan' to become sole ruler. The party was stripped of the very thing Stalin wanted to strip it of: the ability to change its leadership through elections.

Lewin, Moshe 2005, p.38 *'The Soviet Century'*

Extract C

Revolution and Civil War gave birth to a 'politics of permanent emergency'. This had two consequences. In the first place militarization conditioned behavior within the leadership long after the guns fell silent, persuading them that the best way to get results was to utilize the symbols and structures of command and authority. One form of Bolshevism was being selected out by elite perceptions of contemporary realities, and to some extent Stalin's success was due to his adroit use of skills learned in the harsh world of the immediate post-revolutionary years. Second, permanent emergency precluded consensus or coalition, within and outside the party. Stalin was one among many – Lenin included – who were intolerant of dissent and anger and eager to brand opponents as deviationists.

Ward, Chris: 1993, p. 37 *Stalin's Russia*

Further reading

If you only read one book about Stalin's Russia, it should be Christopher Ward (1999), '*Stalin's Russia*', which not only synthesises other historians' views on Stalin, but provides his own convincing evaluation of the era.

If you want to know more about Lenin then Robert Service's (2000) biography is highly acclaimed and paints an interesting portrait of the private Vladimir Ilych and the public Lenin.

Geoffrey Hosking's '*History of the Soviet Union: 1917–1991*' (1992), focuses specifically on the experience of the peasantry, urban workers and professionals under Stalin's regime and traces the evolution of the Soviet regime from its origins in 1917 succinctly.

For further reading about Trotsky you may want to read Isaac Deutscher's '*The Prophet Armed: Trotsky, 1879–1921*':1954: Oxford Paperbacks.

 Chapter summary

After studying this period, you should be able to:

- describe the formal structures of the Communist government in 1941
- compare the political authority possessed by the leaders Lenin and Stalin
- assess how successfully the economic policies of the Communist Party were implemented under Lenin and Stalin
- assess how much society changed under Lenin and Stalin
- evaluate the political, economic and social conditions in Russia in 1941.

End notes

[1] Figes O. *A People's Tragedy: The Russian Revolution, 1891-1924*: Pimlico; 1997

[2] Read C. *War and Revolution in Russia 1914-22: the collapse of Tsarism and the establishment of Soviet power, European History in Perspective*: Palgrave Macmillan; 2013, p.127

[3] Carr E.H. *Bolshevik Revolution,* Volume 2: Macmillan; 1952, p.234

[4] Deutscher I. *The Prophet Unarmed: Trotsky 1921-29*: New York; 1965: p.6

[5] Deutsher I. *The Prophet Unarmed: Trotsky 1921-29*: New York; 1965, p.31

[6] Rosenburg W. *Russia in the Era of NEP: Explorations in Soviet Society and Culture* (eds) Fitzpatrick, S. Rabinowitch, A. Stites R. Indiana University Press; 1991, p.3

[7] Siegelbaum L. H. *Soviet State and Society Between Revolutions, 1918-1929*: Cambridge University Press; 1992, p.8

[8] Tucker R. C *The Rise of Stalin's Personality Cult,* The American Historical Review Vol. 84, No. 2: Apr., 1979, pp. 347-366

[9] Hosking G. *A History of the Soviet Union 1917-1991: Final Edition London: Fontana Press; 1992, p.205*

4 The Stalinist dictatorship and reaction, 1941–1964

In this section, we will examine how the Second World War affected the people of the Soviet Union, consider some of the changes that took place in the final years of Stalin's dictatorship, and how his successors maintained the Soviet system after his death. Key areas we will explore are:

- the impact of the Second World War on Stalin and the regime
- the conservatism of the final years of Stalin's rule
- Khrushchev's rise to power and de-Stalinisation
- economic and social changes under Stalin and Khrushchev
- Khrushchev's fall from power
- political, economic and social conditions by 1964.

Introduction

There is a strong argument to be made that the Second World War ought to have destroyed the Soviet Union which, according to many at the time, had been made inert by stifling bureaucracy and savage repression. Out-manoeuvred by the Panzer divisions of the Wehrmacht and exhausted by protracted battles, the Soviet Union amazed even their allies (Britain and the USA) by prevailing triumphantly against the Nazis in 1945, albeit at a catastrophic human cost. The great paradox

Key terms

A **superpower** is a state with a dominant position in **international relations**. Superpowers are characterised by their unparalleled ability to exert influence on a global scale. This is done through both military and economic strength, as well as diplomatic influence. At the end of the Second World War, the USA and the USSR were the two largest superpowers in the world.

Capitalism is an economic system in which trade, industries, and the means of production are largely or entirely privately owned. A capitalist can be used to describe someone who operates within a capitalist system.

Speak like a historian

The Nazi-Soviet Pact (sometimes referred to as the 'Molotov-Ribbentrop Pact', after the ministers responsible) was signed between Germany and the Soviet Union on 23 August 1939. Under the terms of the pact both countries promised neutrality, should the other side become involved in a war. The pact included a secret protocol that divided the territories of Estonia, Finland, Lithuania, Latvia, Poland and Romania into German and Soviet 'spheres of influence', which anticipated the later carving up of these countries.

was that the Soviet Union emerged from the Second World War as a great **superpower**, but one with spectacular failings. Unable to feed the people or fully stifle discontent, and surrounded by potential competition from those younger men who had achieved heroic status during the war, Stalin resorted to repression on a massive scale, which in some ways echoed the terror of 1937–8.

However, the final years of his dictatorship were marked by conservatism. Stalin did not focus heavily on domestic policy because his attention was distracted by new threats abroad, namely, the **capitalist** Americans. Therefore, the Fourth Five Year Plan was implemented to bring the economy back to pre-1940 levels. It did this to some extent and also provided some stability for the population, who had undergone considerable upheaval during the war years. When Stalin died, the population mourned him as they had Lenin and he was placed beside the architect of the 1917 revolution in the mausoleum of Moscow. Yet it wasn't long before his inner circle jostled for position to assume leadership of the superpower. The least likely candidate, Nikita Khrushchev, won the power struggle using his position as Party Secretary, as Stalin had done, and by opening up criticism of Stalin in his 'secret speech' delivered to the party in 1956. In doing so, Khrushchev transformed Soviet society, even though many of his policies failed, and this ultimately led to his dismissal in 1964. In many ways, his obliteration of the Stalinist cult can be compared to Alexander II's abolition of serfdom, as both bloodless events paved the way for more significant societal changes in the years following them.

Political authority, opposition and the state of the Soviet Union in wartime

The Second World War was, according to historian Chris Ward (1999), 'the greatest calamity ever to befall Russia … The bald statistics … give some hint of the scope of the tragedy but nothing can convey its intensity'.[1] Hitler had certainly planned it this way. Amassing the largest invasion force in history on Russia's eastern borders in June 1941 – supported by 3 million soldiers, 2000 aircraft, 3350 tanks and followed by security brigades known as *Einsatz-Kommandos* – he must have been confident that his grand plan of *Lebensraum* (living space) in the East could be achieved before winter set in.

The effect of the war on Stalin

When the Germans called Operation Barbarossa (the name given to the invasion of the East) into action, the assault was so swift and brutal it left the Soviet forces dazed and confused. Stalin was extremely slow to realise the scale of the catastrophe that lay before him. He simply couldn't believe that Hitler had tricked him, and that Hitler would be foolish enough to risk a war on two fronts. Almost immediately, 2.5 million people began an exodus to the east fleeing the German Wehrmacht, who advanced with astonishing speed. In the first four weeks of the attack, 319 Red Army units were committed to battle and promptly destroyed. Stalin seemed despondent and fled the capital to his country home (*dacha*) for over a week. It is unclear whether he had a mental breakdown or was simply afraid of being arrested for treachery. His minister and long-serving colleague Voroshilov begged him to return, and return he did.

After the initial panic, Stalin set up Stavka as the military command (as Nicholas II had done 27 years ago) and planned the offensives. This was foolish given that the Germans were advancing. The Red Army needed defensive tactics, but they simply hadn't been trained that way. The **Council of State Defence (GKO)** replaced the party's formal mechanisms, including the Politburo, to deal with the invasion. Stalin addressed the people of Russia as 'brothers and sisters' in one of only nine addresses made to the public during the entire campaign. He appealed to popular patriotism, calling the war the 'Fatherland war' rather than one of ideology. It was to save Russia itself. Stalin took decisions to abandon class warfare and focus on uniting the nation. His speech from Lenin's mausoleum (amongst the sounds of German gunfire) sent a strong symbolic message to the people. Nobody, it seemed, doubted Stalin's courage or his iron will.

The brutality of the regime persisted with dogmatic regularity as **martial law** was implemented throughout the country, although the new enemies were spies and fascists. Order 270 was issued in July 1941, which stated that all those who surrendered to the advancing enemies (whether they had any choice or not) were traitors and faced the death penalty. General Pavlov was the first to face the terror of the death squads after his forces suffered heavy defeats in the first few weeks of Operation Barbarossa. Dozens of generals befell the same fate. Even Stalin's own son fell victim: when the Germans captured him, his father refused to trade him in for high-ranking German officers. In Poland, the Baltic states and the Ukraine, the NKVD carried out what historian Richard Overy(1997) [2] has called 'a panic stricken orgy of killing' to punish ordinary citizens who had welcomed the German advance.

Stalin began, at last, to listen to the military experts around him once it had become clear that his own follies in purging 80 000 officers during 1937–41 and ignoring the intelligence communicated to him about German plans had cost the USSR dearly. He allowed the most competent commanders to present their plans, and he adjudicated between them. Stalin made many errors, such as toying with ideas of signing a separate peace with the Germans in 1941 and 1943, both of which strengthened the Nazi's resolve. However, Stalin and the Soviet regime were more resilient. Stalin's policies of removing the disloyal shifted and, instead, he showed no hesitation in jettisoning the incompetent in favour of the young and promising amongst his military advisers.

By 26 June 1941 the Germans had moved in a pincer movement, reaching territory approximately 60 miles from Leningrad, the symbolic heart of the Communist revolution, and by 16 July German forces had reached Smolensk (the last city before Moscow). Strategically this was not so significant, but it is arguable that if the Germans had succeeded in these two cities, the Russians would almost certainly have lost the war, even more quickly than Hitler had planned.

The battle for Stalingrad

The Battle of Stalingrad which followed, from August 1942 to February 1943, proved decisive in the European war. From it followed 'ten Stalinist blows', pushing the Germans back from Kursk to Kiev by 1944, and making victory almost certain. By this time the Allied forces, particularly the Americans, had donated approximately $10 billion of supplies in sugar, spam (tinned meat) and other

Key term

Martial law is the imposition of the highest-ranking military officer as the head of the government, in this case, Stalin. This removed all power from the ordinary executive, legislative, and judicial branches of government.

goods worth about one-fifth of Russia's GDP. These donations proved vital to sustaining the population, as the Soviet Union proved woefully inadequate at feeding the people. It focused on building more tanks to defeat the enemy.

The political impact of the war

The Communist Party yielded to other organs of power during the war; for example, the Central Committee scarcely met between 1941 and 1945. Its normal functions were carried out by the GKO, which was primarily made up of Politburo members. In local areas, party officials had to wade into local economic difficulties and bottlenecks, giving them unencumbered power in many respects. The sorts of crises they faced allowed an **authoritarian** decision-making style to develop, as well as a habitual deceptiveness towards their superiors. Some historians argue that these were the formative years for many of the middle officials who were to struggle with more complex demands of a peacetime economy in the years following 1945.

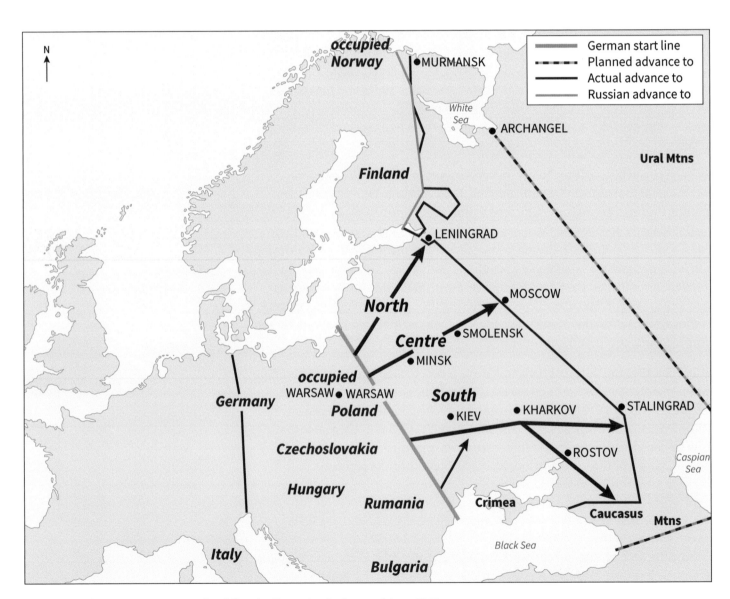

Figure 4.1: The war-torn territories that fell under 'Operation Barbarossa', June 1941.

The losses accumulated during the 'Great Patriotic War' created a need for mass recruitment into the party as turnover exceeded 50% by 1943. Over 43% of those recruited were from the intelligentsia at first. Over 3.6 million new members filled the ranks of the party during the war and a great proportion of these also served in the army or navy. Over 11 million medals were given out to soldiers who had exhibited extraordinary bravery during the war and 74% of these became party members. Those members with technical skills, such as engineers and managers, were transferred to the east to limit the damage done to party operations. The war had a formative influence on those that joined after 1941. Geoffrey Hosking (1985) suggested the Communist Party lost a certain amount of pre-war power and influence because of the dilution in standards caused by mass turnover. However, historian Martin McCauley (1993) has suggested the bond between members, the state and the party was much stronger than previous cohorts.

The economic impact of the war

The Stalinist regime was able to devote a much higher proportion of national income to the war effort than any other country involved. The Soviet Union outperformed Britain and the **Third Reich** in its capacity for organisation, coordination of government systems and infrastructure during the war. This was partly because the decrees, threats and punishments took on a popular legitimacy during the war that they never had in the 1930s; it was this that drove workers to the very limits to pour their energies into the war effort.

Industry
The whole balance of the economy was diverted towards munitions production, starving agricultural production of labour and resources and resulting in a collapse in living standards. In the first year of the war, over 1500 major enterprises

Key terms

Authoritarian in this context means that party leaders dictated policies and procedures, decided what goals were to be achieved, and directed and controlled all activities.

Third Reich was the name given to Germany by Hitler. Reich simply means 'realm'. Hitler thought the first Reich, was the Holy Roman Empire and the second came under the monarchy before the First World War.

Voices from the past

Stalin would not admit defeat, although he called in Georgi Zhukov, the Chief of Staff (a career army officer who had fought in the First World War and for the Bolsheviks in the Civil War) to perform two military miracles in Leningrad and Moscow, perhaps recognising his own weaknesses. Arguably, nobody did more than Zhukov to assure Soviet victory in 1945. He approached Leningrad by flying in the dead of night under the cover of cloud. He immediately started to work with the young Communist leader, Andrei Zhdanov, helping 636 000 citizens to evacuate and ordering the rest to prepare for heavy bombardment. Zhukov ordered the executions of several inadequate officers and organised a special armed regiment that was empowered to shoot anyone who retreated from the perimeter.

After organising Leningrad, Zhukov flew to Moscow in November where only 90 000 soldiers stood between the Germans and victory over the city. Zhukov immediately visited Stalin to beg for more men; to his surprise, there were no heated discussions this time. The haggard leader began to give in to his generals' demands as he began to respect their judgement and expertise, so 58 new divisions, previously kept in reserve, were committed to Moscow. Luckily for the Russians, they had managed to slow the Germans down: Hitler had planned to take the city before the frost set in, and his troops and their machinery were completely ill-prepared for a Russian winter.

By April, the Russians had managed to push the Germans back to Smolensk through a series of counter-offensives, and the survival of Moscow was seen by some as a turning point for the morale of the troops: the Germans could be beaten.

vulnerable to the German advances were evacuated and moved wholesale to the east (beyond the Ural Mountains), along with skilled workers and civilian refugees. They were reassembled in wooden sheds or simply put people to work in the open skies in minus-30-degree frosts.

Mass mobilisation was often achieved more effectively when danger was imminent; further away from the front lines it took much longer, where under-utilised labour reserves consisted of women and children. In February 1942, following mass mobilisation orders of all men aged 16–55 and all women aged 16–45, an exodus of skilled workers left for the front, draining vital branches of industry. By 1942, the total working population had been reduced from 85 to 53 million due to a shift in labour towards the defence sector, as well as catastrophic military losses. Even in priority sections of industry, levels of skill, experience and strength diminished; for example, in Leningrad women made up four-fifths of the workforce. Forced labour became an effective way of plugging some of the gaps, as approximately 3 million were used in mining and munitions work throughout the war and their contribution was clearly significant.

By the end of 1942, output in munitions production was soaring due to the construction of 3500 new large-scale factories and the conversion of civilian industries. Between 1941 and 1942, the number of aeroplanes produced doubled, and the manufacture of rifles rose 2.5 times, machine guns 3.5 times and tanks 5 times. Although German-produced weapons were far superior in terms of quality, the Soviets managed to concentrate production on a limited number of weapons, which meant they could maximise production. Despite these successes, production in areas not related to the war fell markedly; for example, steel production declined from 18.3 million tonnes in 1940 to 12.3 million in 1945, and this had a devastating effect on agriculture.

Lend-Lease Agreements

A significant contribution to the Soviet economic war effort was the Lend-Lease programme enacted by the United States in October 1941. The USA provided $11.3 billion dollar worth of food, trucks, jeeps and communication equipment to the Soviet Union. Although Soviet historians have tended to play down the significance of Lend-Lease to the Red Army's eventual victory, it made a critical difference in easing the civilian economy from late 1942 onwards.

Agriculture

Even more dramatic was the impact of the war on the rural economy. With the best land under German occupation, three-quarters of men drafted into the army or factories, and horses requisitioned for military needs, any progress that had been made in the 1930s collapsed. Mechanisation was abandoned as tractor production fell from 66 200 in 1940 to 14 700 in 1945 and replaced with back-breaking manual labour. Diverting resources and labour to the front served to jeopardise the entire war effort as output plummeted. From a level of 95.5 million tonnes in 1940, the grain harvest fell to 30 million tonnes in 1943 and cattle stock was halved. In April 1942, local authorities were given permission to halt the flow of labour into industry to ensure that food production was maintained. A much wider scope of local initiative was also permitted during the grim years of 1942–3 than had been allowed in the 1930s. Private plots expanded rapidly on collective farms, factories cultivated surrounding land, and city-dwellers worked on private gardens to supplement the pitiful food rations allocated by the government. Women lined the roads bartering food for goods, reminiscent of the 'bagmen' during the Civil War (see Chapter 3).

The social impact of the war

For many years following the war, the people of the Soviet Union were told that their struggle had been for the sake of humanity, to save mankind from annihilation by the fascist Germans. The opening up of Soviet archives after 1988 revealed that the war really demonstrated the astonishing capacity for the people of the Soviet Union to endure hardship and suffering. For this reason, Chris Ward (1999) has suggested the war should be referred to as 'The People's War'. The suffering inflicted on the peoples of Eastern Europe and Russia can hardly be described. Over 500 000 Soviet citizens died from German bombing alone; other causes of death included execution, typhus, starvation; some were even used as human shields in front of advancing German soldiers (when he heard about this, Stalin allegedly uttered 'war is merciless'). Estimates put the total number of civilian casualties at 18 million, with a further 8 million soldiers perishing in combat. Richard Overy (1997) [3] has referred to the war in the east as a 'harvest of death'.

In the early days of the war, citizens hurried to their workplace to ask their managers about news from the front. This spontaneous move to the factory, and people rushing to the banks to withdraw their savings, reveals much about Soviet society at the time and the air of pessimism that surrounded the beginning of the war. Rumours spread that party and police officials were whisking their own families away to safety whilst abandoning the ordinary citizens. The authorities moved quickly to suppress criticism of the party or Stalin himself. Of course, arrests were the primary method, as the NKVD were free to dispense with formal procedures when dealing with threats to security, which Acton and Stableford (2007) [4] have referred to as 'bludgeoning reflex reaction'. The regime carried out practice air-raid alarms to help citizens protect themselves and mass anti-German propaganda campaigns helped to stiffen the resolve of the home front.

Despite these tensions, there are countless stories of genuine heroism from ordinary citizens. Zoya Kosmodenyanska was an 18-year-old living in a village near Tambov, who tried to set fire to anything (such as stables) that might be useful to the Germans. Although villagers denounced her, the Nazi police battalion paraded her through the streets, viciously mutilated her body and publicly hanged her. The brutality with which the Germans treated Soviet citizens certainly helped the Stalinist regime bend them towards patriotism. There is no doubt amongst historians such as Robert Service (1997) and Chris Ward (1993) that without the determination of the people of Russia to defeat the German enemy, the USSR would almost certainly have lost.

National minorities, partisans and Jews

When the war was finally won on 7 May 1945, and when the Germans surrendered unconditionally, the Red Army occupied most of Eastern Europe including Poland, Hungary, Romania, Ukraine and a large portion of Germany. They enacted a heinous revenge on the millions of Soviet citizens who were seen as collaborators with the fascist enemy. Robert Service (1997) argues that even before the Soviet victory, the conquered peoples of Eastern Europe had one of three destinies to look forward to – execution; deportation or forced labour; or starvation. When they occupied territory, German soldiers had applied the rule that for every Wehrmacht soldier shot, 100 civilians would pay the price. The Germans collaborated with nationalists in the east, where one example stands out – Bronislav Kraminsky (a former Soviet engineer) exacted a reign of terror on the Orel region, slaughtering thousands of Poles. In the Ukraine, the people suffered particularly because they were seen as racial inferiors by the occupying forces. Intellectuals, farmers and partisans were all obliterated under the watchful guidance of Erich Koch (a German official), who ensured the people of Kiev were fed one-third of what was needed to sustain them.

The persecution of the Jews

The persecution and attempted extermination of the Jews reached its peak during Operation Barbarossa, because 5 million Jews lived in the Soviet Union in 1941, mostly in the western regions. Although Stalin did not attempt to massacre the Jewish population, in many ways the Russians were complicit in German anti-Semitism during the war. Except for the brief acceptance that allowing Jewish partisans to fight for the Soviet Union in the 'Jewish Anti-Fascist Committee' – set up by Russian Jewish actor, Solomon Mikhoels – hardly anything was done to stop the atrocities that were carried out against this minority. Some of the worst brutalities of the war were carried out in the Ukraine where the population needed no encouragement to seize goods and denounce Jews to the Germans. Approximately 33 771 Jews were massacred in two days at Babi Yar outside Kiev; the dead were thrown into a mass pit, but the gases from the decomposing bodies caused localised explosions, and so local people were used to exhume and re-bury bodies to stabilise the area. By December 1942, it is estimated that the *Einsatzgruppen* had murdered 1 152 000 Jews in Soviet territories by hanging or shooting alone. By the end of the war, almost all of the Soviet Union's Jewish population had been massacred. Stalin refused to acknowledge that the killing of Jews was different to the killing of anybody else.

The role of partisans

The role of partisans grew as the war progressed, particularly in the Ukraine. They were composed of Red Army men, members of the party, local inhabitants and Jews who had nowhere else to go. Their early activity merely consisted of food seizures. Many just sought to survive rather than become heroic defenders of the Motherland. The Nazis reacted with ferocity to these groups, attempting to liquidate them, usually through public executions. Stalin centralised the partisans in May 1942, and individual groups were given lists of German targets to kill. The groups shared a grim existence, constantly living in fear of spies, having poor weapons, no medical supplies and little shelter. The most famous group was founded by the Bielski brothers who managed to save 1256 Jews by sabotaging Nazi operations and living in underground dug-outs for much of the war. As the Russians pushed the Germans back, partisan groups were no longer acknowledged and many were treated to scrutiny from the NKVD. Those that had

Figure 4.2: The Red Army reaches Berlin, May 1945. This striking image shows Soviet troops raising the Soviet flag over the Bundestag.

proven their loyalty to the Stalinist regime were conscripted into the Red Army, but over half were found to be unfit and either sent to labour camps or let go.

At the end of the war it was the Red Army's turn to enact retribution. Over 600 000 Volga Germans were deported to Siberia within weeks of the surrender. Even before this, the Chechnyans had gathered in the main square to celebrate Red Army Day but found themselves surrounded by NKVD officers and were deported to Siberia. In total, it is estimated that 1.5 million people were marched east in this way during the closing months of the war. Beria (head of the NKVD) persuaded Stalin to give medals for those NKVD officers who had distinguished themselves in carrying out the war against traitors to the Motherland. Over 1 million people who had fought for the Germans (including Cossacks and 1400 White Army generals) were given an immediate death sentence towards the end of 1945.

ACTIVITY 4.1

For some historians, the victory of the Soviet Union over Nazi Germany was accidental, for some it was due to Stalin's leadership and the sheer doggedness of the Russians. Go back through your notes and find evidence to support both views. You may want to organise your notes in a table (see below).

The Soviet Union emerged from the Second World War victorious because of …

Luck or accident	Stalin's leadership	The determination and sacrifice of the people of the Soviet Union

ACTIVITY 4.2

Soviet historians tended to emphasise that although the war caused great sacrifice, the population were united behind the cause from the moment Barbarossa was launched. The extent to which this is true has been undermined, yet the driving force of the home front underlining Red Army victories cannot be ignored. Historians still debate the impact of the war on Stalin, particularly as he seemed to emerge from the war stronger than before.

Go back over your notes to collect evidence to assess the impact of the war from different perspectives.

Impact of the war on ...	Positive	Negative
Stalin as a leader		
Support for the Party		
Economy		
Society		

Conclusions

There is no doubt that the extraordinary courage and sacrifice of the ordinary people of Russia helped her to victory in 1945. It was a truly remarkable collective achievement. Historians have debated how and why the people fought with such fierce determination, at times, willing to sacrifice themselves for the Motherland. Most historians agree that it was probably to some degree because of terror and coercion, local patriotism in the case of Leningrad and Moscow, and appeals made by Soviet propaganda to save the very idea of Russia and the cult of sacrifice, which had been cultivated during the Five Year Plans which began in 1929. By the end of the war, the Soviets had lost more than twice as many soldiers as the Germans and ten times as many as Great Britain and the USA combined. The scorched earth policy that Stalin had implemented (June 1941) to destroy anything that might be useful to the Germans as they advanced had left vast tracts of the Soviet Union's western regions flattened. At the end of the war, Stalin called on the Russian people to engage in one last struggle, that of the reconstruction of the 70 000 villages, 1700 towns and 32 000 factories that had been destroyed during the war.

ACTIVITY 4.3

Take time to study an overview of the key military events involving the Soviet Union. Add information from your notes in the third column to show what was happening in the Soviet Union.

Summary of key military events in a timeline

Year	Military events	Other information
1941	Jun: Operation Barbarossa begins Sep: Siege of Leningrad Oct: Battle of Moscow	
1942	Jan: 800 000 citizens of Leningrad are evacuated over the ice road Jul: Germans take Sevastopol Aug: Battle of Stalingrad	
1943	Feb: Liberation of Stalingrad Jul: Zhukov and Vassilevsky given control of operations around Kursk by Stalin. Germans pushed back to starting positions	
1944	Jan: Siege of Leningrad is over as massive two-week offensive pushes Germans back Jun: Zhukov takes command of Operation Bagration Jul: Soviets capture Minsk and Vilnius	
1945	Jan: Warsaw falls to Soviets Feb: Soviets cross into Germany April: Soviets capture Berlin May: Berlin unconditionally surrenders	

Political authority and government to 1953

High Stalinism

Historians have tended to concentrate their works on the emergence of Stalinism and the years before the war, perhaps because the years of '**High Stalinism**' can be summarised as a continuation and deepening of what had already been established in the preceding years. It should, though, be noted that historians such as Chris Read (2001) have described the latter years of Stalinism as the 'bleakest' in Soviet history. It is true that the Politburo was composed of the same members who had staffed it in 1939 (Stalin, Molotov, Voroshilov, and Khrushchev among others). The regime had mutated into a 'court system', rather like that of the Tsarist regime, through which policy was formed over excruciating dinners where Stalin would humiliate those around him. Commissariats were turned back into Ministries as they had once been under the Tsarist system. Soviet politicians lived in an uneasy atmosphere and competed for Stalin's favour. This bureaucratic, centralised and personal form of rule, which characterised Stalin's later years, was nothing new – although, arguably, it had solidified after the war.

There can be little doubt that perhaps the greatest victor to emerge from the terrifying war was Stalin himself. The Soviet victory over Nazi Germany seemed

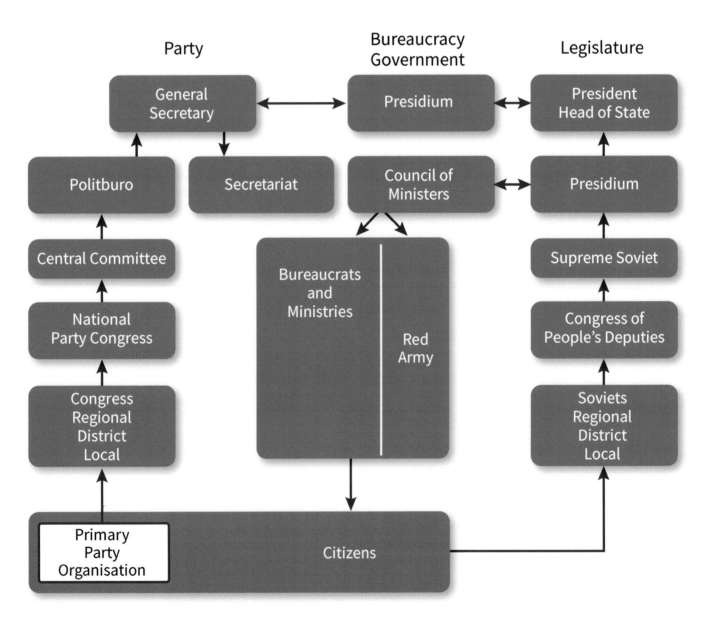

Figure 4.3: The structure of the government under Stalin.

to validate the system he had developed and legitimised his personal rule. In June 1945, he was elevated (after first protesting against it) to the position of *Generalissimo*. In some ways, it is not surprising his authority was consolidated to such an extent because, to many, Stalin had been a great leader during the war. By 1945, he was 65 years of age, but he had spent an inordinate number of hours on affairs of state and had appreciated the need for modern technology. His forced rapid industrialisation programmes had prepared Russia fairly well for the war and he hadn't lost his eye for detail, or the ability to process information. He had also allowed the experts such as Zhukov to devise military tactics when it had become obvious that his own weren't working and many young officers had flourished as talented leaders during the war years.

Key term

High Stalinism can be described as the period when Stalin's power had reached its pinnacle. After the Second World War Stalin's power was unchallengeable and his style of leadership became much more despotic.

Figure 4.4: On 12 August 1945, Generalissimo Stalin cheerfully leads the inner circle for the victory parade: (from left to right) Mikoyan, Khrushchev, Stalin, Malenkov, Beria and Molotov.

Cult of personality; the revival of terror; destruction of 'supposed' opposition

The cult of Stalin

Historians widely agree that the cult of Stalin, which had been assiduously manufactured during the 1930s, put down popular roots during the war. It is paradoxical then, as Acton and Stableford (2007) argue, that he should have so ruthlessly fostered the cult after the war. Whereas early historians blamed the campaign behind 'Stalinisation' on Andrei Zhdanov (hence the period 1946–8 is referred to as *Zhdanovschina*), more recently the archives have revealed the drive coming from Stalin himself. For reasons we may never fully understand, given the lack of rivals or opposition to his premiership, Stalin felt compelled to maintain his personal hegemony. Evan Mawdsley (1998) suggests that with industrial modernisation came mass culture (popular fiction, cinema, radio, spectator sports), and so the regime chose to promote national defence and the leader himself in didactic fashion. The reinvigoration of the Orthodox Church was again suspended after 1946 and cultural uniformity was implemented once more.

Zhdanov was certainly the mouthpiece of Stalin's thinking on literature and the creative arts. Anything that was seen to be kowtowing to the West was denigrated. This was particularly important to the regime because of the fear of Western influence. After the war, soldiers who had fought in Germany, Hungary and other parts of Europe had mixed with Americans and British and brought back with them new ideas, even criticisms of the Soviet model, which could not be integrated into the socialist mould. The post-war period was marked by an end of almost all autonomy for film-makers in the Soviet Union; the heavy control now exerted by the government ended film-making as an art form. Evidence suggests that remarkably low numbers of films were produced from 1945 to 1953, with as few as nine films produced in 1951 and a maximum of 23 produced in 1952.

The popular and talented poet, Anna Akhmatova, was publicly humiliated when Zhdanov referred to her as 'half nun, half whore' after the Western liberal philosopher, Isaiah Berlin, visited her. The satirist Mikhail Zoshchenko was referred to as 'literary scum' because his satires were popular with the public and were deemed dangerous. Even Shostakovich's symphonies, one of which was inspired by the Siege of Leningrad, were banned for not being 'Russian' enough. Sergei Prokofiev, another prolific composer, was accused of the crime of 'formalism', described as a 'renunciation of the basic principles of classical music' in favour of

 Voices from the past

There were some marked differences in the Soviet Union after the war, particularly in the role that foreign policy would play in determining domestic policy. Stalin was increasingly consumed with diplomatic relations and maintaining global superpower status over domestic policy. In some ways, his inclinations towards 'Soviet patriotism' and his meddling in ideological approaches to the economy, linguistics and even genetics can be explained by his distrust of Western 'bourgeois' trends and achievements. Stalinism took on a strong nationalist element after the war in a way that Leninism never had, although Stalin had always leaned this way, even during the Civil War of 1920–4. Stalin's diplomacy can be explained by his concern for state security. The USSR had been invaded three times through its western borders – in 1914, 1917 and 1941 – and Stalin was determined this would never be repeated. Thus, at the end of the Second World War, Stalin sought to create a 'buffer zone' or sphere of influence in Eastern Europe.

This meant either forcing countries to become one-party communist regimes (in the case of Romania and Bulgaria) or 'friendly governments' (as in Czechoslovakia and Hungary). Poland was treated differently because it was the only territory separating the Soviet Union from Germany. Stalin sought to ignore Churchill and Roosevelt's wishes at the Yalta Conference of February 1945, when they called for a free democratic nation, and instead wanted to 'Sovietise' the Poles rapidly. Therefore, Stalin tried to achieve both territorial and political expansion into Eastern Europe whilst still collaborating with the Western allies. These aims were simply incompatible. After 1947, he became more aggressive as it became obvious that the West no longer wanted to co-operate with him. The formation of Cominform (Communist Information Bureau), effectively a military alliance between the Communist countries of the East, saw an intensification of his attempts to control the Eastern bloc and represented the more offensive posture he would take thereafter towards the West.

'muddled' sounds. National myth-making took precedence over truth telling. Even the great Bolshevik film-maker Sergei Eisenstein's '*Ivan the Terrible*' came under considerable scrutiny (from Stalin himself) for portraying the leader's army as a band of degenerates. This was a devastating blow to the film-maker and it is said he died a broken man without finishing the film.

Right up until the early 1950s, Stalin continued to treat questions of theory very seriously and dedicated significant periods of time to writing treatises to discourage any contradictions to his thought or that of Soviet ideology. His commitment to the Marxist-Leninist-Stalinist ideology meant that no area of study was 'apolitical' and this was particularly heightened as the Cold War set in and the supremacy of his beliefs had to be asserted over that of his Western rivals. The most famous example of his foray into academic discipline was in the field of linguistics, when he wrote '*Marxism and the Problems of Linguistics*' in 1950. Stalin rejected the previously held Marxist approach that held that languages developed along class lines. Instead he stressed the specific and special nature of the Russian language that was developed centuries ago. This is not to say that Stalin had become a nationalist; he still held that socialism would one day eradicate languages as it spread across the world. However, he was compelled to defend his socialist state against the capitalist exploiters of the West and part of this was an appeal to Russian nationalism.

It is difficult to pinpoint the beginning of the cult of Stalin. Robert Tucker (1979) suggests it was probably on his 50th birthday in 1929; by the end of the Second World War when Stalin reached 70 (in 1949), it was truly at its zenith. Initially, the promotion of Stalin began by placing him in a succession following Marx, Engels and Lenin – he was a living Marxist philosopher. However, it went much further than this: his views were elevated to the level of sacrosanct dogma and he became the authority in a number of fields. By extension, those who he found appealing were also given authority-figure status, whether their expertise or knowledge demanded it or not – Lysenko (the agronomist) is a good example of this. The history of the Soviet Union had been rewritten during the 1930s to ensure Stalin had been present and influential at all the key points leading up to the Bolshevik revolution and photos had been doctored to support these myths. Accolades to 'Lenin's closest friend and disciple' sprung up everywhere. Vast statues were erected (even in remote parts of the Soviet Union, such as a small village on the river Enisei in Siberia) and operas, paintings and films magnified his role as a national hero.

Terror returns

The coercive measures taken against opponents or critics of the Stalinist regime were nothing new. Neither was the fabrication of material to condemn those that threatened Stalin's premiership. However the 'terror' of the late 1940s cannot be compared to the Great Purges of 1937–8, if for no other reason than there were less executions following arrests and more reliance on forced labour camps instead. The revival of coercion had begun to be applied in the closing months of the war (as previously discussed in the National Minorities section). Practically all those who had any contact with the West were treated as 'suspicious' and segregated from the rest of the population, often by being marched directly to labour camps upon their return. The party was purged of approximately 100 000 members

Speak like a historian

When historians speak of 'hegemony' it is usually in the context of imperialism. Hegemony, in this respect, would refer to the geo-political or cultural dominance of one country over others. However, when historians speak of Stalin's hegemony they are referring to the beliefs, explanations, perceptions, values of Stalin – that it was his world-view that was imposed and accepted as the cultural norm by the people of the Soviet Union.

annually, many falling victim to accusations of plotting, the majority of which the police fabricated.

The heroes thrown up by the war suffered too, the most famous of whom was General Zhukov. After the German capitulation, Zhukov became the first commander of the Soviet Occupation Zone in Germany and had taken part in the Yalta and Potsdam Conferences with the allied leaders in 1945. Rumours circulated that he had taken full credit for winning the war against Germany in a media interview. Stalin was furious and it is highly likely that he was bitterly jealous of his subordinate. However, Stalin couldn't risk executing this popular and world-renowned figure, and there is evidence to suggest Stalin maintained a deeply-held respect for this man who had openly argued with him over military tactics. Therefore, he was stripped of his position and assigned command of the Odessa Military District, far from Moscow and lacking in strategic significance and troops.

Voices from the past

Milovan Djilas recollects a meeting with Stalin in his book entitled '*Conversations With Stalin*' (Rupert Hart Davis, London 1962 p. 44). Born in Montenegro, he was elected to the Central Committee of the Yugoslav Communist Party in 1938 and two years later became a member of its Politburo.

He (Stalin) was of very small stature and ungainly build. His torso was short and narrow, while his legs and arms were too long. His left arm and shoulder seemed rather stiff. He had quite a large paunch, and his hair was sparse, though his scalp was not completely bald. His face was white, with ruddy cheeks. Later I learned that this colouration, so characteristic of those who sit long in offices, was known as the 'Kremlin complexion' in high Soviet circles. His teeth were black and irregular, turned inward. Not even his moustache was thick or firm. Still the head was not a bad one; it had something of the common people, the peasants, the father of a great family about it – with those yellow eyes and a mixture of sternness and mischief.

I was also surprised at his accent. One could tell that he was not a Russian. But his Russian vocabulary was rich, and his manner of expression very vivid and flexible, and full of Russian proverbs and sayings. As I realised later, Stalin was well acquainted with Russian literature – though only Russian – but the only real knowledge he had outside Russian limits was his knowledge of political history.

One thing did not surprise me: Stalin had a sense of humour – a rough humour, self-assured, but not entirely without subtlety and depth. His reactions were quick and acute – and conclusive, which did not mean that he did not hear the speaker out, but it was evident that he was no friend of long explanations. Also remarkable was his relation to Molotov. He obviously regarded him as a very close associate, as I later confirmed. Molotov was the only member of the Politburo whom Stalin addressed with the familiar pronoun *ty*, which is in itself significant when one remembers that Russians normally use the polite form *vy* even among very close friends.

Stalin ate food in quantities that would have been enormous even for a much larger man. He usually chose meat, which was a sign of his mountain origins. He also liked all kinds of local specialities in which this land of various climes and civilisations abounded, but I did not notice that any one dish was his particular favourite. He drank moderately, usually mixing red wine and vodka in little glasses. I never noticed any signs of drunkenness in him, whereas I could not say the same for Molotov, let alone for Beria, who was practically a drunkard.

Discussion Points

1. What are his impressions of Stalin?
2. Do you think he likes Stalin?

Extension: Carry out research on Stalin and his relationship with Yugoslavia in the 1940s and write a report about it.

Anti-Semitism continues

Stalin launched an attack on 'cosmopolitanism', which he associated with intellectuals who were not patriotic. Many were seen as pro-American or imperialist and, in 1947, a strain of anti-Semitism followed in the USSR as 'cosmopolitanism' became a euphemism for Jewishness. Many Jews had fled to the USA during the earlier part of the 20th century (because of the pogroms and terrible conditions they faced in the Pale of the Settlement). An irrational link was made between Jewishness and lack of patriotism. Many Jews had become highly successful in the USA and there was a perception that Jews within the Soviet Union were being supported by them. The Anti-Fascist Committee, which had been set up during the war to fight the Germans, was abolished in 1948 and the leaders were arrested. Mikhoels's position as a leader of the Jewish community led to increasing persecution from the Soviet state. In 1948 Mikhoels was murdered, almost certainly on the direct orders of Stalin, and his body was run over to create the impression of a traffic accident. He was given a state funeral. The cultural and religious life of Jews was severely restricted and schools were closed down, along with Jewish libraries and newspapers. Jewish writers and artists were imprisoned, banished or executed in some cases, on the basis that they were formulating a Zionist conspiracy. Richard Overy (1997) argues that this wave of purges was almost certainly linked to the re-conquest of Eastern Europe, where the Russians had been fighting armed resistance to the Soviet regime – now the enemies were within.

Arguably, 'mass terror' only reappeared on three occasions: the Leningrad affair of 1949; in 1951 with Georgia's Mingrelian tribesmen; and in the 1953 Doctors' Plot.

The Leningrad Affair

The Leningrad Affair was, according to McCauley (1993), largely due to Yugoslavia (led by Josip Tito) being expelled from Cominform due to their unwillingness to be led by Stalin. Zhdanov's untimely and sudden death, in fairly suspicious circumstances, also seems to have been a contributing factor – he had created Cominform, had shared good relations with Tito and had been feted as a war hero during the Siege of Leningrad. Zdhanov's own personal successes were enough to encourage Stalin's attention, and links between Tito and Zhdanov were enough to raise Stalin's suspicions. Zhdanov had worked closely with Nikolai Voznensky (who had been responsible for planning the war economy) and Alexander Kuznetsov

Voices from the past

Late Stalinism must be seen in the context of what historians refer to as 'The Cold War', which was prolonged military and diplomatic tensions between the USSR and the USA that lasted from the latter part of 1945 until 1989. The Cold War dominated international relations during this time as many countries sought to ally themselves with one or other of the superpowers. For the superpowers themselves, mutual suspicion, fear and one-upmanship dominated foreign policy. Yet it is important to note that the events of the Cold War probably had a deep impact on the leaders of the Soviet Union during this period too. Stalin was, for the most part, completely paranoid about capitalist encirclement and the USA trying to buy diplomatic relations with the rest of Europe. This may have been the cause of renewed censorship laws and party purges.

(second only to Stalin in the party hierarchy), both of whom had been tipped to be Stalin's successors. The accusations against Voznensky and Kuznetsov ranged from treachery to debauchery. The initial accuser was Georgy Malenkov, Stalin's first deputy, who almost certainly masterminded the affair. Then, formal accusations were formulated by the Communist Party and signed by Malenkov, Nikita Khrushchev and Lavrentiy Beria. Over 2000 people from the Leningrad city government and regional authorities were arrested on grounds of treason. Also arrested were many industrial managers, scientists and university professors. Public show trials followed and the six main leaders of the Leningrad party were shot, despite them refusing to admit to any crimes. It is estimated that about 2000 other public figures were removed from their positions and exiled from the city.

The Mingrelian Case, 1951

Stalin seemed to be gradually replacing the old guard of the 1930s with new, younger Communists who were more loyal to him than the party. The destruction of the Leningrad arm of the party seemed to mark a revival in fortunes for Beria, head of the security police, and Malenkov, who was principle *cadre* secretary and therefore responsible for the *nomenklatura*. However, even this was tainted for Beria by the splitting of the NKVD into the MGB (Ministry for State Security), responsible for the security police, and the MVD (Ministry of Internal Affairs), responsible for the ordinary police, public order and labour camps. Sebag-Montefiore (2005) argues that by 1951 Stalin had become suspicious of Beria and fired a warning shot across the bows with the Mingrelian Affair. The fabricated accusations of separatism and collaboration with the 'Western imperialists' were followed by a purge, which delivered a devastating blow to the Georgian party organisation and specifically targeted its Mingrelian members (Mingrelian being a sub-ethnic group of the Georgians from which Beria descended).

The Doctors' Plot, 1953

Stalin's paranoia grew almost out of control by the end of his life when he became petrified of death. This might explain the Doctors' Plot of 1952–3 when, initially, 37 prominent Moscow doctors (predominantly Jews) were accused of conspiring to assassinate Soviet leaders; this number grew to hundreds by 1953. In 1951, an MGB investigator reported to Viktor Abakumov, Beria's replacement as Minister of the MGB, that Professor Yakov Etinger, who was arrested for his connections to the Jewish Anti-Fascist Committee, had committed malpractice in treating Zhdanov, allegedly with the intention of killing him. However, Abakumov refused to believe the story. On 4 July 1951, the Politburo set up a commission, which was headed by Malenkov and included Beria, to investigate the issue. Both Beria and Malenkov tried to use the situation to expand their power, by gaining control of the MGB. Abakumov was arrested and tortured soon after being dismissed as head of the MGB. Stalin's death interrupted the trials and so many of the doctors were never executed, and some were even exonerated in March 1953.

Robert Service (1997):[5] argues that there is considerable evidence that Stalin was planning another purge of the inner circles of government just before his death. In the months before his stroke, he extended the Politburo from 6 to 25 persons and simultaneously created a seven-person bureau within this newly named **Presidium**, which would have enabled him to bypass the Politburo and potentially rid himself of all of the Communist party veterans. Chris Ward (1999) reasons that all of the purges in the latter years were a case of Stalin trying: 'to reassert his authority over the military (Zhukov's demotion), the party (the Leningrad Affair), the security apparatus (the Mingrelian case), the upper reaches of the Presidium (the Doctors' Plot) and society at large (the Zhdanovschina)'.

The picture of Stalin that emerges towards the end of his life certainly seems to be that of a sickly despot who was lied to most of the time by terrified subjects, presiding over a stifling and inefficient bureaucracy that was in need of urgent reform.

The power vacuum on Stalin's death

The end of Stalin

There has been much speculation surrounding Stalin's death, because he was left for almost 24 hours without any medical aid after a paralysing stroke. Some have ventured to suggest that Beria had him poisoned, although evidence suggests he almost certainly died of a cerebral haemorrhage. It is plausible that the delay in sending medical assistance could have been a deliberate attempt to hasten the premier's demise; or that his subordinates who were present (Beria, Malenkov, Khrushchev and Bulganin) were afraid of calling for doctors lest he recover and accuse them of attempted murder. Stalin's disdain for the medical profession was infamous. After several anxious days, the end finally came on 5 March 1953.

The Soviet citizens reacted with seemingly genuine grief upon hearing the news of Stalin's death as he had been their leader for almost 30 years. On the day of his funeral, where he was laid next to Lenin, thousands were trampled to death in Red Square in an attempt to get close to his body. Of course, there must have been many who were relieved at the prospect of regime change. The number of labour camp inmates had become excessive and Gulag uprisings, such as those in Koylma in 1949 and Ozerlag in 1952, showed that the Gulag populations were also dangerously high. Stalin had held the peasantry in virtual contempt throughout his personal rule and agricultural yields still couldn't provide plentiful food for the people. The command economy (see Section: 'Changes in industrial organisation from Stalin to Khrushchev) – where industry produced goods according to plan, not need – had in many respects held back innovation; living standards were extremely low amongst most people and consumer goods were in short supply. Stalin's policies after the war had caused embitterment amongst the national minorities and the cult of personality had once again limited the lives of intellectuals. Any reform Stalin's successors made, however, had to be considered in the context of maintaining the Soviet state and the party's monopoly of power over that state. In effect, this meant that any reform would have to acknowledge the wrong-doings of what went before, without admitting responsibility for it. Whoever would succeed Stalin would need to pay these issues serious attention after 5 March 1953.

The successors

Stalin's successors assumed a collective leadership from 5 March 1953 and divided up ministries between them, reminiscent of Lenin's government. Despite their willingness to display a united front, for example having all car doors opened at

171

Summary of key events

- The Second World War had been a catastrophe for the people of the Soviet Union, but a victory for Stalin as he emerged from the war a dictator with mass popularity.

- Many of the systems begun under Stalin in 1928 continued after the war, such as the Five Year Plans and use of repression.

- As Stalin grew older, he retreated from public life and concentrated even more power in his own hands, through fear of enemies.

- Because of the way Stalin had ruled, his succession was problematic and it was unclear how the party would proceed.

exactly the same time when alighting, personal rivalries were barely concealed and huge differences between how far they ought to continue with Stalin's policies or introduce reform, surfaced almost immediately. Lavrentiy Beria promoted himself to Minister of the **MVD** and **MGB**, and so was the prominent figure. He ran the government with his close associates, Georgi Malenkov (Chairman of the Council of Ministers, downgraded from party secretaryship after a reshuffle orchestrated by Khrushchev) and Kliment Voroshilov (Chairman of the Presidium). Nikita Khrushchev (General Secretary of the Central Committee – as Stalin had been in his early career) replaced Malenkov and Nikolai Bulganin (Defence Minister) formed the opposition. Although collective leadership seemed to work for a short time, Stalin's death left a power vacuum at the centre, which his successors struggled to fill. Notably, Khrushchev was the only member who had a position in the Presidium and the Secretariat, allowing him to build a power-base in the party.

Political authority and government

Khrushchev's rise to power

Beria held enormous power, commanding the civil and political police, the border guards and all military and nuclear weapons. Russian tradition had it that prisoners were released when the leader of the country died and so Beria, in order to win popular support, began to dismantle the Gulag system from 27 March 1953, releasing thousands of men and women from the camps in the process. Isaac Deutscher (1955) suggested Beria was instigating a genuinely liberal reform programme, although many historians such as Volkogonov (1998) argue that Beria was trying to score political points and was no reformer. Beria was distrusted by his colleagues in the Presidium and came across as a sinister character but, more than this, posed a threat to all of the leadership because he knew their secrets; he had also worked closely with Malenkov under Stalin. The demotion of Malenkov was almost certainly a concentrated effort to break up the Beria and Malenkov ascendancy. The Doctors' Plot, which had been fabricated in January 1953, was openly criticised, and those still alive were rehabilitated, all under Beria's command. Beria then attempted to tackle the nationalities question; coming head to head with Khrushchev, he promoted natives to top positions in the Ukraine, Belorussia and the Baltic States.

The balance of collective leadership was maintained, at least for a short time. Khrushchev's voice became increasingly important as a result of his position in the party; he seemed to speak for the membership and could, as Stalin had, appoint members loyal to him to build his power-base. Khrushchev received a stroke of luck when Beria's meddling in East Germany backfired with a huge uprising of workers there. Khrushchev's memoirs suggest he masterminded the Beria affair to oust him from power. Whatever the truth, he and the other members of the Presidium needed little persuasion to remove Beria, who seemed to be using his position as head of the MVD to amass troops in Moscow. Khrushchev managed to recruit Marshal Zhukov (the famed Second World War commander) to the Ministry of Defence and he brought other military commanders with him, giving Khrushchev the support he needed to arrest Beria (the MVD were too loyal to have acted against their commander). Fearing a *coup*, the Presidium had Beria arrested on 26 June 1953. He was accused of being an anti-Bolshevik agent during the Civil War (which was probably true), molesting young girls (he admitted to raping four) and of being a double agent for the British after the Second World War (almost certainly nonsense). He was tried in secret and shot. Khrushchev had used Stalinist tactics to rid himself of his greatest rival, for which he was awarded the title of First Secretary of the Central Committee.

The final contest for national leadership would be between Malenkov, whose power base lay in the government, and Khrushchev, who gained authority from the party. Control over the police was significant. The security ministry was split and renamed for the final time. The new MVD would hold responsibility for civil and criminal offences, and the **KGB** (Russian initials for Committee for State Safety) – responsible for state security both domestically and internationally – was firmly put under the control of the party, so that no single person could assume a huge power base in this area again. Therefore, Khrushchev had a say in the new appointment of the KGB chief and he chose to appoint former Komsomol officials such as A.N. Shelepin (1958–61) who had made their career in the party, not the police. The effect was to ensure that, at least outwardly, the police would have to observe what official press reports referred to as 'Socialist legality'.

Why did Khrushchev succeed?

Khrushchev's emergence as supreme leader was not just a response to the question of how the Soviet Union should be run; there were also significant policy and personality differences between him and Malenkov which needed to be resolved. Competition had intensified after Beria's removal and Malenkov had gained the initiative by lowering prices of food and industrial consumer products in April 1953. He then produced a budget which outlined his plans to cut taxes on agriculture, giving peasants more freedom and expanding the consumer industries, but he lacked the charisma to persuade others. Khrushchev had already been making unilateral decisions on a wide range of issues (for example, giving the Crimea to the Ukrainian Soviet Republic) and countered Malenkov's designs with his own plans, announcing the **Virgin Lands Scheme** (discussed in a later section) and an end to police terror. Although Khrushchev's policies won him more friends amongst the military, heavy industry bosses and agricultural experts, ultimately it was Khrushchev's moves to eliminate the 'cult of personality' (referred to in the West as 'de-Stalinisation') and his gregarious personality that won him the leadership.

De-Stalinisation was a process of political reform in the Soviet Union that was initiated by Khrushchev after the death Stalin in 1953.

Key term

Virgin Lands Scheme was **Khrushchev**'s plan, implemented in 1953, to dramatically boost the Soviet Union's agricultural production in order to alleviate the food shortages plaguing the Soviet populace.

Figure 4.5: Khrushchev enjoyed making speeches, about almost anything. He would often depart from the prepared text and make jokes with the audience; the effect was often confusing for those watching.

Khrushchev's policies and ideology; de-Stalinisation

Facing up to the past

The Plenum (meeting) of the Central Committee, held in July 1953, marked a turning point in the governance of the Soviet Union. It was here that members admitted the state faced economic difficulties of grave proportions and open criticism of Stalin first occurred. Members were cautious about the nature of the criticism, but problems such as the lack of meetings of the committee (it had been 13 years since a formal meeting had been held) and abuses of power of their former leader were discussed. Khrushchev wanted to go further than his colleagues in denouncing the excesses of the Stalinist regime, most likely because he was aware that, with Gulag prisoners returning, soon the truth about the repression under Stalin would find its way to the masses and threaten the leadership's position. The dilemma was, how much should the public know and would it prove fatal to the leadership if they found out too much?

Khrushchev managed to convince the Presidium to launch a commission. This was to be undertaken by Pospelov, a former editor of Pravda and, according to Medvedev (1977), another man heavily implicated in the purges of the 1930s. His remit was to explore 'the terror' and particularly 'counter-revolutionary crimes' that had been committed during the 1930s and 1940s. According to his memoirs, Khrushchev was shocked by the extent of the abuses of Stalin's power. This must have been at least, in part, disingenuous, for all of them had blood on their hands. Khrushchev himself had been responsible for up to 250 000 arrests in the Ukraine during the 1930s. In the early 1950s, with Stalin's succession not fully resolved, the garrulous (talkative) former peasant had to tread carefully.

Khrushchev's 'secret speech'

Khrushchev wanted to make a speech to the party about the results of the commission so that he could control the information the party received without implicating any of the inner circle. He managed to persuade Molotov and Kaganovich that he would give a 'secret speech' to a closed session of the Twentieth Party Congress (with only Communist Party members from the Soviet Union present) on 25 February 1956.

Khrushchev spoke for nearly five hours on 'the cult of personality and its consequences', beginning with the suppressed last testament of Lenin. After this he seemed to skip from 1924 to 1934, detailing the fabrication of evidence used to purge party members and implicating Stalin in the murder of Kirov (who was still highly regarded). He even criticised Stalin's blunders at the beginning of the Second World War. Khrushchev carefully avoided the Bukharin, Trotsky, Zinoviev trials, and studiously left out any mention of the brutal treatment of the people under collectivisation or the First Five Year Plan, so that it seemed that Stalin's crimes were limited to the party. By leaving out the people of Russia and placing the blame almost solely on the dead, Khrushchev firmly limited the permissible areas for discussion and criticism, and placed the collective leadership at the forefront in ensuring the future of the party.

Crucially, Khrushchev managed to criticise the worst features of Stalinism without undermining the Stalinist system itself, for that would have undermined the legitimacy of the collective leadership. To achieve this, the commission agents spent sleepless nights rifling through Lenin's works to find appropriate quotations which would condemn the personality cult, thereby diverting attention away from the Socialist system onto the individual leader. However, Khrushchev's revelations sparked uprisings in Poland and Hungary in 1956, as the legitimacy of Soviet control was simultaneously undermined in his speech. The Hungarian revolt resulted in the Soviet invasion of the country. This prompted firm limits on de-Stalinisation, halting the cultural thaw (discussed in a later section) and represents the impact that foreign policy had on domestic trends during this period. Khrushchev did win personal political points amongst the Russian public, by taking time to explain the Leningrad Affair of 1948, carried out largely by Malenkov (on orders of Stalin). This sealed Malenkov's fate as he was too closely associated with the former leader, and cemented Khrushchev's position as party leader until 1964.

Denouncing Stalin

Even though Khrushchev's 'secret speech' was widely discussed, it was not until 1961 that he managed to criticise Stalin the person, prompting a full wave of anti-Stalinism following the Twenty-Second Party Congress. By then, almost 9 million prisoners had been released from the Gulags and special work-camps from across the Soviet Union, and it simply would not do to ignore the ordinary civilians who had suffered under the terror. Thus, it was here that Khrushchev finally acknowledged that the people of Russia, not just the party, had suffered under Stalin. One emotional member listening to the speech suggested she had experienced a dream the night before, where Lenin wept at the thought of Stalin resting beside him. Therefore, for symbolic emphasis, Stalin's embalmed body was removed from the hall he shared with Lenin and buried beneath the Kremlin wall. Donald Filtzer (1993) suggests that the renewed attack upon Stalin may have been used by Khrushchev to detract attention away from his own policies (see Section: 'Krushchev's attempts at agricultural reform') which by this time had become very unpopular.

Political and party change under Khrushchev

Khrushchev's reforms

Against the Presidium's wishes, Khrushchev had transcripts of the 'secret speech' given out to members at the closure of the Congress in 1956 so they could be read to regional party members. The speech was widely circulated and over 25 million members read it worldwide. A London newspaper even managed to acquire a copy of the speech and printed it in full. Yet for all the revelations, startlingly, nobody was dropped from the Presidium, and only two new members were added (Andrei Kirichenko and Mikhail Suslov). The composition of the Central Committee did change more radically, as almost half those elected in 1952 were replaced by Khrushchev's old associates from the Ukraine and Moscow; for example Shepilov replaced Molotov as foreign minister. Khrushchev's hand in this was evident.

Voices from the past

Khrushchev delivered his 'secret speech' on the cult of personality and its consequences at a closed session of the Twentieth Party Congress on 25 February 1956.

… After Stalin's death the Central Committee adopted a strict and consistent line of explaining that it was alien and unacceptable to Marxist-Leninism to elevate a single individual and turn him into some kind of superman with godlike, supernatural qualities. This person supposedly knows everything, sees everything, thinks for everyone and can do anything; he is without fault in his actions.

Such a conception of an individual, specifically, Stalin, was fostered in our country for many years …

Since not everyone understands what the personality cult led to in practice and what immense damage was done by the violation of the principle of collective leadership within the Party and the concentration of unlimited power in one person's hands, the Party Central Committee considers it necessary to report on the matter to the 20th Congress of the Communist Party of the Soviet Union …

It turns out that many of the people working in the Party, Soviet and economic apparatus who were declared to be 'enemies' in 1937–8 were in fact never communists. They had been slandered and sometimes, unable to withstand bestial torture, accused themselves of all sorts of serious and improbable crimes, as dictated by interrogator-falsifiers … It has been established that, of the 139 members and candidate-members of the Party CC elected at the 17th Congress, 98 were arrested and shot, mainly in 1937–8. That is 70%. (*consternation in the hall*) … We know that 80% of the voting delegates to the 17th Congress had joined the party in the days of revolutionary underground or during the Civil War, that is, up to 1920. As for their social position, most of the delegates were workers (60% of the voting delegates).

Taken from Acton, Edward & Stableford, Tom (2007), pp. 308–9 '*The Soviet Union: A Documentary History*', Volume *2: 1939–1991*

Discussion Points

1. How does Khrushchev distance himself from the terror of the 1930s?
2. Why does Khrushchev discuss Leninism at the beginning of the speech?
3. Who, according to Khrushchev, were the main victims of the terror? Why might Khrushchev have sought to create this impression?

Tackling corruption

After the Congress, Khrushchev became Prime Minister in 1958 (according to the wishes of the Presidium) and tried to weed out corruption in the party and the government by ending secret envelopes of cash bonuses, paid to officials who had met their targets. He also ended other perks, such as chauffeurs and private cars for factory directors,. He also instigated 'Rule 25' which limited the number of years any official could stay in office. This caused a higher turnover of regional party structures and seemingly made secretaries less loyal or reliant upon Khrushchev in the long run, as party members sought to cling together to save themselves rather than rely on those above, as had often occurred in the past. The historian Martin McCauley (1995) suggests Khrushchev was an 'evangelist, he was as full of eloquence as he was empty of doubt about the ultimate communist goal.[6]' Khrushchev did all this in the name of a return to true 'Leninism', about which several historians suggest he knew little, and building a true socialist nation in the Soviet Union. Yet, in doing away with abuses of power, Khrushchev almost certainly built enemies within the party who would sow the seeds of his own downfall, particularly as many of his policies sought to concentrate power in his own hands, just as Stalin's policies had done.

Institutional reform

Khrushchev decided, in November 1962, to reform the institutions of the Communist Party that were responsible for economic progress. He split each local party committee in two; half would be responsible for agriculture and half for industry. This was partly because of the reforms that had taken place in industry and agriculture. It caused competition and resentment between the two sectors as now those organising the workers had no interest in helping the agricultural

Voices from the past

POLAND: After Stalin's death and Khrushchev initiating 'de-Stalinisation', many debates arose in the Eastern European territories that had been captured at the end of the Second World War. Although Poland's population was largely happy to pursue Socialism, they wanted to have much more autonomy over their governance. Poznan (largest industrial city) experienced waves of mass strikes in June [1956]– the Soviet officers organised the Polish army, who reacted brutally, killing 57 (although unofficial figures are higher) and over 250 people were arrested.

HUNGARY: In Hungary, spontaneous revolts broke out all over the country against Soviet imposed policies. Students began the protests in Budapest, emboldened by the removal of the General Secretary (former Prime Minister) Mátyás Rákosi – a cruel leader. Very quickly the protests spread across the country. As the government collapsed and Soviet troops rolled in, thousands organised themselves into militias. In November, a large Soviet force invaded Budapest and other regions of the country. Over 2500 Hungarians and 700 Soviet troops were killed in the conflict, and 200 000 Hungarians fled as refugees after 13 000 were imprisoned for their part in the disturbances. Mass arrests and denunciations continued for months thereafter. The USA donated $6 million dollars in aid (after appeals made by the 21-year-old Elvis Presley on the Ed Sullivan show) and the International Red Cross sent approximately $50 million dollars to the Hungarian people. In spite of this, by January 1957, the new Soviet-installed government had suppressed all public opposition.

According to John Lewis Gaddis (2005), pressure from Communist China as well as threats of the revolts spreading into the Soviet Union forced Khrushchev to act with such force to crush the attempted revolutions.

ACTIVITY 4.4

Consider the type of leadership operating in the Soviet Union under Khrushchev. You have seen autocracy under the Tsars, the dictatorship of Lenin and the totalitarian dictatorship of Stalin. How would you describe Khrushchev's leadership?

sector. It had always been a tradition that, at harvest time, workers would return to the countryside to assist peasant farmers in collecting the yield, but now they would not help them. The reform also caused much confusion at harvest time, for example, when it became very unclear whose responsibility it was to provide the transport to collect the foodstuffs to take to the factories for processing. By April 1964 Khrushchev was complaining that the local committees were acting like the organisations they had replaced, which was not surprising given that the staff and working methods were the same. There were no clear lines of demarcation between industrial and agricultural committees and therefore confusion reigned, meaning little, if anything, was achieved by this reform.

Economic and social developments

Changes in industrial organisation from Stalin to Khrushchev

Industry

As he had done in 1929, Stalin instigated another punishing Five Year Plan (this was the fourth plan and ran from 1946 to 1950) which was designed to restore the economy to pre-war levels. It was successful, to an extent, for industry. This was a mammoth task given the calamitous losses incurred during the war, the greatest of all being 26 million or so dead, 70% of whom had been men. This meant many women stayed in the labour force even after the war out of necessity because of the high food prices and low incomes, and few had a husband to support them.

The first year of the plan, perhaps unsurprisingly, failed as it took time to return soldiers to peacetime work, rebuild factories and switch war industry production to traditional goods. The socio-economic and psychological impact of the war also has to be taken into consideration. Almost a million illegitimate children were born in 1949 alone, and war veterans, invalids and displaced peoples crowded the cities looking for work and shelter. In many ways, the chaos after the war was just as punishing as the war itself. The minor miracle in the economic recovery was

 Voices from the past

China had become Communist in 1949 after a prolonged Civil War and Mao Zedong was pronounced the Chairman of the Chinese Communist Party (and leader of the nation). Stalin was broadly supportive and the two countries became close over the Korean War, which began in 1950. The roots of this war were established during the closing days of the Second World War: in August 1945, the Soviet Union declared war on Japan and – by agreement with the United States – occupied Korea north of the 38th parallel. US forces subsequently occupied the south. The occupying powers had set up two separate governments by 1948. Both governments claimed to be the legitimate government of Korea, and neither side accepted the border as permanent.

The conflict escalated into open warfare when North Korean forces – supported by the Soviet Union and China – invaded South Korea on 25 June 1950. When Khrushchev became undisputed leader of the USSR and suggested that the Soviet Union should pursue a policy of **peaceful coexistence** with the USA (to avoid war which the USSR could not afford and would almost certainly lose). Chairman Mao lost respect for him, as he believed they should continue to be belligerent. This not only lost Khrushchev a vital ally in world politics, but caused a great deal of trepidation amongst the Communist leadership too.

undoubtedly helped by the forced labour of at least 2 million prisoners of war and the ability of the Russian people to endure severe privations.

By 1950, it was claimed by the government that industrial production was 73% above the 1940 levels. This was almost certainly an exaggeration, but the achievement overall was astounding. Conditions in the cities were not much better than before the war; in fact, in some cases they were worse as those who no longer had to live in air raid shelters or dug-outs shared cramped apartments. The punitive currency reform introduced in 1947 meant that disposable incomes no longer greatly exceeded the value of goods and services on offer. Cash was exchanged at the rate of one new ruble for ten old ones, so the intelligentsia and peasants with savings were hit hardest. The fifth Five Year Plan (1951–5) was less ambitious than the fourth and essentially brought all of the factories back into production. Russia's scientists had by this time developed the atomic bomb and there had been rebuilding of military armaments and the Red Army itself. Stalin could have rightly argued that by 1953 the Soviet Union had never been stronger.

Industry under Khrushchev

Despite overall growth in industry under Khrushchev, in 1964 the Soviet Union remained an economy of imbalances (see Table 4.1 for figures). This meant that although some areas were successful, others weren't – inflation was hidden from records, as was poor labour discipline, and of course the USSR still lagged behind almost every other developed country in terms of consumer goods. Although Khrushchev had borrowed Malenkov's plan for industry by focusing the Seven Year Plan (1959–65) on light industry and consumer goods, it was again heavy industry that saw the biggest expansion under his premiership. Production had increased immeasurably under Stalin but at the expense of the quality of the goods produced. Gosplan, the highly centralised planning agency, was organised so that each sector of industry was supervised by its own ministry. The ministry communicated plans and targets to factories but without specifying wages, supplies or productivity per workers or directing where finished products should be sent. The system of organisation has been referred to as a 'Command Economy' where industry produced goods according to plan, not need. The weaknesses of this system were manifold: the factories had to compete for resources and fuel just to run; the factory managers competed for low-level assignments so they could over-achieve their targets (and win a promotion to party level operations); figures of production were distorted at every level, there were chronic shortages in almost everything due to plans being created (and stuck rigidly to) five years in advance. Perhaps the largest problem the command system created under Stalin was the 'incompleteness' of almost all products. Often, the majority of the components needed for a product were made at separate factories, then assembled at another, but often something was missing, usually lightweight metals (for example, there were frequent shortages of nails because they were so light and cheap they didn't help factories achieve their targets, so nobody bothered to make them).

Khrushchev's changes

Khrushchev weakened the power of the ministries by creating Regional Economic Councils (*sovnarkhozy*) in February 1957. This meant that regional councils controlled factories according to their location, not by the type of industry they made goods for, which was disastrous. This policy served to add another layer of bureaucracy as enterprises now had to deal with dozens of *sovnarkhozy* to coordinate the production of items, creating what Filtzer (1993) calls 'bureaucratic anarchy'. To overcome these problems, a reorganisation of Gosplan occurred, creating State Committees and Central Councils, all of which worked in parallel to the *sovnarkhozy*, only deepening the chaos. Alec Nove (1977) has pointed out that these reforms tried to solve a problem whilst leaving the basic bureaucratic planning structure in place. Therefore were always likely to fail.

In April 1956 Khrushchev repealed the Stalinist labour laws of 1940, which had made it illegal to change jobs, although it was still almost impossible for managers to sack workers without serious disciplinary violations having taken place. He also restored the power of the trade unions to be able to veto managerial orders to protect their members and he raised the minimum wage. He wanted to narrow the differentials between skilled and unskilled workers. This was an unpopular move and only served to reduce the incentive for higher output. It was even more

	1950	1955	1960	1965
Iron and steel products (million tons)				
Pig iron	19.2	33.3	46.8	66.2
Steel	27.3	45.3	65.3	91.0
Engineering industry				
Metal-cutting machine tools (1000 units)	70.6	117.0	156.0	186.0
Lorries (1000 units)	294.4	328.1	362.0	379.6
Tractors (1000 units)	117.0	163.0	239.0	355.0
Chemical industry				
Electric power (million kilowatt hours)	91.2	170.2	292.3	506.7
Oil (million tons)	37.9	70.8	147.9	242.9
Natural gas (billion cubic metres)	5.8	9.0	45.3	127.7
Coal (million tons)	261.1	389.9	509.6	577.7
Light industry				
Cotton cloth (million square metres)	2745	4227	4838	5499
Wool cloth (million square metres)	193	316	439	466

Table 4.1: Table to show industrial output 1953–64 (cited in Filtzer 1993, page 59).

difficult to narrow the differentials between different industries, as coal and steel workers had gained particular importance under Stalin, leaving those working in food and textiles with pitifully low pay in comparison. Khrushchev has been criticised, perhaps unfairly, for failing to acknowledge the domestic burden of women, therefore never maximising their productivity and limiting production outputs from almost a third of the workforce. In fact, much of the system which had developed under Stalin's Five Year Plans remained under Khrushchev because he tried to reform from within it, rather than change it wholesale.

Agriculture and the Virgin Lands scheme

Many peasants had hoped that by turning a blind eye to private cultivation during the war, the Government would abolish the *kolkhozy* after 1945. In fact by 1946 Stalin halted the drift towards privatisation, and production was once again transferred back to the Machine Tractor Stations (MTS) and its party organisation. This was disastrous given the post-war state of agriculture, practically all horse and mechanical power had evaporated due to the ravages of war and the *kolkhozy* had been severely neglected in favour of private plots. The 1945 harvest produced less than 60% of the pre-war harvests and drought exacerbated issues further in 1946. The following year, as part of the Fourth Five Year Plan, approximately 14 million hectares of land were returned to the collective farms and 140,000 cattle recovered. However, productivity sank lower than 1913 levels and famines swept through the Soviet Union in 1947, partly due to drought, and by 1953 the State had less cattle than in 1916, to feed a population which had grown by at least 30 million. The harvests of 1949 to 1953 were catastrophically low, producing 800 kilogrammes per hectare (even in 1914 it had been 700 kilogrammes). In 1946 the average days labour bought in less than one ruble, not enough for even a third of a loaf of bread; so in order to survive, people stole grain.

As historian Kevin McDermott (2006) convincingly argues, Russian socialised agriculture remained the weak link in the Soviet economy beyond even Stalin's death. In fact the only innovation in agriculture during and after the war came from the pseudo-scientist Trofim Lysenko, a self-proclaimed agronomist (expert in soil management and crop production). He forwarded theories such as hybridisation to create new species of plants resistant to the Soviet climate. His theories implied that organisms could acquire characteristics and pass those on to descendants - for example, the state of being leafless as a result of having been plucked — would be passed on to the organism's descendants. This was ideological pseudo-science, which severely limited any development in agriculture, as criticism of Lysenko was branded 'bourgeois', primarily because of his working class background. Part of Lysenko's influence can be seen in the grandiose twenty-year campaign undertaken by Stalin in 1948 to plant belts of trees across the southern steppe to prevent soil erosion. Over 5.7 million hectares were to be forested, the majority being paid for by farmers; the scheme was a resounding failure as the trees simply did not grow.

Khrushchev's attempts at agricultural reform

Khrushchev's peasant background led him to believe he was an expert in agricultural matters. In fact, it was the area of policy he intervened in most, either through replacing ministers of agriculture or directly influencing policy on crop rotation. He also used agriculture to strengthen the party, reducing the power of the Ministry of Agriculture by putting local party secretaries in charge of Machine Tractor Stations (MTS). Initially, what he wanted was to expand agricultural output, as peasants had been deprived and persecuted by the Stalinist regime for almost 20 years. Output and morale were chronically low by 1953. After visiting the USA (he was the first Russian leader to do so), and seeing Iowa, the corn capital of America, he became convinced of his course. At first, Khrushchev settled for amalgamating the kolkhozy (collective farms) into **sovkhozy** (state farms) which caused severe social distress in some areas and much upheaval in the countryside. Although smaller collective farms benefited from this scheme, many peasants did not like change and were suspicious of it. However, Khrushchev raised pay to incentivise peasants to work as hard on the collective plots as their private plots and donated more livestock as compensation. The number of kolkhozy fell from 125 000 in 1950 to 69 100 in 1958 as a result of Khrushchev's policies and output of grain rose dramatically in the state sector – up 75% in 1953–8.

Khrushchev's policy on opening up 'Virgin Lands' for cultivation was presented as the ideologically pure alternative to Malenkov's idea of enlarging the peasants' private plots. It seems he genuinely believed that the Soviet Union could achieve American levels of grain production using this method. He also knew that industrial bosses would never allow the redistribution of resources to favour agriculture, so he sought short-term measures and took huge risks to increase yield levels. Khrushchev's schema, developed as part of a Seven Year Plan

Key term

Sovkhozy refers to state-owned farms where peasants would be paid a salary, rather than them owning the land collectively (called *kolkhozy*). Some have described this as 'neo-serfdom' as peasants had to have an internal passport to move from the *sovkhozy*, as they had prior to 'Emancipation' in 1861.

(1959–65) involved ploughing 40 million square hectares of 'virgin land' which was situated in the steppelands of Kazakhstan and parts of Siberia, previously uncultivated because of the poor climate and because the Kazakh people had used the land for livestock in the past. Leaders of the Kazakh Communist Party Committee warned Khrushchev about the infertile soil and poor climate, although really they took issue with his idea of sending Russians and Ukrainians to work their land. A huge propaganda campaign ensued, inviting young *komsomol* members to try a new life in the Virgin Lands, and many were taken in by the promises of utopia that Khrushchev promised. The reality was very different: in the first two years over 10 million square hectares of land were taken out of use because the land was indeed unsuitable for growing crops (as the Kazakh leaders had warned). It was not just the land that was difficult. Amenities had not been thoroughly planned before sending the young, inexperienced party members out to these tough lands. Hastily constructed army barracks housed hundreds, not creating the ideal family life many had hoped for; some didn't even have a canteen, forcing them to travel almost two hours to the nearest barracks to get breakfast. The lack of schools, housing, facilities and assistance in farming the infertile lands meant that many left within the first two years of the scheme to go back to the cities to gain jobs there.

Although 1956 yielded an excellent harvest, the following year was disastrous and proved extremely expensive, as specialised chemical fertilisers were needed to cultivate this arid landscape. The chemical industry was simply not able to keep up with the demands; investment had always been weak in this industry due to competing interests from the defence and heavy industries, which always won resources.

Figure 4.6: The plans for the Virgin Lands Scheme, 1956

Figure 4.7: Poster entitled 'Break virgin lands!', published c.1954. Posters showing the effectiveness of the Soviet Union's mechanised farming were common in Soviet propaganda.

Khrushchev suggested that the Soviet Union should grow maize as the Americans did, ignoring the good reasons Russian farmers had for not growing maize before, namely climate and soil. Nevertheless, Khrushchev's enthusiasm for the scheme won the day and thousands of hectares of grain were displaced to cultivate maize. In many cases, it never ripened and over one-third of meadowland was abandoned as a result. This caused a fall in hay production, which also had the knock-on effect of reducing meat production. Khrushchev's mistakes were costly. His solution was to create new ploughs; he suggested that more ploughing would surely help the crop grow in Soviet soil. The new machines were hastily made and did not tackle weed infestation (as the old ones had), so farmers were forced to leave 20% of their fields fallow. This led to mass soil erosion in the virgin lands, creating vast swathes of dusty, infertile fields. Just as Stalin had, Khrushchev sought advice from the charlatan agronomist Lysenko (see Sections on 'Political authority and government to 1953'; 'High Stalinism'; 'Agriculture'), who suggested early sowing would help cultivation in the virgin lands; however, drought plagued the Soviet Union in 1963 leading to the loss of millions of hectares of fields due to soil erosion.

Meat production

Khrushchev promised the people in 1961, at the Twenty-Second Party Congress, that by 1980 the Soviet Union would have overtaken the USA in meat production. This would have meant trebling the figures which, to anyone who knew anything about agriculture, was impossible. Still, it was characteristic of Khrushchev that he didn't heed advice and instructed the local party secretaries to carry out the plan. One particular secretary (by the name of Larionov) was very keen to impress and managed to treble meat supplies in the region of Ryazan within a year. He did this by foolishly slaughtering every animal in sight, even young animals not really ready for slaughter; he even ordered the slaughter of the region's dairy herds and had to buy meat from other nearby regions to complete his targets. He later committed suicide when his actions were uncovered. The upshot of this was to increase levels of bureaucracy by implementing measures that restricted the number of slaughters that could take place on a *sovkhozy*. This had the unintended consequence of livestock building up and being wasted, as they became too old to slaughter in the state farms, and animals often became a drain on resources.

Abandoning the machine tractor stations (MTS)

In 1958, owing to a bad harvest the year before, Khrushchev decided that farms needed access to better equipment, which was in part true. It was decided that the MTS should be abolished. By January 1959, around 8000 MTS had been abandoned, leaving only 39 remaining. The effect of the speed of this reform was devastating: *sovkhozy* were forced to buy the machinery from the MTS, which was often old and damaged. Workers who operated the machinery left agriculture altogether, as working for the MTS had come with benefits, which were not found in *sovkhozy*. This left machines which farmers couldn't operate idle in fields and many state farms returned to harvesting crops by hand, ruining production levels. The machinery was sold to farmers at artificially high prices too, leaving them no money for investment in other projects such as dairy production, which was also desperately needed. Donald Filtzer (1993) offers the example that for a farm to purchase four new tractor tyres, they would have had to have sold 13 tonnes of wheat, putting enormous strain on the *sovkhozy*. The cumulative effect of these policies was to create milk scarcity and force prices up in 1962. This provoked disturbances in Novocherkassk (near the Ukrainian border) so severe that armed garrisons from nearby towns had to be brought in to quell the rioters, killing 22 and injuring 39 of the demonstrators.

Khrushchev's agricultural reforms: an assessment

Khrushchev's policies in agriculture revealed much about the man himself: he was enthusiastic and garrulous, yet had little time for detailed planning, which often led to the failure of his plans. There is no doubt that agriculture was a problem which needed long-term reforms, as it had been neglected since Stolypin's reforms begun in 1906. However, some of the schemes were simply ill-conceived. Khrushchev believed that the decision-making apparatus should be moved out of Moscow and nearer to the rural areas affected, so it moved. The workers, however, didn't move, meaning a commute time of 3.5 hours each way over poorly-laid roads. He also decided, in the interests of equality, that executive staff should carry out menial tasks alongside their manual worker colleagues. Within a year, 1700 of 2200 had handed in their notice, creating a huge gap in knowledge and experience at the ministry. By 1963, another dismal harvest forced the government to dip into the precious gold reserves (which declined from 13.1 million tonnes in 1954 to 6.3 million tonnes in 1963) and purchase meat and grain from the West. Khrushchev's agricultural policies had failed, and he had alienated a great number of supporters along the way.

Social and cultural change from Stalin to Khrushchev

Social change under Stalin 1945-53

Living standards for ordinary Russian people had not substantially improved under the fourth and fifth Five Year Plans. The quota system designed to raise output squeezed the peasants who were forced to live on an income 20% lower than that of an industrial worker. Diets remained poor and housing, services and consumer goods remained well below demands. The working week was maintained at wartime levels of 12 hours per day on average and again it was women who were expected to plug the gaps left by the war dead, making up one third of all workers in the building trade. The Stakhanovite programme, which had begun in 1935 and perpetuated throughout the war, was continued. This meant that workers could be relocated wherever they were most needed. Perhaps the most galling lack of change the people of the Soviet Union had to face was the continuation of wage differentials between party officials and ordinary workers. Due to a devaluation of the rouble in 1947, savings for many people were wiped out, eradicating their chance of providing a comfortable life for their family after the war. Inequality between the Party members and ordinary workers seemed to be growing wider again after the war.

Socialist legacy

Part of Khrushchev's drive to break from the worst excesses of Stalinism was to introduce 'Socialist legality' – that is, he introduced a new criminal code in December 1958. The statutes of December 1958 came into being as a result of a keen sense of dissatisfaction with the state of criminal law in the Soviet Union. The former code, created in 1926, conceived as a daring experiment and a novel approach to the problems of criminal repression, was not a success. It failed to provide a basis for the orderly administration of justice in the Soviet Union and because it had been constantly amended, it quickly became a shapeless mass of penal provisions lacking a central idea and even a formal order. The new code overturned the basis on which trials and convictions could take place and brought in what is known as 'due process' (legal requirement that the state must respect all of the legal rights that are owed to a person). In effect, the code was more of a propaganda exercise than a fundamental shift in legislation, for the Soviet Union remained a police state under Khrushchev, disappointing judges and lawyers who longed for more reform in this area.

It is important to note that after the release of the Gulag prisoners in 1956, the KGB was reformed. This was necessary for Khrushchev if his speech against Stalin was to mean anything. Many of the officials at the top were replaced by *komsomol* members, who had formed their careers in the party, not the police, and to this extent the KGB were a less mysterious and threatening organ. The government also introduced a new punitive 'Parasite Law' in 1957, which effectively created armies of citizens who would inform the authorities of those vagrants who were not undertaking paid work. Khrushchev also moved to restore the death penalty for large-scale economic crimes in 1961; it was even applied retrospectively to two currency dealers who had amassed a fortune of 2 million rubles, and were duly executed on the orders of Khrushchev. In spite of Khrushchev's rhetoric, the security system overall remained politically authoritarian and clearly still

Key term

Polytechnical education was first advanced by Marx and was developed by Lenin as a means of producing a classless society. The purpose was to provide young people with the knowledge and understanding of the means of production, along with providing labour training and skills. It was different to a classical education because much of the training was vocational. It was intended to prepare students to take on careers in an industrialised Soviet Union.

dominated over the legal system. At the same time it was less feared; it never enjoyed the respect or levels of social control that it had before under Stalin.

Pension, education and housing reform

Pensions were raised from 10 to 30 rubles per month, which allowed the elderly to live on the poverty line for the first time. In efforts to tackle disparity in society between the unskilled and skilled workers in factories, Khrushchev attempted two policies. The first was simple wage increase: wages in both the agricultural and industrial sectors increased under Khrushchev (an estimated 7% increase in 1953–64) although consumer goods production remained low, so wages were increasingly spent on food, as there was little else to buy. His second policy aimed at tackling inequality focused on education; he was genuinely shocked at how few officials had a working class background. In 1958 Khrushchev abolished the fees for secondary schools and colleges which had been introduced under Stalin. The number of students enrolled in higher educational institutions rose from 1.25 million in 1950 to 3.6 million in 1964–5. Khrushchev also re-established **polytechnical education**, which Lenin had sought to develop in 1922. The polytechnical elements of education were limited to vocational training with work experience in factories as part of the senior students' timetables. Many workers and factory bosses opposed this policy on grounds of health and safety; students would often get in the way as they wouldn't have a job to complete. Many of the intelligentsia also complained that academic standards were lowered as a result of Khrushchev's tinkering with the system, so work experience was gradually rolled back again by the 1960s.

Khrushchev wanted to improve living conditions for the people and could see that providing housing stock, which was in woeful supply in the towns and cities, was the first step towards this. The new apartment blocks were called *Khrushchoby* (playing on the leader's name and the Russian word for slum, 'choby'). Like much that was produced in the Soviet Union, they were low-cost and looked uniformly dull. Between 1955 and 1964, the nation's housing stock nearly doubled, from 640 to 1182 million square metres. Produced as concrete-panelled or brick three- to five-storied apartment buildings, they did provide families with some form of privacy, unlike those built under the Stalinist regime which had been blocks where kitchen and bathroom facilities were shared. However, for all the social reforms undertaken during Khrushchev's premiership, some policies remained. Churches were systematically persecuted throughout Khrushchev's rule, leaving only 7560 churches standing by 1964. Mosques and synagogues fared slightly better (12 000 mosques and 60 synagogues survived), perhaps because of the continued tensions amongst the nationalities within the union.

ACTIVITY 4.6

Since the beginning of the period under study (1855) personal, political and religious freedom has been curtailed by each leader in various ways. Some historians have suggested that Khrushchev represents a break from the leaders before him in that he allowed more subversive writings to be published. Do you agree?

ACTIVITY 4.5

Go back through your notes and consider how successful Khrushchev was at surmounting the problems facing the Soviet Union. It may help to put your notes into a table

	Successes	Failures
Agriculture		
Industry		
Living conditions		
Education		
The Party		
Opposition		

Opposition to Khrushchev

Cultural dissidents

After the Twentieth Congress (1956), statues and pictures of Stalin were removed from public display spontaneously, and the intelligentsia began to demand greater freedoms, which they were reluctantly given. A weight seemed to be lifted from the ordinary citizens as well as writers; there are stories of families getting together to share poetry or banned literature for the first time, unafraid of repercussions. Once Stalinist conformity had been removed, writers began to move away from the public themes and heroes of 'Socialist Realism' and strived to depict Soviet life with more sincerity and honesty. Illya Ehrenburg's novel '*The Thaw*'(1954) characterises the period well, although much of the cultural thaw at this time has been associated with Malenkov's reforms rather than Khrushchev. As the thaw gathered momentum, the leadership became more concerned about its own power being undermined and so censorship once again set in. The fears were heightened by uprisings in Poland and Hungary and the thaw was halted. The most famous example is that of Boris Pasternak, who was never allowed to print his novel '*Dr Zhivago*', which was set just after the Bolshevik revolution of 1917, and painted a fairly bleak view of Russian life. He was expelled from the Soviet Writers' Union and denounced in the press; those close to him suggested the harassment he suffered brought on his premature death in 1960.

The second wave of de-Stalinisation occurred after the Twenty-Second Party Congress in 1961, where the intellectual thaw seemed to be encouraged by Khrushchev with his usual dynamism. Stalingrad was renamed Volgograd in 1961 (incidentally, never again were cities allowed to be renamed after party members). Perhaps the best-known example of the wave of de-Stalinisation was the publication of '*One Day in the Life of Ivan Denisovich*' by Aleksandr Solzhenitsyn from 1962, which portrays the horror of the Gulags. Khrushchev had endorsed it personally, against the wishes of the Presidium.

Yet again, the cultural climate deteriorated after the Cuban Missile Crisis and in 1963, Khrushchev began publicly to praise Stalin's services to Communism and warned against criticising him too much. Once again, Khrushchev was on the defensive after several policy blunders in agriculture and in foreign policy, and his rivals in the Presidium were keen to protect their positions as they feared that criticism would soon be levelled at them.

In the early 1960s, the Russian literature journal, '*Novy Mir*', changed its political stance from being a Communist propaganda promoter to a more dissident position. In November 1962, the magazine had a circulation of about 150 000 copies per month and became famous for publishing Solzhenitsyn's novella. The magazine continued publishing controversial articles and stories about various aspects of Soviet and Russian history despite the fact that its editor-in-chief, Alexander Tvardovsky, who faced significant political pressure, resigned in February 1970. Solzhenitsyn was eventually expelled from the Soviet Union in 1974, but many others, such as the ballet dancer Rudolf Nureyev, faced so much harassment they simply defected to the West during the 1960s.

Communist divisions: hardliners and reformers

There is no doubt that within a year of the Twentieth Party Congress held in 1956, a significant number of the Presidium felt that de-Stalinisation had gone too far, that 'peaceful coexistence' with the West was humiliating for the Soviet Union and that Khrushchev's economic reforms reduced the power of the ministries far too much. By June 1957 an alliance, which Khrushchev referred to as the 'Anti-Party Group', launched their attack on the high-handed leader. Molotov, Malenkov, Kaganovich and Bulganin led the *putsch* (supported by three others) by calling on the Presidium to replace Khrushchev with Molotov and demoting the leader to Minister of Agriculture. Khrushchev was accused of economic voluntarism (the notion that determination and fervour could generate economic miracles) because of his capricious and rash policies, but the main charge was in condemning Stalin and thereby undermining the CPSU and Communist movement internationally. The military hero, Zhukov, supported Khrushchev vigorously and suggested that the military would follow his orders too, but Khrushchev managed to save himself. He argued that only the Central Committee could remove him from his post. The Central Committee plenum met from 22–29 June and they almost unanimously agreed to support the former peasant leader; only Molotov abstained from the resolution to keep Khrushchev in office.

The Presidium was enlarged again to 15 members, bringing in Zhukov, Brezhnev and Kozlov, who had robustly defended their leader during the plenum. In this way, Khrushchev had shifted the balance of power so that those holding party posts now dominated the inner circle. The way in which Khrushchev dealt with his rivals reveals how much things had changed in the Soviet Union after Stalin's death, for under him they would almost certainly have been shot, and they knew it. Kaganovich is reported to have called the leader fearing for his life, but Khrushchev berated him for measuring others by his own vile intentions. None of

Khrushchev's opponents were expelled from the party, but were simply moved out of Moscow. Bulganin was allowed to stay on as Prime Minister until the following year, when Khrushchev replaced him. Zhukov too, despite his display of loyalty, had proved too independent a Minister of Defence, introducing military reforms in 1957 without consulting the party, and was removed from office. Khrushchev's rivals were demoted in a most humiliating way: Malenkov became the Minister for Electricity and Molotov was posted to Mongolia. After this, it was clear that all the glamorous posts the party could offer would be Khrushchev's; however, his refusal to use coercion against his rivals meant that he needed legitimacy to maintain his status.

Opponents of Khrushchev and his fall from power

Tensions were mounting throughout 1961–2 due to the evident failures of Khrushchev's industrial and agricultural policies; there had even been mass uprisings in Novocherkassk in 1962 due to acute shortages and rising food prices. In spite of these issues, it was Khrushchev's humiliating climb down from the Cuban Missile Crisis and lack of support in the Central Committee which sealed his fate. Criticisms levelled at him were personal ones about his hot-headed impetuosity and recklessness, and condemned his personal rule; even his age was mentioned as a factor (he was 70), which was unfair given his continued energy and good health.

Khrushchev set out the New Party Programme in 1961, which aimed to replace that of 1919. In it he loudly trumpeted successes that had been achieved under his leadership (which were limited) and flamboyantly discussed the speed at which the Soviet system would outperform its capitalist rivals in the West. He was, of course, talking about the final transition of the revolution, from Socialism to Communism, where goods that were already being produced in abundance could now be distributed according to need. With 'breath-taking optimism' (Acton

ACTIVITY 4.7

Study the timeline, which shows some of the key events after Stalin's death. Some domestic developments have been left out. Go back through your notes and use them to complete the timeline.

ACTIVITY 4.8

Carry out research into some of the international events of the Cold War to understand more fully what happened here.

Voices from the past

The young President Kennedy wanted to make an impression in foreign policy so devised the Bay of Pigs invasion (April 1961) to oust the new revolutionary Communist leader of Cuba, Fidel Castro. The CIA and Cuban emigrés made a series of blunders and the invasion failed, pushing Castro towards the Soviet Union for protection. Following this as a sign of strength, Khrushchev built the Berlin Wall, physically separating Western and Eastern sectors of Berlin. The American government, afraid of Soviet superiority in arms production, began a strategic build-up of long-distance missiles. By October 1962, Khrushchev had promised Castro some Soviet missiles and work had begun preparing the ground for their arrival. The Americans discovered the missile sites and imposed a naval blockade around the small Caribbean island to prevent missiles reaching it. A series of tense letters, phone calls and secret negotiations ensued between the adversaries. After 13 days in October, Kennedy secretly agreed to remove all missiles set in southern Italy and in Turkey, in exchange for Khrushchev removing all missiles from Cuba. The compromise humiliated Khrushchev and the Soviet Union because the withdrawal of US missiles from Italy and Turkey was kept secret under Kennedy's instructions. Khrushchev had approached Kennedy worried that the crisis was getting out of hand and therefore the Soviets were seen as retreating from circumstances that they had started.

and Stableford (2007)), Khrushchev proclaimed that this would occur within two decades, even though the Soviet Union was far from material abundance. His sweeping speeches boldly declared that Leninist legality had been re-established when, in reality, he himself was beginning to following some of the same policies, albeit not at the same level, as Stalin had. His days were numbered after this.

The campaign to rid the Soviet Union of Khrushchev's leadership was mounted in February 1964 after a catalogue of blunders, both on a national level and at party level too. He had managed to offend or alienate almost all of his old allies through his arbitrary style of leadership. Meanwhile, the cult of Khrushchev's personality had reached dizzying heights, where his face would appear in newspapers almost daily and a film bearing his name was set for general release in the same month. Reports from those close to him suggest that Brezhnev considered poisoning him and even orchestrating a plane crash to dispose of the leader. Whatever the plans may have been, the eventual removal of Khrushchev was peaceful. Upon returning from a break in the Crimea on 12 October 1964, Khrushchev was warned by his son of a *coup.* McCauley (1995) suggests his naivety was staggering in refusing to believe the rumours. By 14 October a Central Committee plenum was held, indicting Khrushchev on 15 counts. Amongst a host of counts, he was accused of erratic leadership, of taking ill-considered decisions and of developing his own personality cult. Many of the criticisms were entirely justified as workers' welfare had declined, foreign relations were perhaps more tense than ever, industrial production slowed due to excessive bureaucracy and agricultural workers continued to suffer. Khrushchev was pensioned off with a city flat, a country home and 500 rubles per month.

Timeline

Year	Domestic Events
1945	May: Russians declare victory over Germany
1947	Cominform established
1949	**Comecon** founded First Soviet nuclear tests
1952	Doctors' Plot is unveiled
1953	Beria is executed USSR explodes the hydrogen bomb
1954	Virgin Lands Scheme begins KGB established
1956	Khrushchev delivers the 'secret speech' attacking the cult of personality
1957	Sputnik is launched into orbit
1962	*A Day in the Life of Ivan Denisovich* is published
1964	Khrushchev removed from power

The political, economic and social condition of the Soviet Union by 1964

The intensification of the Cold War during the 1950s saw a commitment from the Soviet government to amassing nuclear arms, at the expense of the living standards of average Soviet citizens, which were poor. In this way, the system perpetuated norms that had developed under Stalin. Success was measured in output statistics and political gains for the party, rather than the rights, liberties or values of individuals. The Soviet government under Khrushchev's leadership saw the first successful space flight in April 1961, immortalising Yuri Gagarin's name around the world. But with this glory came other world-renowned disasters, all of which reveal something of Khrushchev's personality and style of leadership, such as the building of the Berlin Wall, the Suez Crisis and the Cuban Missile Crisis. Khrushchev was a contradictory character, and the Soviet Union was a state of contradictions in 1964. Arguably, citizens had gained more freedoms than they'd had since the final years of Tsarism; they had better access to education and training, and enjoyed relatively higher wages than in the previous 30 years. However, living conditions remained pitiful in the newly-created apartment blocks and consumer goods were still a rarity, and only affordable to party officials and factory managers who managed to circumvent Khrushchev's anti-corruption policies to pay themselves bonuses. Levels of corruption would return ten-fold under Khrushchev's usurper, Brezhnev, and the conservatism Khrushchev had tried to reform once again set in.

For all his blunders and reorganisations and interference in policies – referred to by some as his 'petty tyranny', in many ways Khrushchev has been regarded as a great statesman. Geoffrey Hosking (1992) suggests that he, more than any of the collective leadership, had sensed the depth of problems facing the Soviet Union in 1953. However, he must be criticised for being unable to divorce his ideas from the Stalinist mould, particularly in terms of the economy. Nevertheless, it could hardly be imagined that Stalin would have been told to retire because he was too old and his policies annoyed the leadership. Perhaps this was Khrushchev's greatest contribution to the Soviet Union: he removed the fear of vengeful repercussions and allowed a degree of criticism within the party. Volkogonov (1998) argues that his attacks on the personality cult were superficial in many ways, yet it would be 'difficult to find another act of such political importance for the future of the country'.[7]

 Developing concepts

The following concepts have been very important in this section. For each one, write a definition of the concept and give an example of what it means in the context of the Soviet Union between 1945 and 1964.

- Nomenklatura
- Intelligentsia
- De-Stalinisation
- Cult of personality
- Conservatism
- Communist party
- Collective leadership

Summary of key events

- Khrushchev had secured his premiership of the Soviet Union in 1956 by delivering a 'secret speech' which denounced the worst excesses of the terror under Stalin.

- Khrushchev attempted to reform agriculture by opening up new lands and encouraging even larger collective farms, but this was largely unsuccessful.

- The people of the Soviet Union enjoyed better living conditions under Khrushchev, but this may have been due to peace and a maturing industrial economy rather than his policies.

- International relations dominated much of Khrushchev's time and his mistakes here cost him the leadership in 1964.

Conclusion

Orlando Figes (2014) argues that the revelation of the 'secret speech' was the beginning of the third and final phase of the revolution that began in 1917, leading to its collapse by 1990. Stalin's successors had feared that reform would lead to an unravelling of the entire system eventually, and they were proved right. Never again did the Soviet Union exist under a dictatorship, even if Khrushchev had wanted to impose this; he still relied on party votes to retain his position as party secretary and prime minister. Khrushchev had provided the break with the past, but in doing so had exposed fundamental problems with the system and his successors would struggle to find long-term solutions to them.

Practice essay questions

1. 'The lives of the Russian peasants were transformed in the years 1928 to 1964.' Assess the validity of this view.
2. 'The use of repression and terror by Stalin was much more effective after the Second World War than in the 1930s.' Assess the validity of this view.
3. 'Compared to Stalin's policies, Khrushchev's policy of de-Stalinisation had little effect upon the politics and the economy of the Soviet Union.' Assess the validity of this view.
4. With reference to these extracts and your understanding of the historical context, which of these two extracts provides the more convincing arguments in relation to Khrushchev's removal from power?

Extract A

He went not because he was reactionary and not because he was liberal, but because he was erratic, unpredictable, unmanageable, now increasingly dictatorial; because after a solid decade of incessant uproar about agriculture, food production was once more static and showed no signs of rising; because after all his economic plunging, industrial growth was slowing down most dangerously, consumer goods were still in short supply, and the quality of what was turned out was often atrocious; because the country was confused and bewildered, not stimulated any more, by his restless dynamism; …because, in the end he was showing signs of megalomania.

Crankshaw, E. '*Khrushchev*': Bloomsbury: 2011. Chapter 20

Extract B

The decade in the course of which N.S. Khrushchev stood at the head of the Soviet Communist Party and of the USSR was an interregnum and a provisorium. One cannot speak of a 'Khrushchev era' as one speaks of the Stalin era, not merely because Khrushchev was in office only one-third of the time Stalin had been, and exercised not even one-third of the power. Khrushchevism has not represented any great positive idea (or even policy) of its own. It did not even stand for a new canon or myth which might meaningfully express, as Socialism in One Country did, the 'false consciousness' of a real historic situation. Khrushchevism was devoid of any creative aspiration; whenever Khrushchev himself voiced any of the familiar and elementary purposes of socialism, he invariably produced a vulgar parody (a 'goulash communism'). In many respects he continued along lines long set by Stalin, but pretended that he was putting forward his own, breathtaking, innovations. 'Peaceful coexistence' is a case in point. So is the slogan of a 'peaceful transition from capitalism to socialism'. So are the 'national roads to socialism'. These are all refurbished Stalinist concepts dating back to the Popular Fronts of the middle 30s and the National Coalitions of the middle 40s. And Khrushchev was an epigone of Stalin above all in his emphasis on the 'monolithic character' of the Soviet party and state. His determination to tolerate no opposition, no open criticism, no free debate, inevitably led to the 'cult' of his own 'personality', that is to attempt at establishing his own autocratic rule.

(Source: socialistregister.com/index.php/srv/article/download/5945/2841 – accessed on 04/02/15)

Deutscher, I: *The Failure of Khrushchevism* (1965)

 Taking it further

'A substantial difference between theory and practice.' Assess the validity of this view with reference to the official view of social class between 1928 and 1964.

Further reading

If you are interested in literature about the Soviet Union during the Second World War, the best example is by Konstantin Simonov and is called *'Days and Nights'* (1945). The setting is the struggle for Stalingrad and demonstrates some of the tremendous sacrifices made by ordinary citizens during the war.

For an excellent overview of each of the political leaders, Dmitri Volkogonov's *'The Rise and Fall of the Soviet Empire'* (1998) is a clear and analytical read.

Chapter summary

After studying this period, you should be able to:

- evaluate why ordinary citizens suffered so much during the Second World War
- describe how the party changed after Stalin's death
- explain in which ways the Soviet Union was growing economically
- account for the stagnation of agriculture and the impact on Soviet citizens
- compare the Soviet Union in 1964 with that of 1861.

End notes

[1] Ward C. *Stalin's Russia:* 2nd edition: Hodder:1999, p.221

[2] Overy R. *Russia's War*: Penguin: 1997, p.82

[3] Overy R. *Russia's War*: Penguin: 1997, p.125

[4] Acton E. and Stableford T. *The Soviet Union: A Documentary History, Volume 2 1939-1991*: Liverpool University Press: 2007, p.87

[5] Service R. *The Penguin History of Modern Russia – From Tsarism to the Twenty First Century*: Allen Lane: 1997, p.226

[6] McCauley M. *The Khrushchev Era 1953-64*: Pearson: 1995, p.53

[7] Volkogonov D. *The Rise and Fall of the Soviet Empire: Political Leaders from Lenin to Gorbachev*: Harper Collins: 1998, p.201

Glossary

Autocracy — The system of government that existed in Russia until 1917 under the Tsars. All power was concentrated in the hands of the Tsar who had no legal restraints on his power.

Brest–Litovsk — A peace treaty signed on 3 March 1918 between the Bolshevik government of Russia and Germany. It effectively signified a Russian surrender and withdrawal from the First World War.

Comecon — Set up in 1949 in the Eastern bloc under the leadership of the Soviet Union as a response to the USA creating the Marshall Plan. The USA donated $17 billion dollars of aid to Western European countries. Comecon was formed to prevent Eastern European countries moving towards the Americans.

Constituent Assembly — The first democratically elected legislative body in Russian history, formed just after the October Revolution of 1917. It met for 13 hours before the Executive Committee (under Lenin's orders) dissolved it.

Constitutional Democrats (Kadets) — This party was formed of liberals in 1905 just after the announcement of the October Manifesto. Led by Pavel Miliukov, it favoured an eight-hour day but was committed to constitutional monarchy so worked within the Duma.

Council of State Defence (GKO) — This was created on June 30, 1941, a week after the invasion of the Soviet Union by the Nazi Germany. The situation at the front-lines required a more dictatorial form of government. Stalin sat as Chair. Molotov was his deputy (until May 16, 1944) and other members included Beria, Voroshilov and Malenkov.

Duma — Deriving its name from the Russian for 'consider', the State Duma was formed as a result of the 1905 Revolution under Nicholas II. It had legislative and advisory powers, however its power was severely curtailed under the Fundamental Laws issued by Nicholas II just before the opening of the Duma in May 1906.

Epigone — Less distinguished follower of someone

Fundamental Laws — These were a revision of the October Manifesto where Nicholas II sought to restore and restate his autocratic power, but allowing him the power to appoint or dismiss ministers. They were issued in May 1906 just before the state opening of the Duma.

Gulag — The acronym for the 'Main Camp Administration' which was administered by the state police and referred to the Soviet forced labour camp system which emerged in 1930. Although corrective labour camps had been used since the assassination attempt on Lenin in 1918, they were formally instituted under Stalin. The conditions in the Gulags became infamous and immortalised by writers such as Alexander Solzhenitsyn.

Interregnum — A period of discontinuity or a gap in a government or between monarchs.

KGB — Stands for the 'Committee for State Security' and operated from 1954 until the break-up of the Soviet Union in 1991. Derived from the Cheka, NKVD and MGB, it acted as the internal security force or secret police.

Left SRs | The Socialist Revolutionaries were split in 1917 between those who supported the Provisional Government (established during the February Revolution) and those who supported the Bolsheviks (the left SRs). In 1918 they revolted against the Bolsheviks who had signed the Treaty of Brest–Litovsk.

Monolithic character | Large, plain, uniform – not diverse in opinion

Octobrists | A party formed by a group of conservative liberals during the 1905 Revolution and called for Nicholas II to fulfil the October Manifesto, having said that it was fully committed to constitutional monarchy.

OGPU | Supposed to operate with more restraint than the Cheka, the All-Union State Political Administration was the secret police of the Soviet Union from 1922 to 1934. Felix Dzerzhinsky was the first chief of this state security branch, however by 1934 it became reincorporated into the NKVD.

Peaceful coexistence | Khrushchev's theory to deal with the capitalist West in an attempt to reduce hostility and avoid war which they could not afford.

Pogrom | A violent massacre or period of persecution against a minority, particularly Jews. The period 1881–4 saw over 200 pogroms carried out against Jews.

Politburo | An abbreviation of 'Political Bureau of the Central Committee of the Communist Party of the Soviet Union'. Founded in October 1917 by Lenin with seven members who would decide on questions too urgent to await the Central Executive Committee.

Populists | Also known as Narodniks, they formed a movement which sought to encourage the peasants to rise up against the Tsar in the 1870s. Most Narodniks were from the intelligentsia and inspired by the work of Alexander Herzen and Nikolai Chernychevsky. They tried to 'go to the people' to agitate revolutionary fervour in 1874 but the attempt failed.

Presidium | This was the highest body of the Supreme Soviet and became the leading office of the RSFSR between 1938 and 1964.

Procurator of the Holy Synod | Effectively, the lay head of the Russian Orthodox Church and a member of the Tsar's cabinet.

Progressive bloc | Formed when the State Duma was recalled during the First World War – several members, including the Progressists and the Kadets, formed a political front to push Nicholas II to form a 'Government of Confidence' where they could take control of the domestic war effort.

Provisional Government | Formed immediately after Nicholas II abdicated and was intended to be a temporary body until the elections for the Constituent Assembly could take place later in 1917. Initially led by Prince Lvov and latterly by Alexander Kerensky.

Provisorium | Provisional or temporary solution.

The Russian Soviet Federated Socialist Republic (RSFSR) | The name for Russia after the Bolshevik Revolution until 1922, when it became a republic of the Soviet Union.

Social Democrats (SDs) | The Russian Social Democratic Labour Party was formed in 1898 to unite various Marxist groups within Imperial Russia. Members were Marxists and opposed revolutionary populism, believing instead that the agents of the revolution would be the working class.

Socialism in One Country	Stalin's theory that the Soviet Union should strengthen itself to resist capitalist encirclement – it followed the defeat of socialist revolutions in Germany and Hungary. This policy was criticised by Trotsky and Zinoviev.
Socialist Realism	A style of realistic art that developed to further Socialism in One Country. It glorified the working class.
Stakhanovites	Workers who followed the example of Alexei Stakhanov, who over-achieved targets set for him (mining 102 tons of coals in under 6 hours). In 1935, under the second Five Year Plan, some workers tried to equal or better his targets.
Syndicalism	A theory of an economic system. Syndicalism is a form of socialism, considered a replacement for capitalism. It suggests that industries be organized into confederations or syndicates. It is a system whereby industries are owned and managed by the workers.
Totalitarian	Describes a political system where the state retains complete control over society and all aspects of citizens' lives.
USSR (Union of Soviet Socialist Republics)	Formed officially in 1922 and disbanded in 1991, the USSR was a single-party Communist state comprising the RSFSR, Transcaucasian, Ukrainian and Belorussian republics.
Ukase	Sometimes referred to as an 'edict', this was a decree or law passed by the Tsar of Imperial Russia.
Zemstvo	A form of local government that was created during the reforms following Emancipation. Established in 1864, the zemstvo were small elected councils in rural areas to provide social and economic services.

Bibliography

Chapter 1:

Acton E. *Russia: The Tsarist and Soviet Legacy (The Present and the Past)*: Pearson: 1995

Chubarov A. The *Fragile Empire: A History of Imperial Russia*: Continuum: 1999

Dixon S. *How holy was Holy Russia? Rediscovering Russian religion* in Hosking G. and Service R. (eds) *Reinterpreting Russia*: Hodder Arnold: 1999

Fitzpatrick S. *The Russian Revolution*: Oxford: 2008

Freeze G.L. *From Supplication to Revolution: A Documentary Social History of Imperial Russia*: Oxford: 1988

Jones, G.S. in Marx K. and Engels F. *The Communist Manifesto*: Penguin: 2002

Lieven D. Russia as empire: a comparative perspective:. In: Hosking. G and Service. R. (eds.) *Reinterpreting Russia*: Edward Arnold: London: 1991

Lynch M (Accessed website December 2014) http://www.historytoday.com/michael-lynch/emancipation-russian-serfs-1861-charter-freedom-or-act-betrayal

Mosse W.E. *An Economic History of Russia 1856–1914*: London I. B. Tauris: 1996

Pipes R. *Russia Under the Old Regime*: Penguin: 1995

Polunov A. *Russia in the Nineteenth Century: Autocracy, Reform and Social Change 1814–1914*: Armonk, New York: 2005: Cited Peretts E.A. *Dnevnik gosudarstvennogo sekretaria E.A. Perettsa (1880–1883)*: Moscow and Leningrad: 1927

Radzinsky E. *Alexander II: The Last Great Tsar*: Simon and Schuster: 2006

Saunders D. *Russia in the age of reaction and reform 1801–1881*: Pearson: 1992

Seton-Watson H. *The Russian Empire 1801–1917*: Oxford: 1967

Smith D. *Former People: the Last Days of the Russian Aristocracy*: Macmillan: 2012

Tolstoy L. *Anna Karenina*: Oxford World Classics: 1999

Ulam A. *In the Name of the People: Prophets and Conspirators in Prerevolutionary Russia*: New York: The Viking Press: 1977

Waldron P. *The End of Imperial Russia*: Palgrave Macmillan: 1997

Waldron P. *Governing Tsarist Russia*: Palgrave Macmillan: 2007

Chapter 2:

Acton E. *Russia: The Tsarist and Soviet Legacy (The Present and the Past)*: Pearson: 1995

Ascher A. *The Revolution of 1905 Volume 1. Russia in Disarray*: Stanford UP: 1988

Ascher A. *The Revolution of 1905: a short history*: Stanford UP: 2004

Figes O. *A People's Tragedy: The Russian Revolution, 1891–1924*: Pimlico: 1997

Figes O. *Revolutionary Russia, 1891–1991*: Penguin London: 2014

Fitzpatrick S. *The Russian Revolution*: Oxford: 2008

Gatrell P. *A Whole Empire Walking: Refugees in Russia During World War I*: Indiana UP: 1999

Gerschenkron A. The rate of growth in Russia: *The Rate of Industrial Growth in Russia since 1885*: The Journal of Economic History: Volume 7, 1947, pp.144-74

Golder F. *Documents of Russian History 1914–17*: Gloucester, MA: 1964; Read Books: 2008 (reprint of original edition 1927)

Haimson L. 'The Problem of Social Stability in Urban Russia 1905–1917': Slavic Review 23, No. 4: 1964, pp.619-42

Manning R.T. 'The Zemstvo and Politics 1864–1914' in Emmons T. and Vucinich W.S. (eds) *The Zemstvo in Russia: An Experiment in Local Self-Government*: Cambridge University Press: 1982

Marks S.G. *Road to Power: The Trans-Siberian Railroad and the Colonisation of Asian Russia 1850–1917*: Cornell UP: Ithaca, NY: 1991

McKean R.B. 'The Bureaucracy and the Labour Problem, June 1907–February 1917' in McKean R.B. (ed.) *New Perspectives in Modern Russian History*: New York: 1992

Nove A. *An Economic History of the U.S.S.R.*: Pelican: 1969

Perrie M. 'Political and Economic Terror in the Tactics of the Russian SR Party before 1914' in Mommsen W.J. and Hirschfield G. (eds) *Social Protest, Violence and Terror in Nineteenth and Twentieth Century Europe*: Basingstoke: 1982

Pipes R. *A Concise History of the Russian Revolution*: New York: 1997

Read C. *War and Revolution in Russia 1914–22: the collapse of Tsarism and the establishment of Soviet power, European History in Perspective*: Palgrave Macmillan: 2013

Rogger H. *Russia in the Age of Modernisation and Revolution 1881–1917*: Longman: 1983

Service R. *The Penguin History of Modern Russia: From Tsarism to the Twenty First Century*: Allen Lane: 2009

Service R. 'The Russian Revolution 1900–1927', *Studies in European History,*: Palgrave Macmillan: 2009

Service R. *Lenin, A Biography*: Macmillan: 2000

Stone N. *The Eastern Front 1914–17*: London: Hodder and Stoughton: 1975

Thatcher I.D. 'Late imperial urban workers' in Thatcher I. (ed) *Late Imperial Russia: Problems and Prospects*: Manchester UP: 2005

Wood A. *The Russian Revolution, Second Edition – Seminar Studies in History*: Routledge: 1986

Chapter 3:

Carr E.H. *Bolshevik Revolution, Volume 2*: Macmillan: 1952

Clements B.E. *Bolshevik Women*: Cambridge University Press: 1997

Conquest R. *The Harvest of Sorrow: Soviet Collectivisation and the Terror-Famine,* reprint edition: London: 2002

Daniels R.V. *The Rise and Fall of Communism in Russia*: Yale UP: 2007

Davies R.W. Harrison M. and Wheatcroft S.G. (eds) *The Economic Transformation of the Soviet Union, 1913–1945*: Cambridge: 1994

Davies S.R *Popular Opinion in Stalin's Russia: Terror, Propaganda and Dissent, 1934–1941*: Cambridge University Press: 1997

Deutscher I. *The Prophet Unarmed: Trotsky 1921–29*: New York: 1965

Figes O. *A People's Tragedy: The Russian Revolution, 1891–1924*: Pimlico: 1997

Figes O. *Revolutionary Russia, 1891–1991*: Penguin London: 2014

Fitzpatrick S. *The Russian Revolution*: Oxford: 2008

Hosking G. *A History of the Soviet Union 1917–1991* final edition: London: 1992

Landis E.C. *Bandits and Partisans: The Antonov Movement in the Russian Civil War (Pitt Series in Russian and East European Studies)*: University of Pittsburgh Press: 2008

Lewin M. *The Making of the Soviet System: Essays in the Social History of Interwar Russia*: New Press: 1994

Lewin M. *The Soviet Century*: Verso: 2005

McDermott K. *Stalin: revolutionary in an ear of war, European History in Perspective*: Palgrave Macmillan: 2006

Nove A. *An Economic History of the USSR, 1917–1991*: Penguin: 1993

Pipes R. *A Concise History of the Russian Revolution*: New York: 1997

Raleigh D. J. *Experiencing Russia's Civil War: Politics, Society and Revolutionary Culture in Saratov, 1917–1922*: Princeton University Press, 2002

Read C. *War and Revolution in Russia 1914–22 (European History in Perspective)*: Palgrave Macmillan: 2013

Fitzpatrick S., Rabinowitch A., Stites R.: (eds) *Russia in the Era of NEP: Explorations in Soviet Society and Culture*: Indiana University Press: 1991

Service R. *The Bolshevik Party in Revolution. A Study in Organisational Change, 1917–23*: London: 1979

Service R. *The Penguin History of Modern Russia – From Tsarism to the Twenty First Century*: Allen Lane: 2009

Service R. *Lenin, A Biography*: Macmillan: 2000

Schapiro L.B. *The Communist Party of the Soviet Union*: London: 1960

Siegelbaum L.H. *Soviet State and Society Between Revolutions, 1918–1929*: Cambridge University Press: 1992

Smele J.D. *Civil War in Siberia: The Anti-Bolshevik Government of Admiral Kolchak, 1918–20*: Cambridge University Press: 1996

Solzhenitsyn A. *One Day in the Life of Ivan Denisovich*: Penguin: 1963

Tirado I.A. *The Komsomol and Young Peasants: The Dilemma of Rural Expansion 1921–25*: Slavic Review 52.3: 1993, pp.460-76

Tucker R.C. *The Rise of Stalin's Personality Cult*: The American Historical Review, Vol. 84, No. 2, Apr. 1979, pp.347-66

Ward C. *Stalin's Russia*: 2nd edition: Hodder: 1999

Zamyatin E. and Mirsky, D.S. *The Cave*: The Slavonic Review, Vol. 2, No. 4, Jun. 1923: Modern Humanities Research Association, pp.145-53

Chapter 4:

Acton E. and Stableford T. *The Soviet Union, A documentary History, Volume 2 1939–1991*: Exeter: 2007

Deutscher, I. 'The Failure of Khruschevism' *Socialist Register 1965*: Merlin Press, London: 1965 (socialistregister.com/index.php/srv/article/download/5945/2841 – Accessed on 04/02/15)

Figes O. *Revolutionary Russia, 1891–1991*: Penguin London: 2014

Filtzer D. *The Khrushchev Era: De-Stalinisation and the Limits of Reforms in the USSR, 1953–1964*: Palgrave Macmillan: 1993

Gaddis J.L. *The Cold War: a new history*: Penguin: 2005

Hosking G. *A History of the Soviet Union 1917–1991* final edition: London: 1992

Mawdsley E. *The Stalin Years: The Soviet Union 1929–53*: Manchester: 1998

McCauley M. *The Soviet Union 1917–1991*: Longman: 1993

McCauley M. *The Khrushchev Era 1953–64*: Pearson: 1995

McDermott K. *Stalin: revolutionary in an era of war, European History in Perspective*: Palgrave Macmillan: 2006

Nove A. *The Soviet Economic System*: London: 1977

Overy R. *Russia's War*: Penguin: 1997

Read C. *The Making and Breaking of the Soviet System, An interpretation (European History in Perspective)*: Palgrave: 2001

Service R. *The Penguin History of Modern Russia – From Tsarism to the Twenty First Century*: Allen Lane: 2009

Tucker R.C. *The Rise of Stalin's Personality Cult*: The American Historical Review, Vol. 84, No. 2, Apr. 1979, pp.347-66

Volkogonov D. *The Rise and Fall of the Soviet Empire: political leaders from Lenin to Gorbachev*: Harper Collins: 1998

Ward C. *Stalin's Russia*: 2nd edition: Hodder: 1999

Acknowledgements

The authors and publishers acknowledge the following sources of copyright material and are grateful for the permissions granted. While every effort has been made, it has not always been possible to identify the sources of all the material used, or to trace all copyright holders. If any omissions are brought to our notice, we will be happy to include the appropriate acknowledgements on reprinting.

The publisher would like to thank the following for permission to reproduce their photographs (numbers refer to figure numbers, unless otherwise stated):

Chapter 1 opener: Corbis: 1.1 **Alamy Images:** Pictorial Press Ltd. **1.4 Corbis: 1.5 Corbis:** Austrian Archives. 1.6 **Bridgeman Art Library:** The Relief of the Light Brigade, 25th October 1854, 1897 (oil on canvas), Woodville, Richard Caton (1825-55) / National Army Museum, London. Chapter 2 opener **Alamy Images:** Moviestore Collection Ltd. 2.2 **Getty Images:** Sovfoto/UIG. 2.4 **TopFoto:** 2.5 **Getty Images:** Sheridan Libraries/ Levy / Gado. 2.7 **Getty Images:** Hulton Archive. 2.8 **Getty Images:** Print Collector. 2.9 **Alamy Images:** Moviestore Collection Ltd. Chapter 3 opener **Rex Features:** Sovfoto / Universal Images Group. 3.3 **Alamy Images:** Pictorial Press Ltd. 3.4 **TopFoto:** ullsteinbild. 3.5 **TopFoto:** Topham Picturepoint. 3.6 **Corbis:** 3.10 **Getty Images:** Paul Popper / Popperfoto. 3.11 **TopFoto:** ullsteinbild. Chapter 4 opener: **TopFoto:** RIA / Novosti. 4.2 **Getty Images:** Sovfoto. 4.4 **TopFoto:** RIA / Novosti. 4.5 **Alamy Images:** ITAR-TASS Photo Agency. 4.6 **Getty Images:** Universal History Archive

The publisher would like to thank the following for permission to reproduce extracts from their texts:

Extract Chapter 1: Edward Acton: The Tsarist and Soviet Legacy, 1986. **Extract Chapter 2:** Richard Pipes, A Concise History of the Russian Revolution,(1996). **Extract Chapter 2:** ©Alexander Chubarov, 1999, The Fragile Empire: A History of Imperial Russia, Continuum Publishing US, an imprint of Bloomsbury Publishing Inc. **Extract Chapter 2:** Red Petrograd: Revolution in the Factories 1917-1918 by S.A. Smith Senior Lecturer in History, University of Essex (1985). Reprinted with permission of Cambridge University Press. **Extract Chaper 2:** Lenin: A Biography by Robert Service (Pan Macmillan 2000) copyright © Robert Service, 2010. **Extract Chapter 3:** The Soviet Century by Moshe Lewin (2005). Reprinted by kind permission of Verso. **Extract Chapter 3:** ©Chris Ward, 1999, Stalin's Russia. Bloomsbury, Academic an imprint of Bloomsbury Publishing Plc. **Chapter 4:** Excerpts from CONVERSATIONS WITH STALIN by Milovan Djilas, translated by Michael B. Petrovich. English translation copyright © 1962. renewed 1990 by Houghton Mifflin Harcourt Publishing Company. Reprinted by permission of Houghton Mifflin Harcourt Publishing Company. All rights reserved. **Extract Chapter 4:** The Failure of Khrushchevism by Isaac Deutscher. Socialist Register 1965 (Merlin Press, London, 1965). Reprinted with kind permission of Andrew Nurnberg Associates.

Index

Printed in Great Britain
by Amazon